I.O.U.S.A.

I.O.U.S.A.

Addison Wiggin
and Kate Incontrera
with Dorianne Perrucci

Foreword by David Walker

WILEY

John Wiley & Sons, Inc.

Published by John Wiley & Sons, Inc., Hoboken, New Jersey.
Published simultaneously in Canada.

Book design by Figaro.

For general information on our other products and services or for technical support, please contact our Customer Care Department within the United States at (800) 762–2974, outside the United States at (317) 572–3993 or fax (317) 572–4002.

Wiley also publishes its books in a variety of electronic formats. Some content that appears in print may not be available in electronic books. For more information about Wiley products, visit our web site at www.wiley.com.

ISBN   978-0-470-22277-5

Printed in the United States of America.

10   9   8   7   6   5   4   3   2   1

For Jennifer, Meritt, August, and Elizabeth,
who make all the late-night pacing worthwhile

Contents

Foreword

This book will provide you with information on two journeys based on the critically acclaimed documentary *I.O.U.S.A.* The first is a journey through time in which you learn about various key events relating to our country's financial and other affairs since the beginning of the American republic in 1789. This journey also looks forward to what our future would look like in 2040 under a do-nothing or let-the-chips-ride scenario. During this journey you will also learn about four key deficits that threaten America's and our families' futures and what both Washington policy makers and you should do about them.

The second journey follows the efforts of various participants, including myself, in the Fiscal Wake-Up Tour across the United States. As of June 2008, the Tour had traveled to over half the states and about 40 cities. Participants in the Tour state the facts and speak the truth directly to the American people about our nation's true financial condition and fiscal future. They also highlight the failure of Washington policy makers to address a range of large, known, and growing challenges that threaten our future.

The documentary is based in large part on a "Four Deficits" speech that I have given on a number of occasions on the Fiscal Wake-Up Tour, which also draws certain lessons from the fall of Rome, the longest-surviving republic in human history. These and the book *Empire of Debt* (Wiley, 2006), written by Bill Bonner and Addison Wiggin, provide a solid foundation for the documentary's message. These messages are reinforced by a solid cast of bipartisan characters from the political arena. And we hear from three major sectors of the U.S. economy: those who save and invest; those who choose not to save; and those for whom saving is very difficult.

This Foreword, however, covers my own personal journey, including how it evolved during the shooting of the film over the past two years. My journey continues and will until leaders whom we've sent to Washington start focusing on the nation's future rather than their own present need to get reelected and begin to make tough choices. Our leaders need to deliver some real results for the American people. The alternative is unthinkable for many people.

My personal journey started on October 2, 1951, in Birmingham, Alabama. I was the first of three sons of David S. Walker and Dorothy West Walker. As a child I grew up in several towns in Alabama and Florida. In my early years we rarely traveled outside our hometowns and never outside our home states.

I went to college at Jacksonville University in Jacksonville, Florida, where I met my wife Mary. We were married at the end of my sophomore year. In fact, at the early age of 19, we eloped to South Carolina. I subsequently graduated with a B.S. degree in accounting. Thirty-seven years and many moves later, which included homes in Florida, Georgia, Texas, and Virginia, Mary and I are still married. We now have two children and three grandchildren. So far we've beaten the odds associated with marrying at such a young age.

My professional career stated in public accounting with Price Waterhouse and Company. After earning my certified public accountant (CPA) certificate, I changed firms and joined Coopers and Lybrand. Later, I became involved in the recruiting and human resource consulting business before doing public service in the federal government. My career has included serving as head of a global service line for Arthur Andersen LLP before the firm experienced the problems that led to its downfall.

My federal government career started in 1983 with the Pension Benefit Guaranty Corporation and later the Labor

Department. I've had the privilege to lead three federal government agencies, all professional services organizations. Most recently I served as Comptroller General of the United States and head of the U.S. Government Accountability Office (GAO) from 1998 to 2008. I also served as a Public Trustee for the Social Security and Medicare Trust Funds (1990–1995) while I was a partner with Arthur Andersen.

I have been fortunate to receive Presidential appointments from Ronald Reagan, George Herbert Walker Bush (41), and Bill Clinton, each time being confirmed unanimously by the United States Senate. There aren't many people who can say that. In fact, I may be the only person who can.

During my more than 35-year professional career I have spent 20 years in the private sector and 15 years with the federal government. I have been a transformational change agent in many of these positions, so far with very positive results. Hopefully, that will continue.

Other than my professional background, there are things about me and interests that have had a strong influence on my career and actions. For example, my Walker line came to America in the 1600s and initially settled in Virginia. I have several ancestors who fought, and at least one who died, during the American Revolution. I am a student of history and a member of the Sons of the American Revolution. Mary and I live in Mt. Vernon Farms, Virginia, on land that was once owned by George Washington.

Despite my family's long history in America, to my knowledge, I am only the second Walker in my direct line to graduate from college. Most of my ancestors prior to my father worked in the mines, in mills, on farms, or as ministers.

While we rarely traveled outside the state in my early years, I have been fortunate to travel to all 50 states and about 90 countries to date. And, while I am proud to be an American, I also realize that there are many issues that are global in nature and that we must partner for progress with other countries to help make the world a better and safer place. Furthermore, while the

United States is number one in many things, my experience has caused me to realize that we are not number one in all things. In fact, we lag many other industrialized nations in connection with a range of key outcome-based indicators—public finance, education, health care, savings, and research and development, to name a few.

From a political perspective, early in life I was a southern Democrat. Later I was one of the first in Northern Florida who changed my party registration to become a Republican. In 1997, I officially became a political independent, reflecting my frustration with both parties. As a candidate for the position of Comptroller General of the United States, I believed I should be independent both in form and in substance.

I consider myself an American who is an internationalist. I was very involved in international policy and accountability issues during my tenure as Comptroller General. My interest in international issues continues and I was recently fortunate to be elected as the first chairman of the Independent Audit Advisory Committee (IAAC) of the United Nations.

Enough about my background—what about my involvement in the documentary? My involvement began with reading a book. As a history buff and a person interested in financial matters, I decided to buy the book *Empire of Debt* on one of my many trips into a bookstore before boarding a flight. On this occasion, Mary and I were flying to Phoenix to visit our son Andy, our daughter-in-law Meghan, and their family.

During my career, I have become a fast reader and prolific writer. As a result, I was able to speed-read the book on the long flight west. I enjoyed the book, especially the analogies to past history. I have used the analogies in many of my speeches, including frequent references to the challenges that we now face that led to Rome's downfall. At the same time, while I enjoyed the book, I did not agree with everything in it.

When Mary and I arrived at Andy and Meghan's home we had the opportunity to engage in a time-honored tradition for grandparents: reading to our then granddaughter, Grace. She is a very bright young girl. While I took my turn and read her a children's book, as somewhat of a joke, I also read her a single paragraph out of *Empire of Debt*. The paragraph discussed how our current federal policies were mortgaging our future. When I was done, I asked Grace what she thought. To my shock and amazement she said, "Devastating, Granddaddy!" She was only four years old at the time!

If a four-year-old can get it, then why is so hard for a vast majority of current federal elected officials? Are they in denial or just happy to kick the can down the road while they leave key sustainability challenges for someone else?

In large part, I believe the greatest deficit that the United States has right now is a leadership deficit. You'll hear more about this and our nation's other deficits in this book and in the film.

Subsequent to our Phoenix trip, my office at the GAO was contacted by the film crew who requested to meet with me about a documentary they were planning to do on federal deficits and debt. Since I had done a number of electronic interviews and was obviously interested in the topic, I agreed.

The meeting was attended by Patrick Creadon, Addison Wiggin, Kate Incontrera, and others from Agora Financial. They provided an overview of the planned documentary, and when they had finished I said, "Does this have anything to do with the book *Empire of Debt*?" Addison and Patrick looked at each other and hesitated to speak. Evidently, they didn't know whether I liked the book or not. Once they acknowledge that it did, I noted that I had read it and liked it. After that point, things went well and it was the beginning of a great adventure.

While the book was the initial basis for the documentary, over time it evolved to concentrate more on our efforts in the Fiscal Wake-Up Tour. That Tour is coordinated by the nonpartisan Concord Coalition and it also involves scholars from the Brookings Institution, the Heritage Foundation, and me. Successful documentaries, Patrick explained to me early on, usually have one or more persons to focus on in order to help personalize the film. I was fortunate to be selected as one such person.

Patrick, Addison, and their crew followed the Tour to several locations across America, including Omaha, Nebraska; Des Moines, Iowa; Manchester, New Hampshire; Los Angeles, California; and Madison, Wisconsin. They also filmed many other subjects

The Fiscal Wake-Up Tour also took on extra notoriety after the CBS *60 Minutes* program decided to do a segment on it. The program helped increase attendance at our events outside Washington as well as the attention paid to our efforts inside Washington's Beltway. The *60 Minutes* segment also paved the way for a timely introduction to our work in the documentary.

We found in our many Town Hall meetings that the American people were smarter than many politicians realized. Once you state the facts and speak the truth, people get the message. At the same time, the American people are distrustful of Washington. They're starved for two things: truth and leadership.

In November 2007, after many Tour stops, I was fortunate to be recognized as the Concord Coalition's Economic Patriot of the Year. Prior recipients included former president of the United States Bill Clinton, former Treasury secretary Bob Rubin, and former chairman of the Federal Reserve Paul Volcker. Little did I know that in accepting that award, my career path would change once again.

During that evening I made a brief yet substantive acceptance speech. I also had the opportunity to participate in a substantive panel discussion with Rubin, Volcker, former senators Rudman and Kerrey, and the president of the Concord Coalition, Pete Peterson. I must have done all right because about a week later, I received a call from Pete Peterson.

Pete called under the pretense that he wanted my input on his plans to start a new foundation dedicated to trying to address the budget and other key sustainability challenges. It didn't take long before his real purpose became clear: He wanted me to head his new foundation.

Needless to say, I was flattered and surprised. And yet I was very happy with my current job and the work I was doing at GAO. While I noted that fact and raised a number of reasons why I felt it probably did not make sense for me to change, Pete was persistent. A couple of months of discussion later, I decided to accept his offer.

My primary reason for deciding to accept was that I became convinced that at my new post I would be able to do certain things to help achieve changes that I could not do as Comptroller General. As the president and CEO of the Peterson Foundation I would be able to advocate specific policy solutions, build strong and overt coalitions for change, and stimulate and support the various grassroots efforts designed to pressure Washington policy makers to make tough choices—and to hold them accountable if they failed to act.

I was also interested in working in partnership with Pete, who is a great American and in many ways a case study of the American dream come true.

As I said when asked about leaving my position as Comptroller General and head of the GAO, "Committed generals do not leave the fight, although sometimes they change their position on the battlefield." I said that we aim to "keep America strong and the American dream alive by promoting responsibility and accountability today in order to provide more opportunity tomorrow."

After joining the Foundation, I proposed and the directors agreed that the Foundation should purchase the documentary from Agora and finance its distribution. We are excited about its message and feel strongly that the time is right for it to be heard.

We look forward to the theatrical release of the film and to its later premier on television. We also plan to take other steps to make sure that it is ultimately seen by as many people as possible.

In my view, it is time for elected officials to start making tough policy choices in connection with our nation's budget, entitlement programs, spending policies, and tax policies.

Our next president needs to make fiscal responsibility and intergenerational equity a priority. If he does, and if he resists making dumb promises, while using the bully pulpit of the presidency and working on a bipartisan basis to achieve real and lasting change, we can successfully meet this challenge.

If this happens, and a few bipartisan leaders join in the fight, we can make sure that our future is better than our past and that the United States is the first republic to stand the test of time. These are goals worth fighting for. "We the People" can turn things around. If you agree, then join the fight for America's future at www.pgpf.org. You, your country, and your family will be glad that you did.

Honorable David M. Walker
President and CEO, Peter G. Peterson Foundation
Former Comptroller General of the United States

I.O.U.S.A. Cast of Characters

CAST

Hon. David Walker: Former U.S. Comptroller General and President and CEO of the Peter G. Peterson Foundation.

Robert Bixby: Executive Director of the Concord Coalition.

Sen. Kent Conrad (D-ND): Chairman of the Senate Budget Committee.

Sen. Judd Gregg (R-NH): Ranking member, Senate Budget Committee.

Alice Rivlin: The first director of the Congressional Budget Office and on the team that balanced the budget during the Clinton administration.

William Bonner: Bestselling author and founder and president of Agora, Inc., a financial research and publishing group.

The Concerned Youth of America: A grassroots, non-partisan organization whose goal is to increase awareness of the state of the U.S.'s finances among the youth of the nation.

Robert Rubin: 70th Secretary of the U.S. Treasury (1995–1999), one of the key players in the Clinton administration's balanced budget.

Peter G. Peterson: Co-founded the Concord Coalition in 1992, and founder of the Peter G. Peterson Foundation.

Paul Volcker: Chairman of the Federal Reserve Board (1979–1987), and best known for battling the inflation of the early 1980s.

Hon. Ron Paul: Outspoken proponent of "free market" economics and critic of the Federal Reserve System.

Alan Greenspan: Chairman of the Federal Board (1987–2006, and still seen as a leading authority on U.S. economic and monetary policy.

Warren Buffett: CEO of Berkshire Hathaway, and regarded as one of the world's greatest stock market investors.

James Areddy: Correspondent for the *Wall Street Journal* in Shanghai, China.

Paul O'Neill: 72nd Secretary of the U.S. Treasury, who was fired after 23 months, after having a 'difference of opinions' about deficits with Vice President Cheney.

Art Laffer: Former member of President Reagan's Economic Policy Board. He is best known for popularizing his Laffer curve.

CREW

Addison Wiggin, Executive Producer

Patrick Creadon, Director

Christine O'Malley, Producer

Sarah Gibson, Producer

Doug Blush, Editor

Brian Oakes, Graphic Design

Theodore James, Associate Producer

Kate Incontrera, Associate Producer

Acknowledgments

I t turns out that reverse engineering a documentary film into a companion book is not as easy as it might sound. Creatively, you can convey a lot of information with images, music, and dialogue in a movie that require much more background and setup in a book. There are a number of people we want to thank for allowing us to take six weeks in the summer of 2008 to wrap our heads around two and half years of travel, filming, interviews, and research.

First, we want to thank Ian Mathias and Greg Kadajski for holding down the fort in Agora Financial's *5 Min. Forecast* and *The Daily Reckoning*, respectively. Writing, editing, and publishing daily stock market and economic commentary is a daunting task when you're working as a team. Going it alone is much more so. Both have done an admirable job. Thanks to all the folks who work so hard at Agora Financial, including but not limited to Joseph Schriefer, Mark O'Dell, Greg Grillot, Chris Mayer, Eric Fry, Michelle Nickels, John Forde, Chad Barrett, and Mike Pizzo, for relieving us of critical duty during the writing of the book, and to Bruce Robertson for helping negotiate all the paperwork and the labyrinthine accounting process.

We'd like to thank Bill Bonner, too, not just for his insights in *The Daily Reckoning*, but for biting his tongue and giving us the freedom to explore the documentary project at will. Thanks to Matt Turner, Myles Norin, and Bob Compton for supporting the project legally and financially, and to Scott Weiser and Doug Nevin for ably representing our interests in the film acquisition by the Peter G. Peterson Foundation.

Thank you to David Walker for taking such an interest in our work, for helping us get the story straight on the nation's four deficits, and for providing the Foreword to this companion piece. It's worth noting that while David wrote the Foreword to this book and his consultation was helpful in piecing the script together, the words in this book are our own and do not necessarily represent the views and/or opinions advocated by the Peter G. Peterson Foundation. In addition, we'd like to thank Elizabeth Wilner at the Peterson Foundation. Thanks to Bob Bixby and all the folks at the Concord Coalition for the ideas and insights they contributed to the film and subsequently the book.

A big thank-you goes to the amazing crew that put together the movie: Patrick Creadon, the director; Christine O'Malley, Sarah Gibson, and Theodore James, producers extraordinaire; Brian Oakes, who designed all the graphics you see in the film and in this book; and our editor, Doug Blush. We know this subject can be extremely difficult, but this group of talented individuals tackled this project wholeheartedly. We are very grateful for the unique vision and insights each person brought to the table to help shape the story of *I.O.U.S.A.* We would also like to thank Jon Carnes and the One Horizon Foundation for getting the film from just an idea we were batting around to a reality, and to Roadside Attractions for getting *I.O.U.S.A.* out into the public eye. A big thank-you to Dorianne Perrucci and the team over at John Wiley & Sons, especially Debra Englander, Joan O'Neill, and Kelly O'Connor, for all of their hard work on this book and putting up with our unique understanding of deadlines.

We would like to thank the Wiggin and Incontrera families, as well as Craig Stouffer, for their continued support of this project (and of us). Thanks to our friends and co-workers for putting up with our hectic schedules, being a sounding board when needed, and even providing us with a place to write (thanks, Kyle!).

Last, we would like to thank the distinguished group of experts who allowed us to interrupt their busy lives to sit down with us to be interviewed for *I.O.U.S.A.*:

- Alice Rivlin

- William Bonner

- Robert Rubin

- Peter G. Peterson

- Ron Paul

- Paul Volcker

- Alan Greenspan

- Warren Buffett

- James Areddy

- Paul O'Neill

- Arthur Laffer

- Steve Forbes

Part One
THE MISSION

THE MISSION

*Deficit reduction cannot be described as a sexy
topic. Unfortunately, it is hard to break through with
an unsexy message. It comes across as kind of like
taking a cold shower. We come along after the sexy
messages and cool people off.*

—Bob Bixby, executive director,
Concord Coalition, in the film *I.O.U.S.A.*

The *I.O.U.S.A.* project has been one long, cold shower.

As Bob Bixby put it, it's hard to break through with an unsexy message. But we've been trying. The film and the book are the culmination of nearly five years of work. When we began, the potential difficulties of a growing national debt and a struggling currency—both abetted by negligence on the part of the nation's policy makers—were far from the media headlines.

3

Words like *subprime, mortgage-backed securities,* and *inflation* barely piqued the interest of the average American. Gasoline and food prices appeared to be stable. The stock market appeared to have recovered from the tech bust and was on its way to new record highs. It looked like house prices would be going up forever. Interest rates were dropping. Despite the wars in Iraq and Afghanistan, Americans were generally positive about the outlook for the economy and their own prospects within it.

But we had our suspicions.

Along with much of the Western world, the United States is entering a demographic transformation to an older society. But we're doing so at a bad time. Health care costs are rising dramatically. The nation has a falling savings rate. Together they make a very bad combination for the economy. But, as with any extravaganza, it's hard to get people to see that the party's over.

■ ■ ■

In the fall of 2005, after two years of research and writing, Bill Bonner and I published *Empire of Debt,* a look at the history of rising debt in all levels of American society. The federal government had been, and still is, running historic deficits in the federal budget. The national debt was growing at a pace never seen in the nation's history. While the Bush administration waged increasingly unpopular wars overseas, Congress—and, by extension, the American people—was depending more and more on foreign lenders and tapping the Social Security and Medicare trust funds to pay its bills. The national savings rate was about to go negative. And the current account balance—the nation's balance sheet with the rest of the world—was entering historically negative territory as well.

On the surface, the stock market and housing were growing nicely, indeed. Underneath, a review of the numbers told an entirely different story.

We didn't know for sure, but suspected the mortgage market was likely to show the first cracks of a system under stress. We forecasted an implosion in that market and an ensuing recession led by a slowdown in housing, which so many Americans had begun to rely on as their principal source of wealth. As such, we thought it would be a good idea, if a tad impertinent, to send the book *Empire of Debt* to all the members of Congress at their home offices. We sent a copy to the Federal Reserve and another to the White House. At the time, we were under the impression no one in Washington was paying attention. As long as U.S. dollars were rolling off the presses at the Bureau of Engraving and Printing, the record seemed to show no one was inclined to worry.

One serendipitous moment would prove us wrong.

On November 14, 2005, the very day we were stuffing copies of the book into manila envelopes, *USAToday* ran a cover story featuring a press conference that David Walker, then comptroller general of the United States, had given before the National Press Club.

"The United States can be likened to Rome before the fall of the empire. Its financial condition is 'worse than advertised,'" the newspaper said, quoting Walker. "It has a 'broken business model.' It faces deficits in its budgets, its balance of payments (the trade deficit), its savings—and its leadership." That we were mailing a book which effectively drew the same analogy seemed like more than a small coincidence. Little did we know how important Mr. Walker's list of "four deficits" would become to this project. As you'll see, they would provide both the context and framework we were looking for to help bring a difficult, complex, and unsexy message to a wider audience.

■ ■ ■

Before we even had a title for *Empire of Debt*, I got snowed in for several days doing research at Brad and Julie Wiggin's condo in Sugarbush, Vermont. I'd taken a slew of reading material and one documentary along with me, Daniel Yergin's *The Commanding Heights*. Yergin's work follows the ideas of two of the twentieth century's most influential economists, John Maynard Keynes and Friedrich A. von Hayek, during the course of their prolific lives.

Surrounded by the deep snow, and sitting amidst those books, I used the film *Commanding Heights* as a diversion. Call me a masochist. By the second run through, I was impressed with the way the filmmakers had woven together similar themes to our own. They'd even turned economics into an entertaining program for television.

Several months later, the publication of *Empire of Debt* drew moderate interest from the media. We were featured briefly in the *New York Times* magazine. ABC News put us on their 4:00 A.M. slot. The *Economist* listed us as one of their "must reads" for 2005, based on sales from Amazon.com. The book even made it on to the *New York Times* business list. But the housing boom was nearing its peak. Most of the media viewed our work with a jaundiced eye.

Recalling the snowed-in episode in Vermont, I decided at that point, naively, that turning *Empire of Debt* into a documentary would be a good idea. Wouldn't it be easier to hand a friend a DVD and say, "You have to watch this movie," than a 400-page economic tome on the history of debt in the United States? You'd think so. But making a movie, it turns out, involves a few more moving parts than writing a book.

After a few false starts, we got lucky and found the team that would ultimately pull the project together. Jon Carnes, a reader of our *Daily Reckoning* e-letter, responded to an informal proposal of the film we'd written up. Jon, who had founded Eos Funds, a firm providing research for hedge funds, had recently invested in a production company in Hollywood. Jon said he'd met some producers through the process and could introduce us if we were serious. That relationship lead us to Sarah Gibson, who produced a film featured at the Sundance Film Festival in

2006, where she met Patrick Creadon and Christine O'Malley, who were also at Sundance with their film *Wordplay*, a documentary about the *New York Times* crossword puzzle.

The O'Malley-Creadon team didn't come to the project lightly. It took several, five in fact, serious phone conversations and a few face-to-face meetings to help them see we were serious about taking a rather complex and dry economic subject and making it fun and entertaining enough for a wider audience.

Eventually, Patrick and Christine grew interested in the challenge. "We didn't think we could find a more challenging subject for a film than crosswords," Patrick would later tell an audience of *Wordplay* fans in Los Angeles, "until we decided to make this film about the national debt."

With the team assembled, and a fair amount of the budget already on the line, we went to work. Among the first tasks involved in making the documentary was to assemble a hit list of the folks we'd like to interview for the project. Naturally, David Walker's comments regarding the finances of this country resembling Rome before the fall of the Empire put him at the top of our list. Having been engaged in the Fiscal Wake-Up Tour, he accepted a meeting with us.

To our surprise, during our first meeting David revealed he'd read *Empire of Debt* and enjoyed it—even if he didn't agree with everything in the book. We learned we shared an interest in economic and political history.

From the director's perspective, Patrick's talent is clear. He convinced us that if were we to be successful in telling a complicated story to a general audience, we'd need a "real" human story to help carry the viewers' interest. After a few tense, but fruitful, days in a classroom at the American Film Institute, Patrick's alma mater, we grew increasingly interested in David Walker and Bob Bixby as the lead protagonists of the film. They, in turn, grew more interested in working with us.

Readers of this book will likely expect a screen-by-screen "making of" of *Empire of Debt*. But because of the challenge we faced turning that story into a film, what we have now is something quite different. Indeed, the *I.O.U.S.A.* project took on a life of its own. And thus, as you'll no doubt read in the credits, the documentary was "inspired" by the book. After our first meeting with David, we seized on the "four deficits" he had outlined in his Fiscal Wake-Up Tour as a solid structure for telling what may be most important story of our generation.

The film and this book are largely an exercise in literary economics and consequently different from most of the writing we do in our daily letters, or in our other books, for that matter. As we've seen from our discussions, interviews, and chance encounters across the country, the average citizen doesn't have a clue about economics or the challenges we face as a nation. On average, most think Social Security and Medicare, the wars in Iraq and Afghanistan, managing the "money supply," or keeping the government afloat, are somebody else's job—an "expert" in Washington or in New York.

In order for people to feel empowered to institute change, we decided to travel the globe and go visit them. Of course, the film took us to New York and Washington, D.C. But it also took us all over North America—Los Angeles; Vancouver; Omaha; Concord, New Hampshire; Ames, Iowa. It took us overseas to Shanghai, Beijing, London, and Paris.

We interviewed two former Fed chairmen, two former Treasury secretaries, one former commerce secretary, and two former presidential candidates. We talked to the two ranking senators on the Senate Budget Committee and the first director of the Congressional Budget Office.

We aimlessly wandered through the marbled halls on Capitol Hill, each of us carrying a different piece of camera or lighting equipment. In the same fashion, we politely slipped through security at the nation's largest bank. Likewise, we jabbered our way through conversations with the richest man in the world, several best-selling financial authors, leading policy makers, bankers, economists, entrepreneurs, and civic leaders. We badgered journalists and editors of leading financial publications. For 18 months, we bounced our ideas off other filmmakers, writers, and producers.

Everywhere we went—to a fault, some would say—we asked the proverbial "man on the street" what he thought about our mission, the economy, his lot in life.

In the end, what we learned and, by extension, what you'll read in this book, can be boiled down to one statement: No one agrees 100 percent on what the solutions are for the problems we face as a nation. But that we've lived beyond our means for too long is obvious to everyone. "There is no free lunch," Robert Rubin told us in the executive offices of Citibank. We agreed with him.

■ ■ ■

While we have included some numbers and charts to illustrate what we expect will happen if the nation's four deficits are not addressed, to keep the story interesting, we focused on people—the people who are making important decisions about the economy and the finances of the federal government.

Who wouldn't want to hear, for example, Paul O'Neill, the 72nd Treasury secretary of the United States, tell us, in person, his account of the day Dick Cheney, then vice president, told him "Reagan proved deficits don't matter," or later when he got fired for "a difference of opinion" over the Bush tax cuts. What Reagan proved was deficits don't matter if you, the electorate, don't hold them, the office holders, accountable.

Having written a chapter entitled "The Fabulous Destiny of Alan Greenspan" in *Financial Reckoning Day* (Wiley, 2003), we didn't know what to expect when we interviewed him. But we found his explanation for why interest rates remained so low during the 18 years of his tenure as the chairman of the Federal Reserve very interesting. The end of the Cold War, he said, and the fall of the Iron Curtain had created a demand for capital in the East that kept interest rates low in the West.

We met with Robert Rubin, the 70th Treasury secretary of the United States, at the Citigroup executive offices where he was presiding, only five months before the subprime crisis began in earnest. But Mr. Rubin told us, calmly, how difficult it was to reach "political coalescence" when the Clinton administration showed a federal surplus on the budget "for the first time in roughly 30 years."

Warren Buffett joined us in an unassuming meeting room at his Berkshire Hathaway headquarters in Kiewit Plaza in downtown Omaha. Initially, we believed we only had 20 minutes with him; however, when he entered the room he told us he "wasn't doing anything else today." By the end of the interview we had exhausted our list of questions and had over an hour of film with him.

The point of this particular literary exercise is simple. We wanted to show what Alice Rivlin, the first director of the Congressional Budget Office, meant when she said, "People may think somehow that decisions are made by other people far away, but in a democracy that's not really true. It is your representative in Congress or in the Senate that is influencing what happens—so it's pretty important for people to pay attention to it."

■ ■ ■

As the conditions of the once-vibrant U.S. economy began to take a turn for the worse, the American people seemed to be paying more attention to the country's fiscal challenges. And when the debt crisis gained mainstream attention with the near default of Bear Stearns in July 2007, the *I.O.U.S.A.* project took another turn. By mid-September, we were forced to throw out the whole film as we'd conceived it to be up to that point ... and start again. The crisis we had been expecting was no longer "going to happen" but was, in fact, happening right then. We could read it in the headlines every morning before getting settled in the editing bay.

Having gone back to the drawing board, we were shocked when *I.O.U.S.A.* was among 16 out of 935 films to be selected for competition at the Sundance Film Festival in Park City, Utah, in 2008. At the festival it became clear that the audience was in tune with the film's message, as it sold out every screening and we received standing ovations. *Variety*, the film industry magazine, likened the film to *An Inconvenient Truth* for economics. Kenneth Turan, film critic for the *Los Angeles Times*, called it the "scariest film at Sundance." Michael Sragow of the *Baltimore Sun* lauded our project as having come from a "new breed of documentary filmmakers."

We subsequently took the film to Dallas; Philadelphia; Jacksonville, North Carolina; Oregon; and Silver Spring, Maryland. At each festival the film was received with critical acclaim. We screened at the Maryland Film Festival, in our home town of Baltimore, with the help of festival director Jed Dietz, whose office is a stone's throw away from our own. Jed was instrumental in helping us navigate the early phase of the project. Again, we were encouraged by the audience's response. By this time, we began to notice new faces in the crowd. Former senators and members of previous presidential cabinets arrived and took part in question and answer sessions. We hope they were paying attention.

David Walker, as he explains in the Foreword, was inspired by the film's reception. He was persuaded to resign his post at the Government Accountability Office (GAO) to head up the Peter G. Peterson Foundation. His first act at the Foundation was to acquire the film from Agora Entertainment, the production company we founded to produce the film, and subsequently to orchestrate the distribution of the film.

Through the Peterson Foundation's efforts, the film opened in 400 theatres around the country on August 21, 2008. The premier itself was held in Omaha, Nebraska, with a live simulcast satellite feed featuring Warren Buffett, Pete Peterson, and David Walker. During the two weeks following the event, the film was screened at the Impact Film

Festival, and was one of four selected for viewing at both the Democratic and Republican national party conventions.

The timing of the debut of the film on the national scene and the release of this book couldn't be more appropriate. Over the course of the project, the national debt alone has provided ample proof of what negative compounding can do to a balance sheet. At the time we were mailing *Empire of Debt* to Congress, and David Walker was sounding the alarm at the National Press Club, the national debt stood at $4.7 trillion. We didn't want to believe the $8 trillion the Levy Institute projected by 2008. Unfortunately, their projections fell significantly short. On August 31, 2007, the debt hit $8 trillion. As *I.O.U.S.A.* debuted in theatres in August 2008, the debt spiraled over $9 trillion.

The promises on the books for all of the federal obligations, including Social Security and Medicare programs, already exceeds $53 trillion—a number so monumental it makes understanding the scope of the obligation next to impossible.

To meet its current obligations, the U.S. government racks up another $1.86 billion of debt every day. In very simple terms, every citizen already "owes" over $32,000. By 2010, that figure will be $38,000. By 2017, Social Security will no longer run surpluses and, thus, will no longer help fund the government's other activities. From that point forward, the debt compounds negatively—and in dramatic fashion.

What's at stake? The U.S. government is going broke. At this rate it won't be able to do what you believe it can do. One study, conducted by the National Center for Policy Analysis (NCAP), suggests that without meaningful increases in government revenues and reform of the entitlement programs:

- By 2012, the federal government will stop doing 1 in 10 things it's doing now.
- By 2020, the federal government will stop doing 1 in 4.
- By 2030, the federal government will stop performing half of the services it provides.
- By 2050, Social Security, Medicare, and Medicaid will consume nearly the entire federal budget.

- By 2082, Medicare spending alone will consume nearly the entire federal budget.

At the current rate, it's inevitable: Most Americans are going to have to rethink what they expect from their government. Do politicians need to be held accountable for the promises they make during election campaigns? Seems like a natural. But individuals need to take responsibility for their own financial future, too. Planning better, saving, and investing wisely in private life will make it easier for policy makers to make difficult decisions regarding the finances of the government.

■ ■ ■

We have set this book up in a different fashion than *Empire of Debt* or *Demise of the Dollar*. The first part, "The Mission," can be read almost as if it's a play—a tragicomedy of sorts. It's a primer if you're seeking a basic understanding of the nation's biggest economic challenges, both public and private.

If you'd like to dig a little deeper, we've printed the full transcripts of all the interviews we conducted in the second part, "The Interviews." There is no shortage of ideas, fiery discussion, and inflammatory statements. Some readers will want this book to be an attack on one party at the behest of the other. Still others will want us to throw Molotov cocktails at the Establishment and suggest the United States government is a failure and deserves what it has coming. In this book, as in the film, we do neither. We reserve those activities for other more appropriate locales.

Together, the book and film do provide a unique slice of contemporary economic history in the United States early in the twenty-first century. With any luck, we'll make fiscal responsibility hip in Washington again and inject the themes of the book and the film into the national conversation well before and long after the 2008 election.

Or maybe we should just wait for the next bubble.

Chapter 1

THE *REAL* STATE OF THE UNION

I would argue that the most serious threat to the United States is not someone hiding in a cave in Pakistan or Afghanistan, but our own fiscal irresponsibility.

—David Walker, former comptroller general of the United States

O n January 28, 2008, the forty-third president of the United States, George W. Bush, gave the final State of the Union address of his presidency. During the speech, he was interrupted 72 times by applause. Curiously, the president only broached the nation's deficit once, briefly, and then only to reassert the administration's pie-in-the-sky projection that it will be reduced to zero by 2012.

The president asserted his administration's premise that tax cuts would spur economic growth and that growth would, in turn, help the nation "grow" its way out of debt. Yet, even by Congress's own measures, as of late January 2008, the yearly deficit for that year was already on track to increase by $219 billion. It in fact ended the year at $482 billion more than twice the projection. Those figures don't include off-budget spending for the wars in Afghanistan and Iraq. Nor do they include the so-called economic stimulus checks the president and Congress passed out to American consumers in the spring. The economy in the meantime had been teetering towards recession—no "growth" at all—for nearly two years.

During the speech, the President used the word *debt* once, despite the fact that the national I.O.U. had already crossed the $9 trillion threshold in the same month. By the time the Bush administration leaves office in January 2009 it will have tacked on another trillion.

Debt Ceiling:
The maximum borrowing power of a governmental entity; this limit is set, and can therefore be raised, by Congress.

A complicit Congress has already given the green light for such a debt burden by raising the *debt ceiling* to $10.6 trillion. On July 26, 2008, Congress snuck the increase into the Federal Housing Finance Regulatory Reform Act of 2008, which was passed to bail out giant mortgage enablers Fannie Mae and Freddie Mac and to help victims of bank foreclosures.

A short review of contemporary history reveals that the State of the Union is nothing more than political theatre. Congress has interrupted every president with partisan applause since the addresses made their television debut during the Eisenhower administration. We combed the archives looking for examples of leadership in tough economic times but found little more than sound bites and vacuous promises:

> "We must try to break this calamitous cycle." President Eisenhower was referring to the huge explosion in our debt during World War II.

> "We will continue on the path to a balanced budget." Then President Johnson put his stamp of approval on Medicare benefits, one of the most expensive programs in federal history.

> "We have been self-indulgent," President Ford chided Congress in 1975.

"and now the bill has come due. . . . The State of the Union is *not* good."

"We must act today in order to preserve tomorrow." President Reagan looked earnest, but he grew the debt more than two and a half times—from just under $1 billion to $2.6 billion.

"We will solve problems," George H. W. Bush (number 41) said before failing to keep his promise not to raise taxes, "and not leave them to future generations."

"We need a spending discipline in Washington, D.C." said President George W. Bush (number 43) to wild applause on January 28, 2008.

As we have seen, Congress and the presidents bask in the heat of TV camera lights, but behind the scenes—in the committee rooms and oak-paneled bars of Washington D.C.—it is clear that the process for managing the nation's finances is badly broken. When Bush 43 came into office in 2001, the federal debt was $5.6 trillion. He'll leave the next president—and every other American citizen—nearly twice as much. Meanwhile, the real state of the union—or at least the popular perception of it—can be seen by rifling through the headlines of the nation's mainstream media:

December 4, 2007: "Economy moves to fore as issue for 2008 voters," writes the *Wall Street Journal*.

March 4, 2008: "Record High for Oil Socks Economy" states the *Chicago Tribune*. Gas prices, too, have been weighing heavily on consumer balance sheets.

May 16, 2008: "U.S. Consumer Confidence at Lowest Since 1980." reports the *Financial Times*, noting that 1980 was the last year in which concerns about inflation played a major role in a presidential election.

June 30, 2008: "Expect U.S. economic woes to linger into 2009," warns the *Christian Science Monitor*.

July 1, 2008: "It's a Murphy's Law Economy," says the *Baltimore Sun*, referring to the bursting housing bubble, suggesting that "whatever can go wrong" in the economy "will."

Beginning with revelations that the investment bank Bear Stearns was nearly insolvent, in the summer of 2007, the average citizen learned new terms like *subprime* and *inflation* and woke up to the fact that something wasn't right with the economy.

Enter our first protagonist.

The Fiscal Cancer

GAO: *This non-partisan agency is the audit, evaluation, and investigative arm of the U.S. Congress and is in the legislative branch of government. It exists to help improve the performance and accountability of the federal government for the benefit of the American people, according to its most recent mission statement. At the helm of the GAO is the Comptroller General of the United States, which is a 15-year position appointed by the President.*

"Who is David Walker?" Steve Kroft asked on CBS's March 4, 2007, episode of *60 Minutes*, "and why should we care?"

According to Kroft, "He's the nation's top accountant—the comptroller general of the United States. He's totaled up the government's income liabilities and future obligations and concluded that our current standard of living is unsustainable unless some drastic action is taken . . . and he's not alone."

In his capacity as the comptroller general of the United States, David Walker was head of the U.S. Government Accountability Office, better known as the GAO. The office is in the legislative branch of government and, as Walker stated in the documentary *I.O.U.S.A*, is charged with "improving transparency, enhancing government performance, and assuring accountability for the benefit of the American people."

Three months before the *60 Minutes* episode aired, we'd had the opportunity to meet with Mr. Walker and came to see that we shared similar concerns for the state of the economy. Over the next year of filming and producing *I.O.U.S.A.*, we talked to him in numerous locations around the country. This first interview was at his office at the GAO in Washington, D.C.

"I was set to be career military," says Mr. Walker. "I had appointments to the Naval and Air Force Academies but I couldn't go at the last minute because I had a bad left ear and it kept me out of my military career. I knew it was only a matter of time before I decided to serve my country in some way. And I've been fortunate to have three presidential appointments—one from Reagan, one from Bush 41, and this one from Clinton. It's been a pleasure and an honor to serve my country."

Today, however, for Mr. Walker, service to his country includes issuing a dire warning. "We suffer from a fiscal cancer," he asserted on *60 Minutes*. "It is growing within us and if we do not treat it, it could have catastrophic consequences for our country."

> **"We suffer from a fiscal cancer," Walker asserted on CBS's *60 Minutes.* "It is growing within us and if we do not treat it, it could have catastrophic consequences for our country."**

Fiscal cancer? Sounds grave. What's he talking about?

Let's see. When we began making the film the federal debt was $8.7 trillion, and as mentioned in the beginning of this chapter, that number is growing daily at a rapid rate.

With a number this big, it helps to compare it to the overall size of America's economy, or what economists call the *gross domestic product* (GDP). In February 2007, when our federal debt was $8.7 trillion, our GDP was around $13.5 trillion in size. That meant that our federal debt was about 64 percent of our GDP. This level of debt to GDP ratio is not the real problem. It's where we are headed that matters.

"In addition," David Walker says, "as you'll find out soon, this $8.7 trillion number is just a fraction of our fiscal challenge. And it's projected to get much worse in the future."

But Walker isn't banging on his fiscal responsibility drum alone. There are others like him who see an economic disaster of epic proportions waiting for the United States just around the corner, and who are passionate about alerting the American people. Take Bob Bixby, for example, who is the executive director of the Concord Coalition. We first met Mr. Bixby in his office at the Concord Coalition headquarters in Washington, D.C. "Our current fiscal path is unsustainable," he says. "Most people from the left or the right agree

> **Gross Domestic Product (GDP):** *The total market value of goods and services produced by labor and property located within a country in a given year. When talking about how much debt a country owes, it is often helpful to look at the debt-to-GDP ratio. What a country produces is indicative of the country's ability to pay back its debt.*

Concord Coalition: *A nationwide, nonpartisan, grassroots organization dedicated to educating the public about the causes and consequences of federal budget deficits, about the long-term challenges facing America's unsustainable entitlement programs, and about how to build a sound economy for future generations.*

on that. They may disagree on how to deal with it, but most people think that eventually the fiscal policy of the country is headed over a cliff."

To illustrate his point, Bob entreated us to take a look at the federal budget proposals that were sitting on his desk.

We looked first at the federal budget for 1988, which was jam-packed with numbers, figures, graphs, and charts. It's a slim volume, the size of a short beach read. In addition to data, the document contains a few descriptions of the programs that the president was pushing. Pretty cut-and-dried.

Then Mr. Bixby hefted up the budget for 2005. If 1988s was a beach read, this was *War and Peace*. The budget did have numbers—but now it had color pictures and glossy paper. It "is not what it used to be," says Mr. Bixby, "when it was just numbers and descriptions of the programs. The budget proposal document itself is a kind of a metaphor for what's happening with the federal government."

Fiscal Wake-Up Tour: *Since 2005, this joint public engagement initiative, made up of the Concord Coalition, the Brookings Institution, the Heritage Foundation, and the Honorable David M. Walker of the Peterson Foundation, has traveled to more than 30 U.S. states holding "town hall meetings" explaining why the country's long-term fiscal policy is unsustainable.*

The Fiscal Wake-Up Tour

To help voters and the American public understand the gravity of financial crisis facing the nation, David Walker and Bob Bixby have joined together. They've been leading a tour of fiscally minded policy leaders from both sides of the American political aisle. The group hosts a series of luncheons and civic meetings around the country, which they've dubbed the Fiscal Wake-Up Tour.

Early in our coverage of the Tour, David appeared on the *Diane Rehm Show*, a National Public Radio talk show broadcast out of WAMU, the American University radio station. We filmed their discussion from the studio.

"David Walker, the comptroller general of the United States, is here in the studio with us," Ms. Rehm tells her audience. "For the past few years you've gone around the country on what you call the Fiscal Wake-Up Tours. Tell us what those are and why you're doing this."

"There's a coalition of groups that has come together," David says. "The key players are the Concord Coalition, the Brookings Institution, the Heritage Foundation, and myself as comptroller general of the United States. We have many other organizations that are involved as well but those are the four cornerstones.

"What we're doing is we're going outside the beltway to state the facts and speak the truth to the American people, to help them understand where we've been, where we are, where we're headed. Because my view is the only way that elected officials are going to make the tough choices is if the people understand the need for these choices and will not punish them for doing what's right for America's future.

"The facts aren't Democrat or Republican, the facts aren't liberal or conservative—the facts are the facts. And there is broad-based agreement among the Fiscal Wake-Up Tour participants that span the political spectrum: Our financial condition is worse than advertised and we need to act; we need to act soon because time is working against us."

> **The facts aren't Democrat or Republican, the facts aren't liberal or conservative—the facts are the facts. And there is broad-based agreement among the Fiscal Wake-Up Tour participants that span the political spectrum: Our financial condition is worse than advertised and we need to act; we need to act soon because time is working against us.**
> **—DAVID WALKER**

He continued, outlining the four major economic challenges that drew us to his message at the outset of the project: "America faces four serious deficits today. The first is a budget deficit; the second is a savings deficit; the third is a balance of payments deficit, of which the trade deficit is a subset; and the fourth and most serious of all is a leadership deficit."

"How can this be happening to the richest country in the world?" Diane Rehm wanted to know.

"Well, we've lost our way, quite frankly."

The four deficits facing the nation, as outlined by David in over 50 speeches and interviews given since the Fiscal Wake-Up Tour began on September 26, 2005, would ultimately form the framework for the film and subsequently this book.

The National Conversation

We're in agreement on one fundamental fact: Our current fiscal path is unsustainable. These deficits are not predictions of what could happen in the future. They are imbalances within the U.S. economy that are occurring now. As we write this, in the summer of 2008, the American people are slowly awakening from their easy credit and housing bubble-induced slumber. The problem is that now that these problems—record energy prices, skyrocketing food costs, and an overall weakened economy—are staring them in the face, Americans are generally unprepared to engage in the national conversation occurring concerning these fiscal issues.

As we learned though talking with the average man on the street, people feel daunted and overwhelmed by economics. The simple fact is, we've been apparently successful as a nation for so long that the average citizen hasn't felt compelled to understand what's happening in the economy. Fear of gigantic numbers, seemingly indiscernible statistics, debates over theory, and partisan bickering among the national political parties only add to the confusion. When people don't understand something, they tend to dismiss it. What the average American doesn't realize is that what happens at the Federal Reserve . . . in a Senate Budget Committee hearing . . . at a scrapyard in Los Angeles . . . or even in a lightbulb factory in China, directly affects them.

What we hope to do in the next few chapters is arm you with the language and resources necessary to engage in this national conversation so that you can hold your elected officials accountable for their decisions.

Chapter 2

THE BUDGET DEFICIT

*It's not just immoral. It's fundamentally wrong—
and mean—for one generation to spend the next
generation's money.* —Bill Bonner, best-selling author

I n 1992, Warren Rudman, a Republican senator; Paul
Tsongas, the Democratic presidential candidate; and Pete
Peterson, the former Commerce Secretary, founded the
Concord Coalition. At the time, they were very concerned
about the budget deficit and also the long-term outlook of
compounding national debt.

A press conference was held to introduce the organization in front of the National Debt Clock in Times Square.

"We believe the Concord Coalition will be a powerful
grassroots organization that will say to the politicians all

23

across this country that the American people are ready for truth," Paul Tsongas told the group of reporters.

"Let me be blunt," said Warren Rudman, "the two political parties are unable to speak the truth because the American people frankly don't want to hear it. Because they don't understand it."

"We are now borrowing twenty-two cents of every dollar that we're spending," Pete Peterson warned, "and in effect what we're doing is we're slipping this huge hidden check for our free lunch to our children and our grandchildren. And you ain't seen nothing yet."

The Concord Coalition was founded to warn blissfully unaware American citizens about the growing national debt and fiscal challenges faced by a nation that runs persistent budget deficits. Based on its mission, it was only natural that it was on the hit list of organizations that we included in our film.

As mentioned previously, one of our main objectives in the early part of the film was to help Americans to understand basic concepts like the difference between a federal *budget deficit* and the *national debt*. You'd be surprised how many otherwise intelligent human beings couldn't begin to tell the difference between the two. We also wanted to warn people that running persistent budget deficits over a long period of time can be disastrous to the currency—the dollars in your pocket. We figured, armed with this freshly minted knowledge, American consumers would be more likely to hold their public officials accountable for the decisions they make and the legislation they pass.

Bixby Goes to Washington

"The Concord Coalition was formed to address the issue of federal debt," Bob Bixby says while making his way through the Washington, D.C., subway system, "so I do feel a particular responsibility to advance the cause. Things like this (like

Federal Debt: A Brief History—1776 Through 1992

Today's federal debt is the sum of the United States' annual budget deficits and surpluses going back to the beginning of the Federal government. The country's War for Independence created much of the early debt, and by March 4, 1789, the first day of the federal government, America's national debt was $75 million, which was about 30 percent of the economy. This terrified the Founding Fathers and they acted quickly to pay this debt down. By 1835, the federal debt was $0—the only time in America's history that achievement has been reached.

Of course, the United States didn't stay there for long. The Civil War not only had a large human cost, it brought the country to the brink of bankruptcy. However, like before, the debt was paid down quickly. In 1913, the Federal Reserve System was created to help manage the nation's money supply and to oversee national banks. That year also saw the birth of the modern income tax. Several years after the costly first world war, the Great Depression brought with it extreme economic hardship for millions of Americans. The Social Security program was created to help Americans save for the future. World War II was a time of sacrifice, and while the government took on unprecedented levels of debt, Americans bought savings bonds to finance winning the war.

The large military and social spending practices of the 1960s and 1970s were two key factors that led to a major economic downturn by the 1970s. The 1980s saw the rise of such things as *supply-side economics, Reaganomics,* and the controversial *Laffer curve,* which proposed that lower marginal tax rates would eventually generate higher total tax revenues. The theory did have its critics and the debate over supply-side economics continues to this day. However, what is not debatable is that the federal debt exploded during the 1980s. A fundamental shift had occurred: America was becoming addicted to debt. Never before in the country's history had so much debt been created during an era of relative peace and prosperity. Yes, the Cold War ended, but this came at an extremely high price, and people from across the political spectrum were becoming very alarmed.

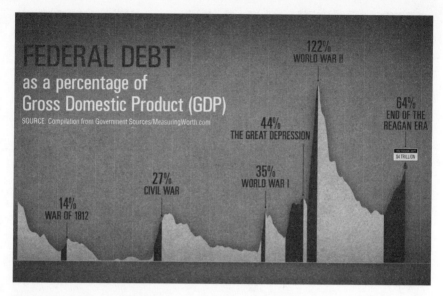

Figure 2.1 History of the Federal Debt as Percentage of GDP
Source: Compilation from government sources and MeasuringWorth
(www.measuringworth.com).

Senate Budget Committee:
This committee is responsible for drafting Congress's annual budget plan and monitoring action of the budget for the federal government. The Committee is chaired by Sen. Kent Conrad (D–North Dakota) and the ranking minority member is Sen. Judd Gregg (R–New Hampshire).

today's hearing) are just a great opportunity to do so. They don't come along all the time."

Bixby is referring to his testimony before the Senate Budget Committee during a hearing on the long-term fiscal health of the federal government.

In an effort to explain the budget deficit in an easily understandable way, Bixby uses various metaphors that resonate with the average American. First, he likens a budget to going on a diet. They only way that you can really lose weight is to get more exercise or to eat less. Similarly, there are really only two ways that you can balance a budget: You can cut spending or you can raise taxes. Not surprisingly, people don't necessarily like those hard choices so they look for easy solutions.

Next, he likens the budget committee to that of a family meeting. He says that the committee is like Mom and Dad sitting at the kitchen table at the beginning of the year, figuring out what the family can afford. Everybody comes to the table with their ideas about the new things that the family needs. Mom and Dad then look at how much income they're going to have that year and how much they can afford to spend.

"The family hasn't been doing too well," Bixby says, chuckling. "We've been running deficits of two hundred to three hundred billion dollars every year, which is quite a bit of money.

"I think everybody realizes this sort of a family budget is unsustainable over the long term. At this rate, the family's going to be in a lot of trouble."

On this particular occasion, four people were testifying at the Senate Budget Committee hearing: Bob Bixby, of the Concord Coalition; Dr. Stuart Butler, of the Heritage Foundation; Jason Furman, of the Brookings Institution and Barack Obama's chief economic adviser; and Joseph Minarik of the Committee for Economic Development.

Senator Kent Conrad from North Dakota was presiding.

"One of the major threats to our economy," began Senator Conrad, "is the budget stresses from the baby boomers as they begin to retire en masse." Conrad quotes Federal Reserve Chairman Ben Bernanke, who recently testified before the same committee: "If early and meaningful action is not taken, the U.S. economy could be seriously weakened. The longer we wait, the more severe, the more draconian, the more difficult the objectives are going to be. I think the right time to start was about ten years ago."

Conrad continued, "We need the will to put our fiscal house back in order . . . the sooner we act, the better."

"We're all involved in the Fiscal Wake-Up Tour," Bixby says, motioning to those who are testifying before the hearing. "Dave Walker is involved, as well. We've been going around the country holding town hall meetings . . . and talking to local media. We are finding the public seems to be willing to hear the tough choices that need to be made. What they want to make sure is that you're serious about them," he added, pointing to the members of the Senate committee.

When we talked to Senator Kent Conrad, the ranking member of the Senate Budget committee, after the hearing, he flipped the coin the other way: "Obviously, if the public doesn't understand, there's going to be no sense of urgency and no pressure on our colleagues [in Congress] or on the White House to act."

> **Obviously, if the public doesn't understand, there's going to be no sense of urgency and no pressure on our colleagues [in Congress] or in the White House to act.**
>
> —KENT CONRAD

The public needs to care and may be moving in that direction.

"There's this perception," says Bob Bixby, "that 'Oh, the public doesn't care about it. These are just numbers, you know; it's boring stuff.' But when we go to our town hall meetings . . . people love it. What they're frustrated with is that they can't get straight answers from politicians, or they're told things that just don't make sense, like, 'We can cut taxes and add a prescription drug benefit to Medicare,' and you know instinctively people think, 'I don't think that really adds up . . . but this guy is telling me that I can have it all so . . . okay, I'll vote for him.'"

> **When we go to our town hall meetings . . . people love it. What they're frustrated with is that they can't get straight answers from politicians, or they're told things that just don't make sense.**
>
> —BOB BIXBY

There's a joke going around Washington that goes something like this: The guy who promises to go to Washington and collect $10 in taxes, then send $10 back to the community, gets polite applause. But the guy who promises to collect $10 in taxes, then send back $11—he gets elected.

Do we really believe the government can function this way?

The Silver Tsunami

If everyone's pointing their finger in a different direction, who is really to blame? That's what *I.O.U.S.A.* aims to find out. Or, at the very least, we hope to get the parties involved to recognize that they, in turn, are each part of the problem and each must come to the table to seek a common solution. Without it, the second-longest-standing republic in human history will fail. That is no small accomplishment.

In the past 40 years, the U.S. government has run 35 budget deficits, and only 5 budget surpluses. (See Figure 2.2.) Lucky for them, at the same time, Uncle Sam has been running large annual surpluses in our Social Security program. Those surpluses are spent every year to help pay other bills the federal government has run up.

Here's where the trouble lies.

If you discount the Social Security surpluses, the government's real track record on spending money it doesn't have looks even worse. By 2017, less than 10 years from now, the Social Security program will start paying out more than it garners in revenue. As the baby boomers retire in larger and larger numbers, the balance sheet of the Social Security trust fund deteriorates.

Beyond 2017, Social Security will no longer help the government pay its bills. (See Figure 2.3.) Deficits in the Medicare

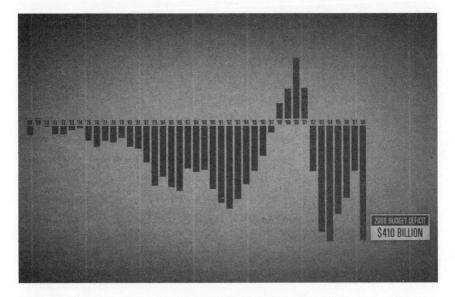

Figure 2.2 The U.S. Budget over 40 Years: 35 Deficits, 5 Surpluses

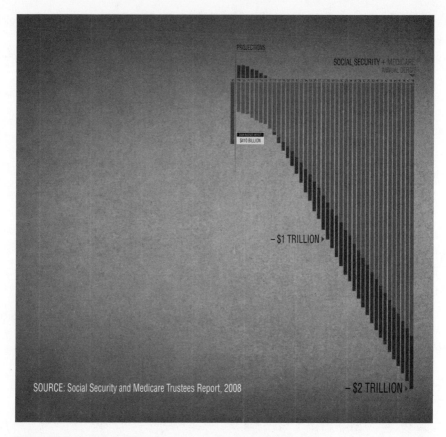

Figure 2.3 Deficit Projections, Including Social Security past 2017
Source: Social Security and Medicare Trustees Report 2008.

program and other federal spending will only serve to make the situation worse.

One second past the stroke of midnight on January 1, 1946, a star was born. The nation's first baby boomer. Kathleen Casey-Kirschling, has had this distinction throughout her life—she even has a boat aptly named *First Boomer*. On October 15, 2007, Casey-Kirschling, applied for Social Security benefits. Over the next 20 years, some 80 million other Americans will follow suit—and the U.S. government is ill equipped to provide for them.

Called the *silver tsunami,* the Social Security crisis is projected to only get worse as the years go on. On October 15, 2007, Reuters reported, "The latest report by the program's trustees said by 2017, Social Security will begin to pay more in benefits than it receives in taxes. By 2041, the trust fund is projected to be exhausted."

The Federal balance sheet is already unsustainable. And the baby boomers have only begun to retire this year. "The baby boomers are not a projection," says Senator Conrad. "They were born, they're out there, they're going to be eligible for social security and Medicare . . . and yet we can't pay our bills now."

Judd Gregg, the Republican leader in the Senate Budget Committee, puts the looming problems of these unfunded liabilities this way: "The only issue more severe than this is the idea that an Islamic fundamentalist would get his or her hands on a nuclear weapon and use it against us. Beyond that there's nothing more severe than this."

Gregg goes on to state that the retirement of the baby boomers represents "the potential fiscal meltdown of this nation . . . and absolutely guarantees, if it's not addressed, that our children will have less of a quality of life then we've had . . . that they will have a government they can't afford . . . and that we will be demanding so much of them in taxes that they will not have the money to send their kids to college or buy a home or just live a good quality of life."

> The retirement of the baby boomers represents the potential fiscal meltdown of this nation . . . and absolutely guarantees, if it's not addressed, that our children will have less of a quality of life then we've had . . . that they will have a government they can't afford . . . and that we will be demanding so much of them in taxes that they will not have the money to send their kids to college or buy a home or just live a good quality of life.
> —JUDD GREGG

These grave warnings from leaders in both political parties have largely fallen on deaf ears, but we believe Americans can no longer hide from them. Simple economics dictate that you may be able to spend more than you take in for a long time, but you cannot do it forever.

What Is a Budget Deficit?

In the 1970s, the members of Congress believed they needed a budget office that would help them look at the federal budget and make decisions about it the way the Office of Management and Budget helps the president make his decisions. So in 1974 they passed a law called the Budget Reform Act of 1974 that set up the Congressional Budget Office (CBO).

The data that the CBO generates, then and now, are the most commonly used numbers in and around Washington. Ostensibly, this Office was created to give the Congress a solid, nonpartisan, professional set of numbers. While there is always some uncertainty regarding the numbers, the CBO does not have any political axe to grind. They work for both the House and the Senate, and they work for the Republicans and the Democrats, and are regarded among those bodies and the press as a reliable source of statistics for measuring the health of the federal government and the economy.

"I was very lucky," Alice Rivlin told us when we met her for the interview in her office in Washington. Ms. Rivlin was the first director of the Congressional Budget Office in 1975. "I was there eight and a half years. I loved it. It was a fascinating thing to do. I loved it in part because I like working for the Congress. It is a very interesting group of people, and the issues are interesting. And I think I also liked it because it was entrepreneurial. I got to set up this whole new organization. That is a little bit like starting a new company."

Ms. Rivlin has been fascinated with the "dismal science" ever since she took a summer school class in economics in college, and hasn't looked back ever since. Passionate about how taxes, budgets, welfare, and public policies affect people and the economy, she is currently an economist at the Brookings Institution, an independent research and policy institute in Washington, which is also involved in the Fiscal Wake-Up Tour.

"Deficits matter," says Rivlin. "A deficit occurs when the federal government is spending more than it's taking in in revenues, and that means it has to borrow money. We are not paying for the government's services we are asking our government to provide."

The government, in turn, borrows the money and passes the IOU or bill on to the next generation.

"Right now," offers Ms. Rivlin, "if you look at the federal budget, [the government] is running a deficit and it will probably run a deficit for the next several years. Those deficits are not off the charts. We have been there before. But what is really worrisome is the longer-run future."

Under current rules, Federal spending for three programs—Medicare, Medicaid, and Social Security—will rise very rapidly over the next few years.

Rivlin continues: "Increases in longevity and rising medical care spending are symptoms of being a rich country. However, we have got to do something about it. Unless we are willing to raise taxes and keep on raising them, or close down the rest of the federal government, we've got a very big problem staring us in the face. We've got to decide, are we getting our money's worth for all of this spending? And who's going to pay for it?"

Bearing these high debt levels and forcing future generations to pay for current programs is at odds with the ideas written and espoused by the founders of the country. "Jefferson went on record saying that it was immoral for one generation to load up the next generation with debt," says best-selling author and friend Bill Bonner. "In private life we don't do that. A person goes to his grave and his debts go with him, more or less." (We met with Bill several times during the filming of *I.O.U.S.A.* His ideas were instrumental in the development of the film.)

"In public we have this system whereby one generation can spend money before it's been earned," Bill continues. "Then somebody's got to pay that money in the future, and that somebody is the next generation. To me that is an immoral situation, and it's not just immoral, it's fundamentally wrong—and mean—for one generation to spend the next generation's money."

> **Deficit:** *A deficit occurs when the federal government is spending more than it's taking in in revenues, and that means it has to borrow money.*

The Concerned Youth of America

The idea that future generations should have to foot the bill for decisions they were too young—or not even alive—to make doesn't sit well with a minority of aware and active young people today.

One group we were introduced to by Harry Zeeve calls themselves "the Concerned Youth of America" (CYA). Rightfully so, the members of the CYA see the deficit spending engaged in by the U.S. government as a modern form of taxation without representation.

"When we thought of the idea of starting Concerned Youth of America," says Yoni Gruskin, one of the organization's founders, "the goal was to be the face of the generation that's going to be affected by the national debt and to try to put a human touch to it."

Concerned Youth of America (CYA): The CYA was created to increase awareness of the United States' finances among the nation's youth. This non-partisan organization now exists on college campuses throughout the country and has been successful in holding a number of grassroots educational activities.

The organization's founding members—Yoni Gruskin, John Gwin, Prateek Kumar, Martin Serna, and Mike Tully—were not your average high school students. In the early months of 2007, as seniors at the prestigious Phillips Academy in Andover, Massachusetts, they took it upon themselves to create this nonpartisan organization to help raise awareness among their generation about the United States' fiscal challenges. After all, they will be the ones footing the bill tomorrow for today's reckless spending.

"It stinks," says the organization's director of communications, Mike Tully. "Our parents talk our ears off from the time we're ten about financial responsibility—this is what you have to do, don't get into credit card debt, you have to pay for what you buy, you have to save your money. Then the politicians who are supposed to represent your values and represent what you want, they just are doing the same thing. They're telling you one thing and then doing another thing. And you want to look at them and say, how can you not realize that this is going to damage our future?"

Specifically, CYA is concerned about the consequences of burgeoning federal debt, and the drain the unsustainable entitlement programs will have on the U.S. economy. They're strategically targeting their peers and seeking to educate the younger generation on the reasons federal budget deficits occur. You get the sense when you talk to them that they've given up on anyone in the older generation calling the shots in Washington or ever making sound fiscal decisions.

"This situation is comparable to my parents incurring serious credit card debt before I was born," says Chrissy Hovde, 23, the northeast regional director for the Concord Coalition, "and through my entire lifetime, and then expecting me to pay for it at some point in the future—and that's insane." The founders are now freshmen at the University of Pennsylvania. But they're building a network of students that are interested in learning more about the United States' fiscal challenges and what it means for their generation down the line. Today, there are chapters of CYA on the campuses of Harvard, Yale, Duke, and the University of Pennsylvania, and they hope to spread their reach throughout the country.

In November 2007, we met and filmed Yoni, Mike, and another member of CYA, Caroline Matthews, while they were gearing up for two events that they, in association with the Concord Coalition, were putting on at Penn. Most of the students unconnected with the movement who attended were more interested in the promise of free pizza. Undaunted, Yoni told the *Daily Pennsylvanian*, who had sent a reporter to cover the event:

"For us, it's not about raw numbers. It's about our future."

"Whenever you talk to someone about the federal debt," Mike Tully told us, "they're always like 'Yeah, that's really interesting, that's awesome,' but that's about it. It's hard to really, really get kids inspired, but I think we're starting to do that. We're starting to get a lot of interest, especially with the 2008 election and the youth starting to realize that they do have a voice. Kids are now starting to take the extra step. It sort of gives you hope."

Is Anyone Listening?

While Concerned Youth of America are throwing a lot of energy at the prospect of getting their peers in the younger set to pay attention, you have to wonder if anyone else is paying attention. In fact, while we were filming in New England, we captured a perfect example of why and how the story doesn't get more traction among politicians.

We had followed the Fiscal Wake-Up Tour to Concord, New Hampshire, and beyond. In one day we did a radio interview; met with the editorial boards of the *Manchester Union Leader* and the *Concord Monitor*; held a luncheon for business leaders and members of the State House of Representatives at the Capitol Arts Building in Concord; and later that evening held a Town Hall session at St. Anselm's New Hampshire Institute of Politics.

Scott Spradling, the political reporter for WMUR TV, an ABC affiliate in New Hampshire, came to the luncheon in Concord with a TV crew.

"Yankee frugality is alive and well here in New Hampshire," Spradling commented, "and when it comes to numbers and crunching the dollar signs, this is the state where this type of dialogue makes a lot of sense. Off the top of my head, it's the type of story that we'll probably put into the middle of the newscast. It's a red meat dialogue, something that we'll try to just bring some attention to—what this effort is, what the tour is—and I'm sure it will get some moderate play in the news."

Later that evening, a major snowstorm blanketed the area. Dave and Bob just barely made their flights back to Washington. Spradling and his cohost opened the show with coverage of the storm. Then the "red meat dialog" of the program covered a man from Hollis, New Hampshire, who swallowed his wife's diamond ring rather than handing it over to the police. The Fiscal Wake-Up Tour segment didn't make the news that night.

Similarly, the members of the House of Representatives did not attend the luncheon at the Capitol Arts Building. They were holed up debating a ban on smoking cigarettes in public areas in the state.

The story was featured in the *Concord Monitor* and the *Manchester Union Leader* on February 14, 2007. But the message they were delivering seemed to have been missed, as evident in commentary stated by Isabel Sawhill of the Brookings Institution and Allison Fraser of the Heritage Foundation.

> Isabel Sawhill: "It's not a wolf at the door," she said to a reporter from the New Hampshire *Union Leader*. "It's termites in the woodwork."

> Allison Fraser: "What we're talking about, the things that need to occur—either restructuring of entitlements or restructuring the tax structure—are going to affect the middle class."

While two local papers covered the story, the exclusion of the Fiscal Wake-Up Tour story from other media points to a larger problem with the media in America. How can the average American be expected to know anything of the budget crisis their country faces when the nightly local (and more often than not, national) news favors stories on the latest socialite to be incarcerated for drunk driving, or, in this case, an engagement proposal gone awry?

The Committee to Save the World

During a brief period in the 1990s, politicians and the media appeared to recognize the challenge and got together to try to fix the nation's finances.

"Our federal financial problem is worse today than it was in 1992," says David Walker, "but back then the media, business leaders, and several presidential candidates made fiscal responsibility a key issue. The country woke up, recognized the challenge, and demanded change."

Both the Republicans and Democrats worked toward balancing the budget in the 1990s.

Six weeks before the 1994 Congressional election, a group of Republicans released a document called the "Contract with America." The Contract, which was built upon a large amount of text taken from Ronald Reagan's 1985 State of the Union address and ideas that originated at the conservative think tank the Heritage Foundation, detailed the actions the GOP would take if they became the majority in the House for the first time in 40 years. Seen as revolutionary by many, the document laid out major policy changes, including 10 bills to implement major reform in the federal government. Though most of the bills died in the Senate, there were a few notable exceptions, including the Fiscal Responsibility Act.

This Act contained two budgetary reforms: a constitutional balanced budget and a permanent line item veto. Those on the right saw the Contract as not only a triumph for GOP leaders Newt Gingrich and Tom DeLay, but also as a major stepping-stone for the balanced budget that occurred in 1998 and as a jumping-off point for the ensuing bull market in the U.S. economy. Those on the left often gave credit to then Treasury Secretary Robert Rubin, Deputy Treasury Secretary Larry Summers, and Federal Reserve Chairman Alan Greenspan, aka "The Committee to Save the World."

We interviewed Robert Rubin about the political coalescence that took place during the 1990s. We met Rubin in the corporate offices of Citigroup in New York City, where he was presiding over the Citigroup executive committee.

"Politics of sound fiscal policy are very difficult," says Rubin, "because the natural inertia in the political system is toward federal programs, most of which are very useful. Therefore the inertia is toward spending on the one hand and tax cuts on the other."

But, the former Treasury secretary went on to explain, "in order to have sound fiscal conditions, it is necessary to not only constrain spending, but to also provide for adequate revenues. What ultimately is involved are very difficult trade-off decisions involving federal programs and what the American people want their government to do . . . then providing the means to pay for it.

"I left Treasury in July 1999. In 1998, the federal government of the United States had a fiscal surplus for the first time in, roughly speaking, thirty years. The projections forward based on the fiscal policies then in place were for continued surpluses for long, long time into the future. I thought that what had happened—well actually, I'm not going to say what I thought. What *had* happened was that a political coalescence had occurred or developed around maintaining fiscal discipline, which is a very difficult thing to do politically because it requires spending constraint and adequate revenues. And I thought we were on that track."

> **I thought that what had happened was that a political coalescence had occurred or developed around maintaining fiscal discipline.**
> —Robert Rubin

Unfortunately, as you'll see, that didn't last long.

What Were They Thinking?

With the projections for surpluses well into the future, the owners of the debt clock in Times Square decided to turn off the debt clock that real estate mogul Seymore Durst had erected in 1989 to show the amount of money owed by the government. "It happened this week," said one reporter, "something few of us thought we'd ever see. The national debt clock was turned off at noon last Thursday, having outlived its purpose. While the national debt has hardly disappeared, it stands somewhere in the five trillion dollar range; it is slowly winding down, having dropped by over a hundred billion dollars since the first of the year."

"When the debt clock was turned off," says Bob Bixby, "I thought, 'This is going to get ugly.' It sends a signal that the problem is solved, and those of us that were looking at the long-term numbers knew that the problem really wasn't solved, and frankly weren't very surprised to see the debt clock go back on again a few years later."

The National Debt Clock: First erected in Times Square in 1989, the national debt clock was the brainchild of real estate developer Seymour Hurst, who had grown increasingly despondent over the growing national debt. By the end of 2008, the Durst family will have to order a new clock because the current one doesn't have even spaces to show $10 trillion.

In July 2002, just two years after it had been turned off, Douglas Durst, son of Seymore Durst, decided to start it up again. At that time, the clock showed the United States government owed more than $6 trillion, or $66,000 for every American family.

Mr. Durst turned the clock back on because he thought the American people needed to be reminded that the surplus of the late 1990s was long gone—and the era of deficit spending was back.

"My father had many ideas of how to bring out the growing danger of the debt," says Durst. "At one point he sent out a New Year's card to all the people in Congress, saying, 'Happy New Year: You owe the Federal Government thirty thousand dollars.'

"When we put this sign up we moved it from around the corner and we put it up over the entrance to the IRS, which we thought was very appropriate.

"The clock we had during the Clinton presidency could not run backwards so we covered it up with an American flag. This new clock will be able to run backwards. Hopefully, we'll get to a point where we can do that."

The Real Pain

When the Fiscal Wake-Up Tour hit Ames, Iowa, in July 2007, we met up with David Yepsen, a political columnist with the *Des Moines Register.*

"The most important issue in the election is Iraq," says Yepsen, "but [the state of the nation's balance sheet] is really the most important issue facing the country. But why should we care? Isn't this money we basically owe to ourselves? What's the effect of all this?

"We are talking about running deficits and compiling debt burdens at a rate that is clearly unsustainable," David responds, "that will threaten our future economic growth, will threaten our future standard of living, and could potentially threaten our national security if we don't do something about it.

"There are no good solutions," Yepsen comments. "You're talking about raising some taxes, cutting some spending, maybe reinflating the economy. No matter where you turn, there's nothing but painful solutions, there's no easy way out of it, and so candidates are reluctant to talk about these ideas for fear they're going to make people mad. It's going to take a crisis before America responds to this.

"This is America. We don't do anything until something reaches a crisis, whether it's military rearmament before World War II or this question now. We're not going to be willing to take this pain until it gets to be a real problem."

While the "real" pain Mr. Yepsin refers to isn't quite here, we've seen over the life of this project an increasing level of anxiety over gas and food prices, employment opportunities, and the sagging stock market. The anxiety over the economy immediately spills over into the political arena. Consumers, accustomed to easy credit conditions and low prices, begin to ask tough questions of their elected officials. They expect answers.

> **This is America. We don't do anything until something reaches a crisis, whether it's military rearmament before World War II or this question now. We're not going to be willing to take this pain until it gets to be a real problem.**
> —DAVID YEPSEN, DES MOINES REGISTER

Solutions

On the budget front, there are several things leaders in the government of the United States need to do to fix the current budget deficit problem. First, Congress needs to bring back tough budget controls, like those in the 1990s. For example, between 1991 and 2002, members of Congress imposed on themselves so-called "pay-go" rules which required them to pay for every spending increase before it was enacted into law. Those rules expired in 2002. Since 2002, spending increases have gone unchecked. The nation has seen an historic rise in its federal budget deficits and the national debt has skyrocketed.

Second, Congress needs to address the long-term financial imbalances by reforming the current Social Security, Medicare, and Medicaid programs. "We can't afford to pay our bills now," says Kent Conrad, the leading Democrat of the Senate Budget Committee. "What's going to happen when these entitlement bills come due?"

Third, federal spending needs to be constrained. America's federal government has grown more quickly in recent years than it has over the past several decades. The country needs to engage in comprehensive health care reform, which will assure that the biggest future expense for America's medical expenses don't continue to grow out of control.

Lastly, comprehensive tax reform is necessary to insure that there are adequate tax revenues to pay the government's bills and deliver on the promises the U.S. government plans to keep.

It goes without saying that all of these solutions are highly charged politically. Addressing the long-term fiscal challenges of the country will only be successful if both parties can put aside their differences and work toward a common goal.

Chapter 3

THE SAVINGS DEFICIT

*Too many Americans are following the bad example
of their federal government. They're spending more
money then they make. They're taking out home
equity loans. They're charging up their credit cards.
They're building up compound interest.*

—David Walker

For two years in a row, in 2005 and 2006, American households spent more money than they took home. That's a negative savings rate. The last time the country had a negative savings rate was back in 1933 and 1934—admittedly not good years for America or the world.

It wasn't always this way for the United States. Previous generations didn't believe that they could live on credit and borrow their way into prosperity.

"Children of the Great Depression," Bill Bonner said, "didn't have the delusion that you can get away with spending more money than you earn forever and ever. They thought that not spending too much was the way to go, they thought that savings were important."

But times have changed. In 2007, the savings rate was again historically low, but not in the negative range—hovering somewhere around 1 percent. Personal savings in the United States only amounts to 2 percent of the economy. In China, an economy gaining much of the world's attention over the early part of the twenty-first century, personal savings is equivalent to 40 percent of GDP.

In the United States, the concept of sacrifice and building for a better tomorrow has been pushed aside by our live-for-today, easy credit and consumption-oriented society. As many are beginning to see, low savings rates can be a problem. In healthy, productive economies, savings result in increased investment, additional research and development, a stronger overall economy, and an improvement in the average citizen's standard of living. (See Figure 3.1.)

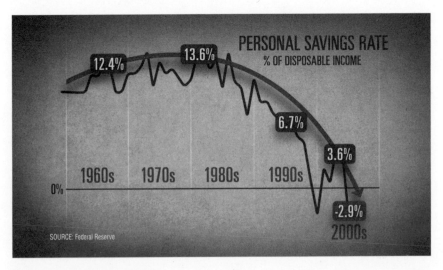

Figure 3.1 Falling Savings Rate
Source: Federal Reserve Bank.

What Americans Bought and Lost

Historically, low levels of savings mean that not only are people spending more than they've earned, but they are also increasingly borrowing money to finance purchases. What have Americans been buying? Since the beginning of the new century, a home-buying frenzy hauled the economy in the United States and much of the Western World. Following the collapse of the tech stock bubble on Wall Street, Americans began to look at their homes not as a place to live, or a long-term investment, but as an ATM. Through refinancing, they believed that they could take money out of their home at any time—and that the ATM would never run out of money. That's all well and good as long as home prices are rising.

Many first-time homeowners entered the market via *subprime* and other adjustable rate mortgages. These mortgages were set at a low teaser rate and the borrowers often put little or no money down.

In 2007, $375 billion in subprime loans reset to higher payments, and in 2008 another $340 billion will reset.[1] Many of the homeowners were not prepared for this jump in monthly payments and found themselves falling behind on their mortgage payments. They also found that contrary to popular delusion, home prices do, in fact, decline.

As Figure 3.2 shows in dramatic fashion, home prices fell in the United States in 2007 for the first time in 40 years.

Many homeowners awoke one day to find that they owed more than their house was worth. Consequently, during the first six months of 2008, 343,159 Americans lost their homes, up 136 percent from 145,696 recorded during the same period in 2007, according to RealtyTrac, an online marketer of foreclosed properties.

There are very few people in the world today that can afford to live like Americans. Too bad Americans are among them.

—BILL BONNER

---

[1]*Bloomberg News,* January 30, 2008.

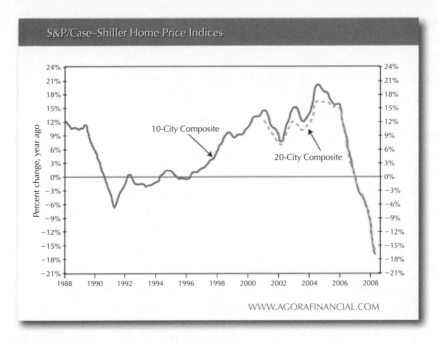

Figure 3.2 S&P Case-Shiller Home Prices Indexes

As home prices continue to fall, oil hits a new record high each day, and the prices for food skyrocket, American consumers will learn to tighten their belts. The days of "buy now, pay never" thinking are going out the window.

But is America's low savings rate simply a matter of personal choice? Or are there also other forces at play here?

The Federal Reserve

Fiat Money:
Money that has no intrinsic value and is not convertible to any commodity, such as gold or silver. It is made legal tender by a government decree.

In 1913, President Woodrow Wilson was successful in pushing the Federal Reserve Act through Congress. The act allowed the government to establish the third central bank in the nation's history.

Think of the Fed as the bank of banks, and the government's bank—the gatekeeper of the U.S. economy. The board, which is run by seven governors and presided over by a chairman and vice chairman, is charged with managing the supply of money and credit to the economy. By manipulating interest

rates and creating money, the Fed can either stimulate or sti-
fle the economy. The Federal Reserve is the primary force in
determining our nation's money supply. The Fed's two main
goals are (1) to help stimulate economic growth and (2) to try
to keep inflation low. These goals often conflict.

The central bank Federal Reserve System has a tremendous amount of power and a monopoly control over money
and credit. The chairman of the Federal Reserve is more powerful than even the president because he has so much control
over the economy. The Fed is the key to how much money and
credit is in the U.S. economy in any given time. This is due
to the fact that the United States currency is a *fiat money*—in
other words, it is not backed by anything tangible, and therefore it can be created out of thin air.

The U.S. dollar was not always a faith-based currency.
There was a time when for every dollar in circulation, there was
a coinciding amount of gold to back it up—a *gold standard.*

"In the nineteenth century, starting with the Napoleonic
Era, all the major money systems of Europe were anchored by
gold," Bill Bonner explains. "All of these countries had gold
lining their systems, so when they traded with one another they
could either trade their gold, or if you traded paper money, it
was certain that there was gold backing their currency.

"And that system was very, very successful. The prosperity
of the nineteenth century was amazing," Bonner continues.
"But that system broke down in World War I; the governments, as they always do, spent too much money. Britain borrowed too much, the French borrowed too much, and then
they couldn't pay it back because they didn't have enough
gold to pay that kind of expense."

Even so, that gold-backed system lingered on throughout
the twentieth century—but not perfectly—and the last stage of
this system was called Bretton Woods, which lasted until 1971.

Bonner tells us: "Prior to 1971, we had the Johnson
administration, we had the Great Society and the Vietnam
War, and those things were very, very expensive. And somebody told Johnson, 'Wait a minute, you can't have both guns

and butter. You can't have a huge domestic spending program, the Great Society, at the same time that you have a huge war going on in Asia. That won't work, we can't afford that.' At the time the Democrats, led by Johnson, said, 'Oh yes we can; we're a big rich country, we can afford both guns and butter.' Well, sure enough it wasn't true, and they couldn't afford that much without raising taxes, and they didn't want to raise taxes because then they wouldn't be reelected. So they had this big problem. And what resulted from that was a run on America's money."

Other countries, especially the French, led by Charles de Gaulle, noticed that the dollar was weakening. So de Gaulle told then-President Nixon that he wanted to exchange the dollars France had for gold. Nixon examined the situation and realized that if France took all of that gold, the United States would not have much gold left, and in turn decided to close the gold window. That was August 15, 1971, and since then, no foreign government could trade dollars for gold.

Money Supply:
The amount of money (coins, paper currency, and checking accounts) that is in circulation in the economy.

Money Supply and Inflation

Now, with the Bretton Woods System a thing of the past, when the Fed determines that the economy needs a stimulus, interest rates are lowered, borrowing becomes easier, and more money flows into the economy. This is known as *opening the Fed window,* and the result is an increase in the money supply. If the money supply is increasing, consumers are feeling wealthier and more money is changing hands as they buy goods and services.

This puts a chain of events into motion. Businesses see increased sales and therefore order more materials and increase production. This, in turn, increases the demand for labor and goods. What happens after that, in a buoyant economy, is that prices of stocks rise and firms issue equity and debt. If the money supply continues to expand, the prices for these goods and services begin to rise, especially if output growth reaches capacity limits—in other words, a bubble is formed. As the public begins to expect inflation, lenders insist on higher interest rates to offset an expected decline in purchasing power over the life of their loans. When inflation is rising, the dollar is quickly losing value, and the Fed raises interest rates, which means borrowing becomes more expensive and money eventually flows out of the economy.

When the supply of money falls, or when its rate of growth declines, economic activity declines and either disinflation (reduced inflation) or deflation (falling prices) results. *Closing the Fed window* decreases the money supply.

In a worst-case scenario, the economy can become stagnant and inflation can rise simultaneously, a situation called *stagflation*. The Fed is then faced with an extremely difficult choice, because it can't raise interest rates and lower them at the same time. It must choose either to stimulate the economy or to fight inflation. This last happened in the United States in the late 1970s, and it proved to be a very difficult time for the country.

The forces of inflation had been picking up steam throughout the 1970s, and the prices of just about everything were hitting record highs. Pete Peterson, then secretary of Commerce under the Nixon Administration, remembers this period in U.S. history clearly. "I was in the Nixon White House," Peterson recalls, "first as an economic adviser to President Nixon and then as secretary of Commerce. History will record that the Federal Reserve was part of the problem. They let money supply get out of control. When Paul Volcker took over he realized he had to take truly courageous action. And he did."

Dr. Volcker's office in New York City is adorned with poster-size caricatures depicting the former Fed chairman as a warrior, battling runaway inflation. And these cartoons are hardly exaggerating. Over the din of the ice skaters enjoying themselves at Rockefeller Center, 20-odd stories below, Dr. Volcker told us of the tough medicine he had to spoon-feed the United States when he took the helm of the Federal Reserve in 1979. Inflation had reached a "crisis point," he said, and in less than a year, the Fed's key rate rose from 10 to 19 percent.

"Inflation," explained Dr. Volcker, "gets built into expectations, and when people think it's going to happen it affects their wage demands, it affects pricing policies, and it has a certain built-in momentum, which clearly happened during the 1970s."

While his raising rates to an all-time high certainly caused some controversy, Dr. Volcker did what was necessary to achieve and sustain stability in the U.S. economy—and found that, overall, the country was ready for him to step in.

"I think the mood of the country was willing to accept action, which ten years earlier they wouldn't have been willing to accept," he told us. "And once the country got caught up in an anti-inflationary effort, while they were difficult years, I think there was a certain acceptance of a willingness to take, among other things, very high interest rates and eventually a rather severe recession, [because] there was this underlying core that the country had not been on the right path economically and that it needed to be shaken up, in a sense, to restore stability. And that faith not only sustained me, it sustained the country.

> **One of the lessons of the early 1980s is don't let inflation get started because once it gets momentum it's very difficult to deal with, but it's also destructive for economic growth and prosperity. If that happens—and right now it seems like there is a little flavor of it—we will all find ourselves back in the days of stagflation and unacceptable economic performance.**
>
> **—PAUL VOLCKER**

"One of the lessons of the early 1980s is don't let inflation get started because once it gets momentum it's very difficult to deal with, but it's also destructive for economic growth and prosperity. If that happens—and right now it seems like there is a little flavor of it—we will all find ourselves back in the days of stagflation and unacceptable economic performance."

As Dr. Volcker suggested, current economic indicators show we're entering a similar cycle in the economy. In the second half of 2008, American's inflation expectations have jumped to their highest level since 1981, according to the Reuters/University of Michigan Surveys of Consumers. Not only that, but growing concerns over the country's two largest buyers of U.S. home loans, Fannie Mae and Freddie Mac, drag down the already hurting U.S. stocks; the price of crude oil hits a new high every day; and consumers are seeing their grocery and energy bills grow by leaps and bounds.

"With respect to the fiscal crisis looming out there in the future," says Paul Volcker, "We'll see whether a democracy can deal with an obvious problem that's going to be present in not too many years. The earlier we take action to deal with it, the better."

The First Panacea

"The first panacea for a mismanaged nation," the writer Ernest Hemingway once famously said, "is inflation of the currency; the second is war. Both bring a temporary prosperity; both bring a permanent ruin. But both are the refuge of political and economic opportunists." As the lessons Dr. Volcker shared with us show, inflation can ravage an economy.

"Inflation is very simple," explains the Honorable Dr. Ron Paul. "It's when government arbitrarily prints money—creates money and credit—out of thin air. When I talk to many teenagers, grade-schoolers, they seem to have no problem comprehending the fact that if you just create a lot of money it will be like monopoly money and won't have value."

Dr. Ron Paul has had a long and checkered career within the U.S. government, including two presidential campaigns. When the United States went off the Bretton Woods System in 1971, Dr. Paul, a student of the Austrian school of economics, was inspired to run for Congress on a platform of a return back to "sound money." He is incredulous of the United States' current paper money system, and believes that

Inflation:
An increase in the amount of currency in circulation, resulting in a relatively sharp and sudden fall in its value and a rise in prices.

a currency based on faith alone, that can be printed at a push of a button, is set up to fail.

He believes that America's system discourages people from saving, because as the dollar depreciates in value, the consumer can't keep up.

"A negative savings rate is very, very detrimental," the congressman told us when we met with him in Washington, D.C. "True capital comes from savings. You should have what you can earn over and above what you have to use to run your business or live on. This should be savings and that should be used to be loaned out to create more jobs and more wealth; but today, the dollar loses its value, and then it if earns a little interest then we go ahead and tax people for the interest they've earned. So in order to regenerate savings, you should have sound money, get rid of the devaluation of the currency, and get rid of all taxes on savings, and then people would go back to savings again. At the same time, we should prohibit the Fed from creating money out of thin air."

During the mid- to late 1990s, Dr. Paul was one of the only government officials who was speaking out about the flaws that he saw in the U.S. monetary system. And when Dr. Paul spoke out, he went directly to the source: Alan Greenspan, then chairman of the Federal Reserve. His debates with Alan Greenspan at Congressional hearings were legendary in D.C. – and Paul was becoming quite well-known, especially in the libertarian circles, for asking the Fed chairman quite pointed questions about the Fed's role in the depreciation of the U.S. dollar, inflation, and money supply.

In one such debate, Dr. Paul told us, "I was complaining about the negative savings rate and he [Greenspan] says, 'Yeah, but housing prices are going up, and therefore people have savings.' I told him that he was getting savings confused with inflation, because as a consequence of inflation the nominal price of houses were going up, but that really isn't savings because as something like that can go up in price, it can also go down.

"Today, because we don't have any savings," Ron Paul explains, "we depend on the Fed, and the Fed creates too much money, lowers interest rates too much, and then they create a bubble. How long has it been that many, many good economists have been predicting that the consequence we're facing is the collapse of the housing bubble? When the markets finally realize how damaging this is and how pervasive it is and how it's going to affect all of our other markets, we're going to have a lot more unwinding to do and it's going to affect our whole economy, because housing is a significant part."

When we met with Dr. Paul in the summer of 2007, the housing market was only just beginning to show cracks in its foundation. Now, in one year's time, the U.S. housing market has collapsed upon itself—and has taken many financial institutions and U.S. home owners down with it.

The society has become addicted to cheap and easy credit. "We've been so wealthy. We're still doing pretty well on the surface. But the tragedy is it's all on borrowed money now. The finances are in such disastrous shape because we can't survive without borrowing two and a half billion dollars every day from overseas. Eventually that will create big economic problems."

> We've been so wealthy. We're still doing pretty well on the surface. But the tragedy is it's all on borrowed money now. The finances are in such disastrous shape because we can't survive without borrowing two and a half billion dollars every day from overseas. Eventually that will create big economic problems.
>
> —RON PAUL

Ron Paul's Historic Love Affair with Alan Greenspan

Ron Paul and Alan Greenspan have had a long and tumultuous relationship, as Dr. Paul took every opportunity to grill the former Fed chairman on his monetary policy decisions, most of which he did not agree with. What follows is testimony from February 17, 2000, at a Congressional hearing on money supply.

(continued)

(continued)

Paul: Good morning, Mr. Greenspan. I see you have stayed on the job in spite of my friendly advice last fall. I thought you should look for different employment but I see you've kept your job.

At least you remember the days of sound money, even if it's only nostalgia, so I'm pleased to have you here.

We have talked a lot about prices today, but for the sound money economist the money supply is the critical issue. If you increase the supply, you create inflation.

If we aim at a stable price level, we're making a mistake. Technology and other factors can keep prices contained, but if you're increasing the money supply we still have malinvestment, excessive debt and borrowing.

Someone mentioned that the Fed might be too tight with money. I disagree. The last quarter of 1999 might be historic highs for an increase in Fed credit. . . . Everyone likes it now because the bubble is still growing. But what happens when it bursts? Can you reassure me it won't?

Greenspan: Let me assure you we believe in sound money. We believe if you have a debased currency you will have a debased economy. As I've said earlier, the difficulty is defining what money truly is. We have been unable to define a monetary aggregate that will give us a reliable forecast for the economy.

Paul: So it's hard to manage something you can't define.

Greenspan: It is not possible to manage something you cannot define.

A Short Visit with the Maestro

As chairman of the Federal Reserve for 18 years, Alan Greenspan presided over (among other things) the "Black Monday" stock market crash of 1987, the dot-com boom, and a minor recession in 2001. He is simultaneously lauded and criticized for his "EZ credit" policies that fueled the housing bubble of the past few years. Love him or hate him, it is clear even now, two years after his tenure at the Fed ended, that when Dr. Greenspan talks, the country—and most of the world—listens.

The financial media gobbles up his every word, straining to decipher what has been coined *Greenspeak*, in reference to his painstakingly crafted and coded language, for which he has become famous. Having such a carefully honed language comes with the territory when everything you say not only must be reinterpreted and reported throughout the press, but also has the weight to impact global financial markets. For this reason, that Maestro gives very few interviews, even now.

That's why, when we were granted the privilege of sitting down with the former Fed chairman, we were highly aware that we had been awarded a unique opportunity. While there were many questions we could have asked him, his opinion on the savings problem in the United States was number one in our minds. What did he think, we asked him, of Ron Paul's claims that the blame for America's lack of personal savings rests at the door of the Federal Reserve?

"The Federal Reserve has had very little to do in that particular scenario, and therefore, Ron Paul, with whom I agree on a number of issues, is mistaken in this area," he told us. "If fiscal policy is lax or savings are exceptionally low, there is nothing monetary policy or any central bank can do about that. All it can do is try to protect the system from being excessively affected by what would be an irresponsible policy on the part of the government."

The explanation Dr. Greenspan gave for the era of low savings and high spending over which he presided was very interesting:

"The issue of rising wealth in the past 15 years or so is essentially a global phenomenon, and one that results because of the consequences of what was seen when the Cold War came to an end. The extraordinary amount of economic devastation behind the Iron Curtain induced a very large part of the so-called Third World to move significantly towards competitive market capitalism, the effects of which are twofold: one, a major decline in the rate of inflation, and two, a huge increase in the propensity to save around the world, but most dramatically in those areas of the world which ordinarily save a great deal but were saving increasingly more. The effect of that was a major decline in long-term interest rates, which in turn have always had the effect of lowering capitalization rates on real estate, commercial, and on stocks and bonds, obviously.

> **If fiscal policy is lax or savings are exceptionally low, there is nothing monetary policy or any central bank can do about that. All it can do is try to protect the system from being excessively affected by what would be an irresponsible policy on the part of the government.**
>
> —ALAN GREENSPAN

Although Dr. Greenspan asserts that there is no way for the Fed to target all Americans—especially the ones that haven't prepared for a rainy day—Fed decisions do directly impact all U.S. citizens. But not everyone is convinced that the Fed is blameless in the current state of U.S. economic affairs. In an interview on *The Daily Show*, host Jon Stewart asked Dr. Greenspan about U.S. money supply and its effect on the economy.

Dr. Greenspan replied: "The more money you have relative to the amount of goods, the more inflation you have, and that's not so good."

"So," Stewart said, "we're not a free market then. There is an invisible, there is a benevolent hand that touches us."

"Absolutely, you're quite correct to the extent that there is a central bank governing the amount of money in the system. That is not a free market, and most people call it regulation," answered Dr. Greenspan.

"And so," points out Stewart, moving in for the kill, "when you lower the interest rate and drive money to the stocks, that lowers the return people get on savings."

"Ah, yes indeed, yes indeed."

"So they've made a choice," says Stewart, pithily, "we would like to favor those who invest in the stock market and not those who invest in a bank. That helps us."

"That, no . . . that's the way it comes out," says Dr. Greenspan, "but that's not the way it is."

Solutions

If the Federal Reserve is successful in carrying out its mandate of maintaining strong economic growth while keeping inflation low, everyone can benefit. However, if the economy grows but inflation rises, people who have less income and self-worth will suffer more.

Americans must start to save again. And they need to invest those savings to help create a better future for themselves and their families. At the same time, Americans need to know that the money they are saving will hold its value.

Too much easy credit for too long can create a false sense of wealth, as we saw in the tech and real estate bubbles. No one plays a more important role in all this than the Federal Reserve.

Chapter 4

THE TRADE DEFICIT

In the last six or eight years, the United States has been consuming considerably more then it produces. It has relied on the labor of others to provide things that are used every day. Because the country is so rich, this can continue for a long time, and on a large scale—but not forever.

—Warren Buffett

lthough still seen as the world's economic superpower, the United States has found itself with a myriad of problems: a skyrocketing federal debt, growing annual budget deficits, an almost nonexistent personal savings rate, and the dubious honor of being the country with the largest *current account deficit,* of which trade makes up the largest part.

A trade deficit occurs when you are importing more than you are exporting—in other words, you are consuming more than you are producing. So the next time you are at Wal-Mart or Target, take a look around. Just about everything you can purchase there comes from another country.

Economists are generally split over what the economic impact of a trade deficit is on a country. Those who defend running a trade deficit argue that when the United States sends money to another country for its goods or services, that country will take that money and invest it back into the United States, in one way or another. In economist Milton Friedman's opinion, having a large trade deficit meant that your country's currency is desirable. He believed that a trade deficit simply meant that consumers had an opportunity to purchase and enjoy more goods at lower prices; on the flip side, a trade surplus implied that a country was exporting goods its own citizens did not get to consume or enjoy, while paying high prices for the goods they actually received.

However, as those on the other side of the argument point out, countries with large and long-term trade imbalances also maintain a low national savings rate. Conversely, those countries with trade surpluses (such as Germany, Canada, and Japan) have a high national savings rate. Those arguing against trade deficits believe that GDP and employment will be pulled down by a large trade deficit over the long run. As goods flow into the United States from other countries, the country is losing opportunities to produce these goods domestically, which subsequently has an adverse effect on U.S. jobs.

Trade Deficit:
When imports exceed exports. In other words, when you are buying more from other countries than you are producing.

Somewhere in the middle of these two sides is the world's richest man, Warren Buffett. Mr. Buffett believes that, on a whole, trade is a good thing for America, but that over the long term, running "large and persistent" trade imbalances will be problematic for the United States.

The Road to Squanderville

Mr. Buffett realizes the importance of having the average American understand big economic issues, like the trade deficit. As a result, he wrote an article in 2003 for *Fortune* magazine, called "Squanderville vs. Thriftville." This parable of sorts was designed to simplify for the readers the problems inherent in trade imbalances.

"Economics tends to put people to sleep," Mr. Buffett told us when we sat down with him in his office at Berkshire Hathaway, where he is CEO and largest shareholder. "And I thought by creating a couple islands with inhabitants of quite widely different activities that it might get across a point that otherwise they get lost on."

In Buffett's story, he outlined two side-by-side islands: Thriftville and Squanderville. On these islands, land is the capital asset, and these primitive people only need food and produce only food. At first, the citizens of both islands work eight hours a day and produce enough to sustain themselves. However, as time passes, the Thrifts realize that if they work harder and put in longer hours, they can produce a surplus of goods and then trade what they produce with the Squanders. The people of Squanderville like the idea of working less—and all the Thrifts want in exchange for these goods are "Squanderbonds," which are denominated in "Squanderbucks."

As time goes on, these Squanderbonds begin to pile up and it is clear that the Squanders will have to put in double time to eat and pay off their growing debt. "Meanwhile," writes Buffett, "the citizens of Thriftville begin to get nervous. Just how good, they ask, are the IOUs of a shiftless island? So the Thrifts change strategy: Though they continue to hold some bonds, they sell most of them to Squanderville residents for Squanderbucks and use the proceeds to buy Squanderville land. And eventually the Thrifts own all of Squanderville."

"At that point, the Squanders are forced to deal with an ugly equation: They must now not only return to working eight hours a day in order to eat—they have nothing left to trade—but they must also work additional hours to service their debt and pay Thriftville rent on the land that they so imprudently sold. In effect, Squanderville has been colonized by purchase rather than conquest."

In a nutshell: Buffett's story illustrates that any short-term actions have long-term consequences that sometimes people don't think about in the short run. This is true of the United States.

"Our country's 'net worth,'" Buffett writes in the introduction of his *Fortune* article, "is now being transferred abroad at an alarming rate. A perpetuation of this transfer will lead to major trouble." And it may be more than just economic trouble. History shows that countries with similar trade and debt problems are fertile ground for political movements we're not accustomed to in a democratic society.

In 2007, the total U.S. trade deficit was $738.6 billion, which is down 9 percent from 2006. Much of the decline could be attributed to a decline in the value of the U.S. dollar. The popular argument suggests that a lower dollar makes production of goods in the United States cheaper and therefore more attractive to buyers of U.S. goods overseas. Exports would go up. And in fact they are, each year.

Some would argue that the dollar is being kept weak to help close the trade gap. "If I could finance all my own consumption today by handing out something called Warren Bucks or Warren IOUs and I had the power to determine the value of those IOUs over time, believe me, I would make sure that when I repaid them ten or twenty years from now that they were worth less, per unit, than they are today. So any country that piles up external debt will have a great temptation to inflate over time, and that means that our currency, relative to other major currencies, is likely to depreciate over time."

And this is just what the United States is doing. From November 2002 through August 2008, the dollar has fallen more than 50 percent aganist the euro. Some experts will argue that a weaker dollar benefits the United States—at least where the trade deficit is concerned.

What is not pointed out in this argument is that a falling dollar paired with low domestic productivity means that the country is consuming more than it produces. In that sense, since the dollar is losing purchasing power, Americans are paying more for these imports, and the rise in these import costs erases any sort of benefits the country would have seen because of a falling dollar. In other words, America is getting fewer goods for the same amount of money—but that isn't slowing down the rate of American consumption. "In the past six or eight years," Buffett explains, "the United States has started consuming considerably more then it produces. It's relied on the labor of others to provide things that are used every day. Because the country is so rich, this can continue for a long time, and on a large scale—but not forever."

Purchasing Power: *What money is considered to be worth, as measured by the quantity and quality of products and services it can buy.*

Buffett likens it to a credit card. "My credit's pretty good at the moment," he says, which usually draws snickers from the audience. "If I quit working and have no income coming in but keep spending, I can first sell off my assets and then, after that, I can start borrowing on my credit card. And if I've got a good reputation, I can do that for quite a while. But at some point, I max out. At that point, I have to start producing a whole lot more than I consume in order to clean up my debts."

The trade deficit aside, Buffett doesn't believe that the economic situation in the United States is as dire as many of the other experts with whom we've spoken have made it out to be. While he warns to not "bet against America" because he believes that we have an overall healthy economy, what does keep the Oracle of Omaha up at night is the imbalance between imports and exports.

"The rest of the world is buying more and more of our goods all the time, but at an even greater rate, we're buying more and more of theirs. More trade, overall, is good—as long as it's true trade. If it's pseudo trade, where we're buying but not selling, I do not think that's good over time."

The rest of the world is buying more and more of our goods all the time, but at an even greater rate, we're buying more and more of theirs. More trade, overall, is good—as long as it's true trade. If it's pseudo trade, where we're buying, but not selling, I do not think that's good over time.
—WARREN BUFFETT

This is why the U.S. trade deficit remains high. The United States is consuming more than we are producing. The country's dependence on foreign oil, automotive parts, and cheap consumer products from China accounts for almost the entire deficit.

Welcome to Thriftville

Although the United States is China's largest export market, it is importing far more Chinese products than it is exporting to the Far East. In order to fuel America's consumption, the Chinese are the second-largest holders of U.S. Treasury Securities after Japan. In less than 10 years, China's ownership of U.S. securities has gone from around $50 billion to more than $500 billion. And the economic ties between the two countries are getting tighter every day. (See Figure 4.1.)

In the past few years, China has become the country to watch. In Jonathan Fenby's book *Modern China: The Fall and Rise of a Great Power, 1850 to Present* (Harper Perennial, 2009), he points out that "in 2007, for the first time since the 1930s, another country contributed more to global growth than the United States. A Gallup poll in early 2008 reported that 40 percent of Americans considered the [Peoples' Republic of China] to be the world's leading economic power, while only 33 percent chose their own country."

And who could blame them? China has been the world's leading producer of commodities such as steel, copper, aluminum, and coal for years. The country has edged out Japan as the second-largest importer of petroleum—and this from a country whose vast majority, just a decade ago, didn't even own cars! The Chinese manufacturing sector is putting the United States to shame—and in 2007, the country had the largest trade surplus in the world (the United States ranked dead last).

Of course, the idea of China "taking over the world" has provided those in the financial media with plenty of fodder over the past three years or so. One such writer is James Areddy,

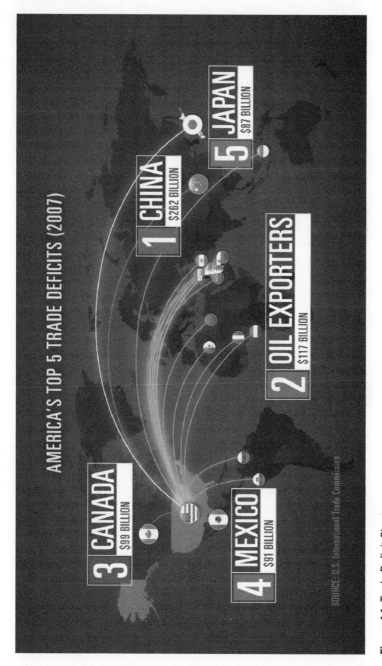

AMERICA'S TOP 5 TRADE DEFICITS (2007)

3 CANADA $99 BILLION

1 CHINA $262 BILLION

5 JAPAN $87 BILLION

2 OIL EXPORTERS $117 BILLION

4 MEXICO $91 BILLION

Figure 4.1 Trade Deficit Chart
Source: U.S. International Trade Commission.

who was part of the Pulitzer Prize–winning team at the *Wall Street Journal* that chronicled the effects of China's rush to capitalism.

"China's probably the biggest global economic story that there is going right now. It affects everything from big business, Wall Street, to down-home America," Mr. Areddy told us in his office in Shanghai.

We traveled to Shanghai, China, to get a firsthand glimpse of this economic boom. The country was bounding with energy. As we walked through the streets, we got the feeling this is what it would have been like to witness the United States' Industrial Revolution. Around every corner was a construction crane, putting in new skyscrapers.

While we were in China, we were introduced to one gentleman, David Chia, who embodied what most would consider the American entrepreneurial spirit.

"I have a mission," he told us, while we drove to visit the worksite of his new factory. "We want to make a brand name, we want to make a good factory. We want to make some nice products. We want to catch up with somebody in front of us. We know what our future is, and frankly, I never imagined I could own such a land and make such a big building."

We noticed something that is uniquely Chinese: By and large, they save their money— even if it means living with a sort of frugality that would never cross most Americans' minds.

While the Chinese may embody the pursuit of the American Dream, we noticed something that is uniquely Chinese: By and large, they save their money—even if it means living with a sort of frugality that would never cross most Americans' minds.

While touring Mr. Chia's existing factory, where they made light bulbs, we sat down with a young Chinese couple to ask them what everyday life is like for them. The young man told us, "Saving money is one of the Chinese traditions. We each make ten dollars a day. After paying our bills, we can save more than half our earnings. We know what a rainy day looks like so we know how important it is to save. Everyone should have a goal in life. Our goal is to live in a quiet neighborhood. Or maybe have a car."

Although the Chinese had different attitudes about saving their money and were much more willing to live a very simple life, without many personal belongings, there are some striking similarities between the Chinese and American people. Our visit to Shanghai showed us that Chinese people are worried about the same things that Americans worry about: their health care, their retirement, and how to boost their income. However, what scares a lot of Americans about China's growing prowess—and the $1 trillion-plus in foreign exchange reserves—is that a lot of that money is invested in U.S. Treasury bonds and U.S. government debt.

"A lot of people worry that somehow China's going to suddenly ask for its money back and walk away from the U.S. economy," said Mr. Areddy. "One wouldn't exist without the other, and I think, increasingly, the relationship between China and the United States is growing tighter—at least economically."

> A lot of people worry that somehow China's going to suddenly ask for its money back and walk away from the U.S. economy. One wouldn't exist without the other, and I think, increasingly, the relationship between China and the United States is growing tighter—at least economically.
>
> —JAMES AREDDY

We Think, They Sweat

In China, the emphasis is very much centered around saving and preparing for the future. We know that in America, the opposite is true. The United States is focused on consumption and living in the now. However, if the country is going to finance its debt and have any chance of meeting its long-term obligations to its retiring elderly or underprivileged, the United States should be hard at work producing more than it consumes. But, as we learned when we visited a scrap processing facility outside of Long Beach, California, that is simply not the case.

Kramer Metals buys scraps—we saw mostly metal and aluminum in the yard—and processes it in a form that steel mills, aluminum mills, and copper and brass foundries can consume in their furnaces to produce new metal. This material then goes to China, Korea, Thailand, and is now starting to ship into Vietnam, India, and some into Japan. This scrap metal is being consumed by what would otherwise be a U.S. mill—now those materials are going to foreign mills.

"We've killed our industrial base," the owner of the facility, Doug Kramer, told us. "We've killed, or are killing, what made us a great nation. We're giving it to China, to India, to all the other nations of the world to produce our goods. We're a net importer when we should be a net exporter.

"The only thing we're net exporting is scrap."

In 2007, the largest U.S. export to China was electrical machinery. Right behind it was nuclear machinery, and coming in third was scrap metal. Instead of producing things of value, the United States is consuming products from all over the world and sending back scrap.

For a time, there was a theory circulating among economists suggesting that the United States could innovate its way out of a slowing economy. "We think, they sweat" was a popular refrain. Unfortunately, there's a lot at play in the global economy. Who's to say the Chinese won't think and sweat, too? As China, India, Brazil, and the Middle East economies develop their own domestic demand, they are less and less dependent on U.S. consumption to fuel their economies. The United States, however, is increasingly dependent on cheap goods from abroad.

The bottom line: The United States is not manufacturing goods the way that it used to. And this is having a very real and very serious effect on the economy and on the citizens'—especially the working class's—quality of life. A recent study by the Economic Policy Institute showed that between 2001 and 2007, the United States lost 2.3 million jobs, including 1.5 million manufacturing jobs. As the China story is illustrating, part of being seen as a strong nation is showing that you bring something to the table. Production in the United States is dwindling, and with it goes the strength of the U.S. economy.

Likewise, as trillions of dollars have been shipped overseas to buy goods, a different, more ominous threat has arisen.

The Nuclear Option

Given the stagnant pool of savings in the United States, every year that we run budget or trade deficits, we have to borrow that money from somewhere.

In the past, when we ran large budget deficits, for example, our government turned to Americans to borrow that money. After World War II, almost all the federal debt was owed to Americans. Today, with our extremely low national savings rate, we have no choice but to turn to foreigners to finance our debt.

U.S. debt held by foreigners totaled $2.5 trillion as of March 2008, the Concord Coalition recently told the Mankato, Minnesota, *Free Press*, and we borrow $711 billion more from the rest of the world than we lend to it. Just as the citizens of Thriftville became wary as their amount of Squanderbonds began to pile up, foreign investors are becoming increasingly concerned with the U.S. debt that they hold—especially as the dollar falls in value.

During World War I, the U.S. government (and, occasionally, celebrities) turned to its citizens to help finance the country's debt that had been incurred during the war through the purchase of *war savings bonds*. While popular decades ago, savings bonds have become all but obsolete in recent years, and direct investments in the United States provide only about a tenth of what is needed to finance the country's debt. This said, the U.S. government has become increasingly dependent on overseas investment and the foreign purchase of U.S. Treasury bonds to finance their burgeoning debt.

Foreign ownership of U.S. debt and foreign investment in U.S. companies in and of itself is not harmful—it is what the *free market* theory is based on. However, as a larger and larger percentage of U.S. assets are owned abroad, combined with a

Free Market Theory: *A market is governed by the laws of supply and demand, and not by regulation or government interference.*

low or negative national savings rate, this situation becomes problematic.

Former Treasury Secretary Robert Rubin explains that although this occurrence is a side effect of the United States' current fiscal situation, as more and more of these Treasury bonds pile up in other countries, "it will create unease abroad and in foreign capital markets, which would then translate back into higher interest rates in this country and a lower currency than would be the case if we were dealing only with our own domestic markets. The bottom line is that it creates a somewhat greater risk of adverse interest rate effects and currency effects than if the debt was domestically held." (See Figure 4.2a and 4.2b.)

"There's nothing inherently wrong with this in the short-term," says David Walker, "and the truth is America lends money to other countries. However, as our reliance on foreign lenders increases every year, one might ask, what are the longer-term consequences?"

In August 2007, the United States almost found out the answer to that question, when China threatened to liquidate

Figure 4.2a Public, Private Debt: Debt Held by Foreigners—1945
Source: President's 2008 budget.

Figure 4.2b Public, Private Debt: Debt Held by Foreigners—2007
Source: President's 2008 budget.

its $1.3 trillion in U.S. Treasuries if the U.S. government continued to insist on placing tariffs on Chinese exports. Basically, the Chinese were flexing their economic muscles. Since 2005, when China depegged its currency, the yuan, from the U.S. dollar, the United States has been on China's case to revalue the yuan, or make the dollar value of the yuan higher. "Instead of a dollar being worth 8 yuan, for example, Washington wants the dollar to be worth only 5.5 yuan," explains Paul Craig Roberts in an article called "China's Threat to the Dollar is Real," published by CounterPunch on August 9, 2007." "Washington thinks that this would cause U.S. exports to China to increase, as they would be cheaper for the Chinese, and for Chinese exports to the United States to decline, as they would be more expensive. This would end, Washington thinks, the large trade deficit that the United States has with China."

In order to force the yuan revaluation, the United States was threatening to impose trade sanctions on Chinese goods. In response, China threatened to dump its Treasury holdings—a move that the media coined China's "nuclear option," since this act would destroy the U.S. dollar. This struck a cord with

U.S. officials who were well aware that the Chinese had them over a barrel.

Paul Craig Roberts continues: "Despite China's support of the Treasury bond market, China's large holdings of dollar-denominated financial instruments have been depreciating for some time as the dollar declines against other traded currencies, because people and central banks in other countries are either reducing their dollar holdings or ceasing to add to them. China's dollar holdings reflect the creditor status China acquired when U.S. corporations off-shored their production to China. Reportedly, 70 percent of the goods on Wal-Mart's shelves are made in China.

"China has gained technology and business knowhow from the U.S. firms that have moved their plants to China. China has large coastal cities, choked with economic activity and traffic, that make America's large cities look like country towns. China has raised about 300 million of its population into higher living standards, and is now focusing on developing a massive internal market some four to five times more populous than America's."

In other words: China gets what it wants.

Financial Warfare

Financial warfare similar to what China was threatening in the summer of 2007 isn't unheard of. In fact, it has happened before.

In the fall of 1956, the world was on the brink of a major international conflict. America's allies, Britain and France, were engaged in a battle against Egypt over control of the Suez Canal, a large man-made canal in Egypt. Russia was threatening to intervene on the side of Egypt.

America wanted to avoid military action at any cost, and demanded that the British and French allies withdraw from the region. When the United States' request was denied, it turned to financial warfare. America, which at that time owned much of England's debt, threatened to sell off a significant part of its

(continued)

> *(continued)*
>
> holdings in the British pound. This would have effectively destroyed England's currency.
>
> As a result, all British and French military forces withdrew from the Suez region within weeks. Some historians consider this the exact moment that the British Empire ceased to exist.

Solutions

Last year, the United States borrowed 65 percent of all the money that was borrowed in the world—10 times as much as the next biggest borrower.

"If fifteen or twenty years from now two or three percent of the GDP," says Warren Buffett, "is being paid abroad merely to service the debts or the ownership of assets that occurred because we're overconsuming, that will be politically unstable."

"It took forty-two presidents two hundred twenty-four years to run up a trillion dollars of U.S. debt held abroad," pointed out Senator Conrad. "This president has more than doubled that amount in just six years."

> **"It took forty-two presidents two hundred and twenty-four years to run up a trillion dollars of U.S. debt held abroad," pointed out Senator Conrad. " This president has more than doubled that amount in just six years."**

"We can't pay our bills now—that's why this debt is jumping so dramatically. It just fundamentally threatens our long-term economic security," continued the senator. "If we don't deal with this, our children and grandchildren are going to have a much different life then we have enjoyed. We'll be in such deep pot to the rest of the world, we'll be dependent on the kindness of strangers, we'll be dependent on other countries continuing to loan us vast amounts of money."

David Yepsen posed a question: "We finance these deficits and this debt by borrowing money from other countries, China for example. What implications does this have for our foreign policy if we're in hock to other governments? Does that give American presidents flexibility to make foreign policy decisions, or do we have to worry about what our bankers think?

Bob Bixby answered: "We have to worry about what our bankers think."

With increased savings, the United States can reduce its reliance on foreign capital and be sure that the nation's mortgage is held primarily by Americans. The United States needs to stabilize the dollar and stimulate foreign exports, especially in its small business sector, if we want to maintain our competitive posture and be successful over time.

Chapter 5

THE LEADERSHIP DEFICIT

After the Second World War we started running budget surpluses and did that through the 1950s and into 1960. Only in the past forty years or so have we accepted that it's a bipartisan thing not to have fiscal discipline.

—Paul O'Neill

Do you think there is a risk of a recession?" a reporter asked President Bush 43 at a press conference in September of 2007. "How do you rate that?"

"You know, you should talk to an economist," answered the leader of the free world, leaning on the podium, and laying on the "aw, shucks" Texas charm. "I think I got a 'B' in Econ 101," President Bush continued with a chuckle. "I got an 'A,' however, in keeping taxes low and being fiscally responsible with the people's money."

Since the Bush administration began in 2000, the U.S. economy has been on a rollercoaster ride. Still, even if the

The Laffer Curve:
The core concept behind the supply-side economics followed by both the Reagan and Bush 43 administrations. The theory suggests that with tax rates at an optimum level, the government can help grow the economy out of deficits. Thus far, the theory remains unproven.

United States was in recession between March and November 2001, a report from the U.S. Congress Joint Economic Committee showed that "the U.S. economy outperformed its peer group of large developed economies from 2001 to 2005. The United States led in real GDP growth, investment, industrial population, employment, labor productivity, and price stability." But, by the end of 2006, cracks were starting to show in the façade of the U.S. economy. Fears that the real estate boom couldn't possibly last forever, as many American home owners had believed, began to surface. The U.S. dollar continued its long, slow slump against other currencies, and interest rates began to edge up again.

Up to this point, the Bush administration was following the economic script set out by Ronald Reagan almost 20 years before. We talked to Arthur Laffer, who sat on Reagan's Economic Policy Advisory Board. Arthur Laffer is most associated with the term *taxable income elasticity,* or what has become popularly know as the *Laffer curve.*

Ultimately, the theory goes, government can maximize tax revenue by setting tax rates at a level low enough to spur economic activity and "grow" the economy out of any fiscal crises that may arise. If, for example, the tax rate is low and the economy grows, tax revenues for the government will increase. Conversely, if taxes are high, there will be no capital for businessmen to reinvest in the economy; therefore tax receipts to the government will be low.

The theory is sound, but even Laffer admits it has its limitations. "Sometimes tax cuts are good for the economy," he told us when we visited his office in Nashville, "sometimes they're not. Sometimes governments behave excessively and raise taxes way beyond what they should."

At the moment, "we're running a completely schizophrenic tax and spending policy," Harry Zeeve, the

We're running a completely schizophrenic tax and spending policy right now. We've got a big government-spending program, and a small government tax program, which is a recipe for deficits as far as the eye can see.

—HARRY ZEEVE

national field director for the Concord Coalition, points out in the film. "We've got a big government-spending program, and a small government tax program, which is a recipe for deficits as far as the eye can see."

The first round of tax cuts, in 2001, were titled the Economic Growth and Tax Relief Reconciliation Act of 2001 and hoped to take the Clinton era surplus and put it back in the hands of American taxpayers. And it worked—for a while.

But by 2003, the United States faced a stagnant economy, falling employment rates, and two impending, expensive wars. The administration believed that pushing through another round of tax cuts, the Jobs and Growth Reconciliation Act of 2003, would give the economy the boost it needed to grow its way out of any financial difficulties.

The second round of tax cuts were, by and large, opposed by economists—Bush's own economic advisory board included. In fact, in February 2003, approximately 450 economists, including 10 Nobel Prize laureates, signed a statement opposing the Bush tax cuts. This petition of sorts urged the president not to enact the proposed tax plan as it would not only hurt the economy in the near term but deepen deficits down the line. The statement, released by the Economic Policy Institute, was printed as a full-page ad in the *New York Times* on February 11, 2003 and read as follows:

> The tax cut plan proposed by President Bush is not the answer to these problems. Regardless of how one views the specifics of the Bush plan, there is wide agreement that its purpose is a permanent change in the tax structure and not the creation of jobs and growth in the near term. The permanent dividend tax cut, in particular, is not credible as a short-term stimulus. As tax reform, the dividend tax cut is misdirected in that it targets individuals rather than corporations, is overly complex, and could be, but is not, part of a revenue-neutral tax reform effort.

Passing these tax cuts will worsen the long-term budget outlook, adding to the nation's projected chronic deficits. This fiscal deterioration will reduce the capacity of the government to finance Social Security and Medicare benefits as well as investments in schools, health, infrastructure, and basic research. Moreover, the proposed tax cuts will generate further inequalities in after-tax income.

To be effective, a stimulus plan should rely on immediate but temporary spending and tax measures to expand demand, and it should also rely on immediate but temporary incentives for investment. Such a stimulus plan would spur growth and jobs in the short term without exacerbating the long-term budget outlook.

In the end, the legislation was pushed through on May 23, 2003, by a tie-breaking vote from Vice President Dick Cheney.

What's the Right Level of Government?

One of the most outspoken critics of this legislation was the Bush administration's own Treasury secretary, Paul O'Neill. Mr. O'Neill has a reputation for having a rather direct way of presenting his ideas and opinions—a trait that would eventually cost him his job.

In 2001, President Bush asked Mr. O'Neill to leave the private sector to join his administration as Treasury secretary. O'Neill, who has had a long and decorated career in Washington, having served in the Kennedy, Johnson, Nixon, and Ford administrations, was initially excited at the prospect of working under Bush 43.

"I saw lots of things in our economy and our society that needed to be done, and I was encouraged to believe that Bush 43 was up for the difficult political things that needed to happen to make course corrections," he told us when we met with him in Washington, D.C., in the spring of 2007. "Those course corrections still include fixing the Social Security and Medicare trust funds, and fundamentally redesigning the way the federal tax system works. I thought there was some prospect that President Bush would entertain the difficult political choices that needed to be made in order to act on these things, and I had spent a lot of time thinking about these things over a period, the better of part of forty years, so I was anxious to have a go at it."

O'Neill told us that he agreed that the economy was up to the first round of tax cuts. When these first cuts came through, the United States was in surplus condition, and on top of that, taxes had crept up above 20 percent of GDP. Historically, 18 percent of GDP is healthy for the economy, provided the government can keep its spending in check. Even more would be healthier.

However, as Bush began to argue for further cuts, O'Neill became concerned. "I honestly didn't think that was the right thing to do because I continue to believe we needed the revenue that we were then collecting to work on the Medicare/Social Security problems," he explained. "To work on fundamental tax redesign after 9/11 while worrying about whether there was going to be another attack or a series of attacks would cost hundreds of billions of dollars.

> **I argued during the second half of 2002 that we should not have another tax cut because we needed the money to work on important policy issues that would shape the nation going forward, and we needed to have, in effect, "rainy day money" for the prospect of Iraq and another set of attacks like 9/11.**
> **—Paul O'Neill**

This was not a popular view, and it led to the now infamous discussion that the former Treasury secretary had with Vice President Cheney on the effect of tax cuts on deficits.

O'Neill tried to warn the administration that the budget deficit was expected to top $500 billion in 2002 alone. Since Americans were paying low taxes now, he argued that their children and grandchildren would have to pay off their debt by paying higher taxes in the future. He also argued that Social

Ronald Reagan proved deficits don't matter?
During Reagan's tenure at the White House, the United States ran very large deficits, and those within that administration believe that there was very little short-term effect on the economy. More importantly, there was no political backlash from running these large and persistent deficits. The government and the American people had become desensitized to the numbers.

Security and Medicare were in dire need. Since the economy was going to be in the positive territory and would likely stay that way for the next couple of years, why risk a budget deficit and add more to the national debt?

At this point in the conversation, the Vice President cut O'Neill off and uttered the now infamous words: "When Ronald Reagan was here . . ." According to O'Neill, Cheney said that "he proved that deficits don't really matter and so it's not a consideration or a good reason not to have an additional tax cut.'"

"I was honestly stunned by the idea that anyone believed that Ronald Reagan proved in any fashion that deficits don't matter," said O'Neill. "I think it is true on a temporary basis that a nation can have a deficit and have a good reason for having a deficit. I think with the Second World War there was no way we could avoid having a deficit, but when we came out of the Second World War we started running budget surpluses again and did that through the 1950s and into 1960. It's interesting, it's really only been in the past forty years or so that we've accepted the notion that it's a bipartisan thing that we don't have to have fiscal discipline."

This heated conversation over further tax cuts carried on until the end of 2002, until O'Neill received a phone call from the vice president telling him that the president had decided to make some changes—and he was one of them. He requested that O'Neill come and meet with the president and then issue a release saying that he had decided to go back to the private sector.

"You know, for me to say that I've decided to leave the Treasury is a lie," O'Neill told us candidly, "and I'm not into doing lies and so that was it. I went back to my office, packed up my briefcase and went down to the parking space that's reserved for the secretary of the Treasury, got in my car, and drove back to Pittsburgh.

"It was the first in my life . . . I've ever been fired before. I'd only been promoted to ever higher levels of responsibility, but it was okay with me. I would have really been uncomfortable arguing for policies I didn't believe in."

O'Neill believes the path the United States is heading down—burdening our children with a massive national debt and soaring deficits—is unsustainable, to say the least. Americans need to understand what is happening in this country, he told us, because the government doesn't have any money "that it doesn't first take from its taxpayers."

"A year ago [in 2006] there was this signing ceremony in the Rose Garden for the new prescription drug entitlement and it's going to cost us trillions of dollars," O'Neill recalled. "This event was not unlike any of the others in the Rose Garden on a nice sunny day, with the president sitting at the signing table with a bunch of grinning legislators behind him taking credit for this 'great gift' they're giving the American people. There was no mention of the fact that this in effect was a new tax on the American people, and we didn't know how we were going to pay for it. It was only grinning presidents and legislators taking the credit for a gift, which strikes me as a ridiculous continuing characteristic of how we do political business in our country.

Medicare:
Initiated in 2006, this federal drug program subsidizes the costs of prescription drugs for Americans who are Medicare beneficiaries. Since its inception, the program spending is running around $40 billion per year (2008 is projected to be $36 billion) and the total unfunded liability for this program is greater than the entire Social Security trust fund.

"When we, the Bush 43 administration, took over, we had something over $5 trillion, maybe $5.6 trillion worth of national debt. Today, the number's $8.8 trillion. That's not an innocent change, it is a monumental change in the debt service that we have to do in addition to and on top

We only need to look at the fate of other countries who've lived beyond their means for a long time you inevitably get into trouble. When you get extended to the point that you can't service your debt, you're finished.

—Paul O'Neill

of all of the other things that our country needs to do. We only need to look at the fate of other countries who've lived beyond their means for a long time before you inevitably get into trouble. When you get extended to the point that you can't service your debt, you're finished."

The United States runs a great risk of following in the footsteps of other democracies that have descended and decayed.

"If you look at what's happened to great republics in the past," says David Walker, "they generally have not fallen because of external threats. They've fallen because of internal threats. Let's look at Rome as an example, which is the longest-standing republic in the history of mankind. The Roman republic fell for many reasons but three seem to resonate today: declining moral values and political civility at home; overconfident and overextended militarily around the world; and fiscal irresponsibility by the central government. You know we need to wake up, recognize reality, and make sure that we start making tough choices sooner rather than later so that we can be the first republic to stand the test of time."

"Washington Is Badly Broken"

Paul O'Neill refused to compromise when it came to making decisions that he knew would affect not only Americans today, but also future generations. David Walker and the Fiscal Wake-Up Tour participants have a similar goal. By warning Americans about what is ahead for their country if action isn't taken now, and educating them on the fiscal problems the United States has, they hope to empower the average citizen to become involved in insisting that changes are made. And from what we saw, the attendees at the town hall meetings they were hosting were ready for a change.

By the time we joined them at a town hall meeting in Los Angeles, after 18 months of intermittent filming, the Fiscal Wake-Up Tour had visited 23 cities.

"It's a lot of fun being able to get out and meet people," says David Walker. "It gives you a lot of energy and it gives you a lot of hope. When you state the facts and speak the truth to the American people, they get it and they're ahead of their elected officials. We can't borrow our way out of this problem. Anyone who tells you we can does not study economic history and is probably not very good at math."

"Here's the thing about the future," Bixby chimes in. "If you knew that a levee was unsound and you knew people were moving into the area and you knew they were at risk, would you stand by and do nothing and say nothing about it? Of course not—that would be irresponsible. Yet that's what we're doing as a nation to the future. We know we have this problem, we know that the fiscal/federal levees are unsound, we know that the structure's not sound for the long term. And yet we're ushering future generations in and saying nothing about it, doing nothing about it, and that's the immoral part of it."

Indeed, Washington is "badly broken," as David often says in his presentations at the town hall meetings and in interviews. Americans can't continue to rely on their government to make the tough choices that are needed to restore the U.S. economy. When many Americans think of debt and deficits, their knee-jerk reaction is to blame it on the war in Iraq, or on defense spending. Some people think that we can solve the country's financial problems by stopping fraud, waste, and abuse, or by canceling the Bush tax cuts. The truth is, the United States could do all three of these things and still would not come close to solving the nation's fiscal challenges. (See Figure 5.1.)

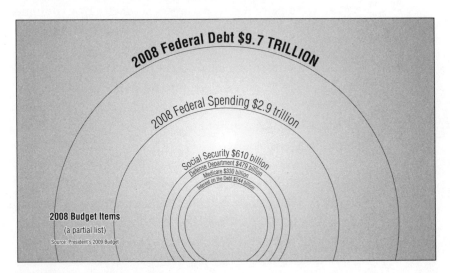

Figure 5.1 Where the Money Goes

The United States already has $11 trillion in fiscal liabilities, including public debt. To this amount, add the current unfunded obligations for Social Security benefits of about $7 trillion. Then add Medicare's unfunded promise: $34 trillion, of which about $26 trillion relates to Medicare parts A and B, and about $8 trillion relates to Medicare D, the new prescription drug benefit which some claimed would save money in overall Medicare costs. Add another trillion in miscellaneous items and you get $53 trillion. The United States would need $53 trillion invested today, which is about $175,000 per person, to deliver on the government's obligations and promises. How much of this $53 trillion do we have? Nada.

"By the time today's college graduates are ready to retire forty years from now," says David Walker, "the only things our government will be able to pay for are interest on the federal debt and some of the Social Security, Medicare, and Medicaid benefits. All other parts of the federal government will be closed and out of business!"

As far as taxes go, the United States would have to raise income tax rates across the board by about 2.5 times today's levels to close the financing gap—and some politicians complain when there is any talk of tax increases. Americans are facing a 150 percent increase in federal taxes if they continue down this road. By the year 2048, the United States' debt-to-GDP ratio will be over 400 percent, more than two times the debt levels we hit at the height of World War II. Good luck trying to get any country to lend the United States money then. No matter which way you slice it, whether you are a Democrat or Republican, the magnitude of this fiscal challenge is much larger than most realize.

For example, let's assume that the Bush tax cuts expire at the end of 2010. That would only solve about 10 percent of the country's federal financial hole. And what about Iraq? Even if the Iraq War ended in 2009, the ultimate estimated cost over time is less than 3 percent of our total financial problem.

America's budget, savings, trade, and leadership deficits individually are bad enough, but in combination they create

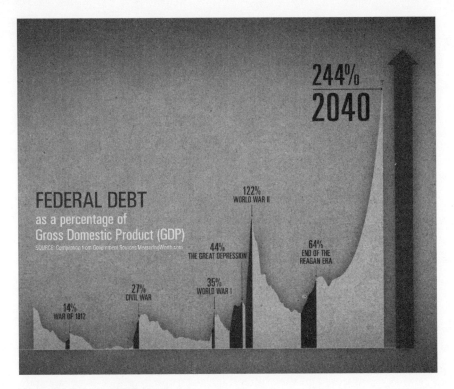

244%
2040

FEDERAL DEBT
as a percentage of
Gross Domestic Product (GDP)
SOURCE: Compilation from Government Sources/MeasuringWorth.com

122%
WORLD WAR II

44%
THE GREAT DEPRESSION

64%
END OF THE
REAGAN ERA

35%
WORLD WAR I

27%
CIVIL WAR

14%
WAR OF 1812

Figure 5.2 Debt-to-GDP Projection

a toxic mix that threatens the country's and each American family's futures.

"And yet," says David, "there is little talk about making these tough choices today. The longer we wait, the harder the choices become. As the baby boomers begin retiring, this tidal wave of spending is about to reach our shores and we are not prepared for it. And trust me, it could swamp our ship of state. Unlike many other problems facing our country, this one is ours alone. We can and we must solve this one. The question is: When will we? As our nation's Founding Fathers said, it's really up to us: 'We the People.'" (See Figure 5.2).

Wake Up, America!

The four deficits we've addressed in *I.O.U.S.A.* cannot be ignored.

Americans need to adjust their expectations of what the government can do. And they should only expect it to do what they can pay for it to do. Given the nation's dynamic economy, many countries and individual investors have thus far been willing to finance the national debt and enable the nation's personal consumption habit. However, should we continue to run persistent deficits and continuously pile up debt obligations, this won't last.

The dollar figures used when discussing the debt are mind-boggling. As of October 1, 2007, the unfunded liabilities of the U.S. government were calculated by the Government Accountability Office to have reached $52.7 trillion. To put that into perspective, the GAO broke it down this way:

- $175,000 per person living in the United States
- $410,000 per full-time worker
- $455,000 per household

By way of comparison, in 2007 the median sales price for a house in the United States—at the height of the real estate boom, mind you—was $217,000. Median income during the same period was just under $50,000 a year.

The numbers just don't add up.

And at the current rate, the numbers only get worse. By January 2009, the U.S. federal debt will be over $10 trillion. The federal fiscal hole will be around $56 trillion. And with each passing moment, your share, your children's share, and your grandchildren's share goes up. Whatever measuring stick you care to use, the long-term finances of the federal government and, by extension, the national economy are dismal and getting worse at an alarming rate.

In July 2008, the Peter G. Peterson Foundation published a "Citizens Guide to the Financial Condition of the United States" to help focus critical public attention on the financial challenges facing the nation. What follows is a summary of the publication's "What's at stake" section, and the accompanying box lists the Foundation's recommended solutions.

- Tax and spending policies in place today lay claim to future resources. Without significant changes, policy makers in the future will—and in some cases already do—have their hands tied.

- Today's deficits reduce national savings, which dramatically decreases productive investment and wealth-creating activities. Increased indebtedness to foreign lenders puts future financial decisions in the hands of people who may or may not have our interests in mind when they make them. Further, interest payments that have historically stayed at home now provide more and more income to investors abroad.

- At the current rate, with existing laws, by 2040 the federal government will be spending twice as much as it takes in from taxes. Just 12 years after that, in 2052, spending will outpace tax revenues by more than three to one. While we're accustomed to dismissing these dates as far off in the future, decisions being made today are all but locking in these outcomes.

- Our children and grandchildren already face a more competitive, challenging, and uncertain world than most Americans have grown accustomed to. Failing to recognize the fiscal crisis represented by falling savings rates and rising deficits is tantamount to throwing in the towel and leaving them to clean up a doozy of a fiscal mess.

All is not lost, though. Bob Bixby, during one of our first interviews, echoed the sentiments of the entire team working on the project. He said, "Some people say, well this is all gloom and doom. You're talking about all these terrible numbers and statistics. But if this were gloom and doom, we wouldn't be doing it."

Some people say, well this is all gloom and doom. You're talking about all these terrible numbers and statistics. But if this were gloom and doom, we wouldn't be doing it.

—BOB BIXBY

The Hit List

According to the Peterson Foundation's "Citizen's Guide," here's a hit list of actions that we should take.

We as a nation must wake up and take some challenging, yet necessary, steps to put our fiscal house in order:

- Demand that Washington policy makers address these deficits and that candidates for office disclose their proposed solutions.
- Rethink our priorities. We should not expect the federal government to do what we're not willing to pay for.
- Recognize there are no easy answers. Economic growth is essential, but these problems are so big, we'll never be able to grow our way out of them.
- Face up to critical policy trade offs:
  - Reinstitute tough budget controls, like the "pay-go" rules that expired in 2002. The government needs to stop digging the fiscal hole deeper.
  - Reform the entitlement programs—Social Security, Medicare and Medicaid—to reign in spending growth. With the onslaught of retirees now beginning to use the system it needs to be more efficient, effective, and sustainable. Otherwise it's going to gobble all the revenues the government needs to perform day-to-day operations.
  - Eliminate low-priority programs to cut spending growth.
  - Reform the tax code to make it simpler and generate more revenues.
  - Set enforceable fiscal policy goals and then hold elected officials accountable for their actions—or inactions.
- Ask tough questions of elected officials:
  - Do they support balancing the budget? Do they support creating a law requiring a balance budget?
  - If they're proposing new programs, how is the government going to pay for them?
  - If they're proposing new tax cuts, how is the government going to pay for them?
  - How do they propose to simplify the tax system?

(continued)

(continued)

On a personal level, here's what you can do:

- Establish a personal budget and stick to it.
- Form a financial plan that considers the following questions:
  - What are my short-term and long-term financial needs?
  - What major milestones do I need to prepare for? Education? Family? Retirement?
  - How much do I need to save and invest in order to retire at a comfortable level that can be maintained over time?
- Put that plan into immediate action—don't wait.
- Be responsible in your use of credit. Save and invest wisely.
- Teach your children the importance of planning, saving, budgeting, investing, and making responsible use of credit.

Source: Peter G. Peterson Foundation, "Citizens Guide to the Financial Condition of the United States."

The Mt. Rushmore Curtain Call

During the course of the *I.O.U.S.A.* project, we were very fortunate to meet with what we see as some of the heaviest of Washington's economic heavy hitters. This is why, throughout the production of the movie and this book, our whole team referred to our interview subjects as the economic "Mt. Rushmore crowd."

While their views on the economy and specific solutions on what to do about the United States' fiscal dilemma vary, they can agree on one thing: Americans cannot live beyond their means forever. That is as true for the government as it is for individuals.

Here we give you the Mt. Rushmore crowd's parting thoughts:

Alice Rivlin: "People may think somehow that decisions are made by other people far away, but in a democracy that's not really true. It is your representative in Congress or in the Senate that is influencing what happens—so it's pretty important for people to pay attention to it."

Ron Paul: "We can't afford to pay all these bills, and if we just pay for these bills by printing money, it will destroy the currency—and that will be a much, much more painful reaction than us just tightening our belts and living within our means."

Warren Buffett: "I do think that piling up more and more and more external debt and having the rest of the world own more and more of the United States may create real political instability down the line and increase the possibly that demagogues come along and do some very foolish things."

Peter G. Peterson: "Has something fundamental happened to the character of our people or our societal structure, or has no one stepped up to provide the leadership? We're not going to know that until we try."

Alan Greenspan: "What these various different deficits are suggesting is that we are trying to consume more than we produce. We can do that in the short run, but over the long run, it is a course impossible. Without savings, there is no future."

Without savings, there is no future.
—ALAN GREENSPAN

Bill Bonner: "In America we're spending debt; in foreign countries they're creating goods and services, they're building economies, they're building factories. They are creating real wealth in China, in India; but in America it's kind of a phony wealth, it's a wealth we get by spending money we don't really have, for things we don't need. And it's putting us in the hole, rather than putting us ahead of things."

Paul Volcker: "We don't want to have to go through big recessions to teach lessons. We'd like to anticipate what needs to be done while maintaining the growth of the economy. And the threat always is an unstable economy, an unstable currency; and that it's destructive not just to economic life, but it can be destructive of America's position in the world, which is a concern to me more generally."

Paul O'Neill: "We need presidents who are so devoted to doing the right thing with and for the American people, that they're prepared to lose for their values and to hang their values out in public for everyone to see them."

Robert Rubin: "It's actually not that complicated. You know there's this old saying, 'There's no free lunch.' I think that almost captures the whole thing. Just as for an individual in the final analysis, there is no free lunch, there's no free lunch for a national economy."

EPILOGUE

When you have children, you want to see them grow up and have the best possible chance to succeed in life. You raise them with values and send them off to college. When they leave, it's a painful experience, but you hope they're equipped to make good choices and meet good people.

In this case, we sent our film to the best Ivy League school in the nation. A week before the Vancouver conference, the film was acquired by the Peter G. Peterson Foundation. Pete Peterson, the founder, is the CEO of the private equity firm Blackstone. Last year, when Blackstone offered a piece of itself up to the public, the Chinese sovereign wealth fund bought about 10 percent of the company. Pete's share of the offering was $3 billion, $1 billion of which he's donated to the Foundation. Its mission, among other things, is to rein in rampant waste, fraud, and irresponsibility in the federal government.

Further, Pete wooed David Walker away from his post as the comptroller general of the federal government—the nation's top accountant—to help create the foundation. David agreed to take the job and left the GAO on March 11, 2008. His first act as the CEO of the Peter G. Peterson Foundation was to buy and orchestrate distribution for our film.

Upon announcing his resignation, David Walker explained his reasons for leaving the government during an interview with Federal News Radio. His thoughts follow:

Reporter: "You will remain comptroller general of the United States until mid-March, is that right?

David Walker: Yes, I love my job as the comptroller general and I love the GAO, and by working together with my colleges here we've made a huge difference in the nine and a half years that I've been here. At the same point and time I believe that our country is at a critical crossroads. There are practical limits as to what I can do as the comptroller general. I can't advocate specific policy solutions. I can't be as aggressively involved in grassroots efforts as I think will be necessary in order to achieve meaningful and lasting change."

Reporter: "Tell us about the Peterson Foundation."

David: "Well, I'm going to be creating this foundation from scratch to make a difference for this country. The mission of the foundation is to get the message to millions of Americans and to propose sensible and workable solutions to address these challenges and to build public will to do something about them. I'm still going to be involved in the Fiscal Wake-Up Tour. You know, generals don't leave the fight, but sometimes they change their position on the battlefield. And that's what I'm doing. . . .

"It was a very difficult decision for me. It's something that really has just come together in the past month because I'm very concerned about the future of our country and I think I'm going to be able to make a bigger difference 'cause we're going to need some more aggressive and alternative tactics to achieve change in Washington. 'Cause Washington is badly broken.

"This is about the future of our country, our children, and our grandchildren, and ultimately I'd like to think that politicians will rise above partisan politics to do what's right for the country."

Part Two
THE INTERVIEWS

THE INTERVIEWS

We interviewed two former Fed chairmen, two former Treasury secretaries, one former commerce secretary, and two former presidential candidates. We talked to the two ranking senators on the Senate Budget Committee and the first director of the Congressional Budget Office. We talked to the richest man in the world, several best-selling financial authors, leading policy makers, bankers, and businessmen. We talked to journalists and editors of leading financial publications.

We came to refer to the list of experts who agreed to sit for the movie interviews as the "Mt. Rushmore Crowd" for their contribution to American economics. Those who accepted, frankly, exceeded our expectations. Because they gave us a wide range of opinions far beyond the scope of the film, we've published the complete transcripts of their interviews right here in this book.

Although this group of economic heavy hitters comes from a wide range of educational backgrounds, political persuasions, and economic training, something the illustrious cast of *I.O.U.S.A.* can see eye-to-eye on is this: The U.S. economy cannot sustain its current path. And if we don't do something now, our children and grandchildren are going to have to pay for our mistakes.

Featured Interviews

Alice Rivlin

William Bonner

Robert Rubin

Peter G. Peterson

Ron Paul

Paul A. Volcker

Dr. Alan Greenspan

Warren Buffett

James Areddy

Paul O'Neill

Bonus Interviews

Arthur Laffer

Steve Forbes

Alice Rivlin

Alice Rivlin has been surprising teachers and peers since college, when she switched majors to study economics after taking a summer school class. Known as a "deficit hawk" with Robert Rubin on the team that balanced the budget during the Clinton Administration, she served as the first director in 1975 of the Congressional Budget Office, an impartial, quasi-governmental agency created by the Congress as a source of reliable, untainted numbers on the economy. Today she works at the Brookings Institution, a liberal think tank in Washington, D.C.

Q: The field of economics feels like a very male-dominated world. How did you get into this?

Alice Rivlin: I got into economics sort of by accident, but maybe everybody does. I took a course in summer school, when I was between my freshman and sophomore year, and I loved it. I had a charismatic teacher who was very good at explaining, and sort of turned us all on to economics. And then I went back to my regular college and said, "Here I am. I want to major in economics." And I did.

Q: What is it about economics that you find interesting?

Alice Rivlin: Well, I think what fascinated me is not so much economics, per se, but public policy. I really care about how things like taxes and budgets and policies on welfare or health policy, how they affect people and how they affect the economy.

Q: Do you ever feel that the American economy and the world economy are something you are never really going to completely figure out? Is that part of what makes it appealing, or is that part of what makes it frustrating?

Alice Rivlin: I do not think anybody thinks they can figure out everything in economics. It is very complicated. Economies are complicated. They are the result of what individual people and companies do. And nobody is ever going to be able to predict that absolutely. But that is why it is interesting. In a way, I think it is like medicine. The human body is very complicated, and doctors are always trying to figure it out, and they are never certain. And that is why economics is interesting to me.

Q: You were the first director at the CBO. How did that come to be?

Alice Rivlin: The Congressional Budget Office, which has been around now for quite a long time, more than 30 years, was brand-new in 1975. The Congress did not have a budget office that helped them look at the federal budget and make decisions about it the way the Office of Management and Budget helps the president make his decisions. So they thought they needed one. They passed a law called the Budget Reform Act of 1974 that set up the Congressional Budget Office. And I was very lucky; I got to be the first director of that office. I was there eight and a half years. I loved it. It was a fascinating thing to do. I loved it in part because I like working for the Congress. It is a very interesting group of people, and the issues are interesting. And I think I also liked it because it was entrepreneurial. I got to set up this whole new organization. That is a little bit like starting a new company.

Q: Let's jump ahead to 1993 and the Clinton administration. What was your title during the Clinton administration, and can you explain to me how the policy was determined in January of 1993? How did that battle go about, and how do you feel the results turned out?

Alice Rivlin: In early 1993, I was the Clinton administration's designated deputy director of the Office of Management and Budget. The first director was Leon Panetta. Somewhat later he became Chief of Staff for the president, and I became the Office of Management and Budget director. But in the early period, even before the inauguration, when we were working out of Little Rock, we were really focused, the whole economic team was focused on what the president thought was the highest priority: Figure out what I am going to do about the budget. The budget was in deficit, [and] everybody was worried about it. We knew that if it stayed on the track that it was on, that the budget deficits would keep rising. We would have to borrow more and more money. And we would be paying higher interest rates on that government debt. So it was a high priority among the economic team to figure out how we were going to get the budget deficit to come down. We had a lot of discussion about how fast it should come down.

The president had made promises during the campaign. He had said he was going to have a big infrastructure program to improve roads and bridges. He had said that he was going to have a middle-class tax cut. He had said that he was going to do health care reform which, indeed, he tried to do. And that he was going to do welfare reform, which eventually we did achieve. But we could not figure out exactly how we were going to do all of that and still have the budget deficit coming down. So we had a lot of discussions about it, first around a big table in the Governor's Mansion in Little Rock, and later around an even bigger table in the White House. And there was controversy within the Clinton team about how fast the budget deficit could come down. I was one of the so-called hawks, along with Bob Rubin and Secretary Benson at Treasury, and Leon Panetta. We all thought that getting the budget deficit down was extremely important to the future of the economy, and that making a strong move on the budget deficit would bring interest rates down. So we were focused on that. Others were focused on two things: One was whether the president's campaign promises could be paid for. And the other was whether bringing the deficit down too quickly would be bad for the economy, because we thought that the recovery from the recession was a bit shaky, and nobody wanted to derail the economy and bring it to a screeching halt. As it turned out, the economic recovery was actually stronger than we thought it was going to be. So we were not skating on quite as thin ice as we thought. But that was a worry.

Q: Are you proud of what you were able to accomplish as a team and as an individual?

Alice Rivlin: I am extremely proud of what happened as a result of the Clinton budget reform. We made some really hard decisions in 1993. The president was very much into it. We spent hours and hours in the Roosevelt Room in the White House with the president discussing how we were going to cut spending, and what we were going to do about taxes. We put together a package that passed the Congress with great difficulty, by one vote in each house. That was a squeaker. But in retrospect, it worked. Interest rates came down, and the economy improved. I am not saying that was all because of the Clinton plan, but it certainly helped. And by about four years later, we not only had a balanced budget, the budget was moving into very substantial surplus.

Q: Can you tell me, was it just the White House that was able to get those victories in the late 1990s? Or did you benefit from having a Republican-led Congress, and if so, how?

Alice Rivlin: I think almost all progress on fiscal responsibility has been as a result of a bipartisan compromise. That was quite obvious in 1990, when President Bush Sr. made a deal with the Democratic Congress to reduce the budget deficit and to put in place some rules about how the Congress could consider the budget. And it was even more obvious, I think, in 1997, when the Clinton administration had to cut a deal with the Republican Congress to keep progress on the deficit going. It was not fun. It was a very difficult negotiation that went on for several years, actually, between the Republican-led Congress and the Democratic Clinton administration, with the president vetoing frequently and using the veto as a weapon. But we cut a deal. And the Budget Act of 1997 was the one that really pushed the budget from deficit into substantial surplus.

Q: On the Fiscal Wake-up Tour, and just around Washington in general, there are many sets of numbers that refer to the same thing. Why is it that the numbers generated by the CBO

tend to be the most commonly used numbers in and around Washington?

Alice Rivlin: The Congressional Budget Office was created to give the Congress a solid, nonpartisan, professional set of numbers. And it has existed for more than 30 years through lots of different administrations, but working for the Congress. The [CBO] produce the best numbers that they can. There is always some uncertainty, but they do not have any political axe to grind. They work for both the House and the Senate, and they work for the Republicans and the Democrats. So their charge is, just give us the best numbers that you possibly can. It is not that they do not ever make mistakes, but they are a reliable source.

Q: So did you ever have a congressman or senator call you after a report and say, "These numbers just do not help me at all"?

Alice Rivlin: When I was running the CBO, now quite a long time ago, there were lots of controversies. It was during several presidencies, of Ford, Carter, and the beginning of Reagan. So there were different administrations and different control in the Congress. And I thought it was a success when we were being criticized from both sides. And it often happened that we were cited. The CBO's report was cited in a debate over energy policy or defense policy or health policy, on both sides or several sides of the argument. And that I considered was a success because we were raising the content of the argument to a higher level.

Q: Numerically speaking, what does life look like in a recession as opposed to what life looks like during economic growth and good times?

Alice Rivlin: From a budgetary point of view, recession is a very difficult thing. Now, it is difficult for everybody. People lose their jobs and companies cannot make a profit in a recession because they are not selling as much. But from the point of view of the federal budget, the result is since people are not earning as much, they are not paying as much tax, and some of the programs that the government has actually increase automatically when there is a recession—unemployment compensation, for example. More people are making unemployment compensation claims because more people are out of work. So that spending goes up, and the tax revenues go down, and you have an automatic larger deficit in a recession.

Q: In a recession, what are the key numbers that you are looking for and hoping not to see?

Alice Rivlin: The thing that economists watch all the time is the unemployment rate—how many people are losing their jobs. If the unemployment rate is going up, clearly, that is bad. It is not always the first sign of a recession. Sometimes a recession will start with profits going down, and sales going down. Those things happen before the job layoffs happen. But the thing that is hardest on most people, of course, is a rise in the unemployment rate.

Q: Let's imagine for a moment, though, it is 1999 and 2000. If someone were to tell you what our federal debt would be, and what our deficit would be today, would you be surprised? Can you characterize the road that we have been on financially for the past six or seven years?

Alice Rivlin: In the late 1990s, the economy was growing very strongly. The stock market was rising fast—as it turned out, too fast. And all kinds of signs in the economy were positive. Unemployment was very low. And even with low unemployment we did not have much inflation. So the whole economy looked very, very good. And the federal budget looked terrific. It had a large surplus in those years in the late 1990s. It had such a large surplus that people were even beginning to worry about the surplus. My then colleague Alan Greenspan worried that the surplus was so large that we would pay off the whole national debt. I never thought that was a very serious worry, but he was genuinely worried about it.

Q: Why would that be a problem?

Alice Rivlin: Well, he thought it would be a problem because then if the government kept running a surplus, it would have to buy private securities. And that would mean that the government would end up owning bonds of states or corporations or even conceivably stock. I did not think we would ever get to that point, so I was not worried about it. But that was what was concerning him, or that is what he said at the time.

Q: But wasn't there a flip side to that argument that we should be bolstering our entitlement programs?

Alice Rivlin: Well, when we were running a surplus in the federal budget, [that] was exactly the moment when we should have taken strong measures to shore up the Social Security system. And, indeed, President Clinton suggested that. He had a slogan for it: "Save Social Security First." He wanted to invest in the Social Security system to make sure that it was solvent for the future, before we cut taxes or did anything else with this surplus. And in retrospect, that was a very good idea. But we did not do it. People were not sufficiently concerned about the future to take the prudent measures that we should have taken to invest in the future so that we would have plenty of money to pay for the benefits that we know are going to be needed as the baby boom generation retires.

Q: It seems there is a different song that people are singing today, seven or eight years later. How would you characterize the road that we are on? Are we heading toward some severe financial difficulties?

Alice Rivlin: Right now, if you look at the federal budget, it is running a deficit and it will probably run a deficit for the next several years. Those deficits in the near term—the next three, four, five years—are not huge. They are not off the charts. We have been there before. But what is really worrisome is the longer-run future. If you look at just three programs, Medicare, Medicaid, and Social Security, the spending for those programs under current rules will rise very rapidly over the next few years—indeed, for the foreseeable future. And that is for two reasons. It is mostly because the medical programs are growing, because we are all using more medical care, more medical care per person, per patient, per anything. That has been growing over several decades, and will continue to grow.

The other aspect is the baby boom generation retirement, and the fact that we are all living longer. That is the thing that most people emphasize, but it is not actually the most important thing. It is part of the problem of federal spending going up in the future, but the medical care programs are going up even faster, and they are the biggest part of the problem. What that means is that since spending on those programs will go up automatically unless we change the rules, we will have to do something. The spending on those three programs by sometime in the 2030s is likely to be about one-fifth of everything we produce. Now, one-fifth of everything we produce is about what we now spend to finance the whole federal government. So unless we are willing to raise taxes and keep on raising them, or close down the rest of the federal government, we have got a very big problem staring us in the face in the next couple of decades.

Q: Is there a solution, and what does that solution look like? A lot of people think it is almost hopeless. How do we dig our way out of this?

Alice Rivlin: I do not think anyone should see the fiscal future as hopeless. In the first place, we are not the only country with this problem. Everybody is facing rising medical care spending. That is true all over the world. And all successful countries are facing an aging population, people living longer. So these things are part of life in all kinds of countries. And we have a good, functioning democracy. We can get together and solve these problems. We are not a poor country—it would be much harder if we were. We are a rich country. And increases in longevity and rising medical care spending are symptoms of being a rich country. However, we have got to do something about it. We have got to decide, are we getting our money's worth for all of this spending? And who is going to pay for it? And we have to figure out how to balance the federal budget in the long run, or come very close to balancing it, because if we do not, we will just keep on borrowing, and passing the bill on to future generations who did not create this problem.

Moreover, we cannot borrow that much. We can borrow $200 billion a year as we are now doing. The rest of the world seems quite willing to lend us that much money. But when we get to the really big deficits of the future, nobody is going to be willing to lend us that much money. So we are going to have to figure out what to do.

Q: What is a deficit and do they matter?

Alice Rivlin: I think deficits matter. A deficit occurs when the federal government is spending more than it is taking in revenue. And that means it has to borrow money. Now, right now we are borrowing some $200 billion a year. That means we are not paying for the government services we are asking our government to provide. We are borrowing the money and passing that bill on to our grandchildren. Now, I do not think that is a moral thing to do. I think the real reason to not run a deficit is that it is not fair to our grandchildren or our children, future taxpayers, whoever they are, to pass them the bill for the things we want to do now. Economically, it is also risky. If you borrow a lot of money, then you have to pay interest on it. The interest becomes a bigger and bigger percentage of what the government spends, and that is really wasted money. You do not get anything for it. And then there is the problem that people might not want to go on lending to the United States government forever. Now, much of our borrowing is from other countries, particularly from central banks in Asia, who are willing to lend us large amounts of money—but they might not be willing to do that for a long time. If they begin lending us less, then we would be in some economic trouble. Interest rates would go up. We would have to pay more to borrow from somebody else, and if it really got out of hand, we might have a spike in interest rates and a recession.

Q: How would you characterize the U.S. economy in comparison to other economies around the world? Where do we fit into that?

Alice Rivlin: Well, the U.S. economy is just a word for everything that everybody does, that is production or sale or getting paid for what you do. It adds up to everybody's spending, whether you are an individual or a corporation, or a nonprofit institution.

The U.S. economy is the largest and most productive in the world. It has really been quite amazing. We have a higher standard of living than most other countries. And we have continued over a long period to be very productive.

Q: **Are you hopeful that the economy is going to stay strong, and it is going to provide benefits to people who live here? Or are you concerned about the challenges that lie ahead? How do you characterize them?**

Alice Rivlin: I am an optimist about the American economy. We have done very well for a long time. We have some threats at the moment. One of them, I think, is that we have made more promises to older people than we can afford to pay for, unless we change the rules. I think we will change the rules, or we will raise taxes, or we will do some of each. I am also worried about the distribution of income, about the fact that some people make a lot of money, and some people are struggling just to make ends meet. And those differences have widened over the past few years. I think that is not good for us. We should make it easier for people at the bottom of the income distribution to make a good living and to have jobs where they earn a living wage. But in general, this is a very strong economy.

Q: **Why should someone who lives in this country, and has no interaction with the government or in, say, Wall Street, know about economics and the federal government and how they work? Why should they care about it?**

Alice Rivlin: Everyone should care about what their government is doing because it affects their lives very directly. If taxes go up or if spending is cut for something that you really care about, like roads and bridges, or education or health care, then you are going to feel it right away. It is not remote. People may think somehow decisions are made by other people far away, but in a democracy that is not really true. It is your representatives in Congress or in the Senate that are influencing what happens to the U.S. economy and what happens to the federal budget. So it is pretty important for people to pay attention to it.

Q: And as for the economy, do you think it as complicated as people think it is, or no? Is it an approachable topic for most?

Alice Rivlin: I do not think the economy is nearly as difficult to understand as many people seem to think. I think it is a little bit like math phobia. People say, oh, well, you know, I never was good at math. But the economy does not involve much math. People know about taxes. They know about spending. They know about unemployment. If it hits them, it is a disaster. So those are things that people can figure out.

Q: What does an institution like Brookings do?

Alice Rivlin: The Brookings Institution does public policy research. That is, we write books and articles and other kinds of publications, and we talk on the air about public policy problems, like taxes and international trade, and budget deficits, and the war in Iraq, all kinds of public policy issues. We are a nonpartisan organization. We try to do the best job that we can to do fair and impartial research. That does not mean people do not have opinions. Of course they have opinions. But we are dedicated to doing fair and impartial research.

William Bonner

William Bonner founded Agora Inc., a financial research and publishing group, in 1979 in Baltimore, Maryland. Bill is the author of the *Daily Reckoning*, a daily free e-letter about contrarian investing that is read by 500,000 subscribers. He is also the author of three bestselling books; *Empire of Debt*, his 2005 New York Times bestseller with Addison Wiggin, was the inspiration for *I.O.U.S.A.*

Q: Why you were drawn to economics and why do you enjoy it?

Bill Bonner: I was never really drawn to economics. I didn't like economics, and when I studied it I found it very boring. But as I began to read and pay attention to what people were actually doing in life and how economies worked, gradually I became aware that I had become an economist. I was not studying the economy or economics in the way that it's traditionally taught or studied. I was trying to understand why people did what they do. And that, as I found out later, really is classical economics.

Q: In *Empire of Debt*, you say that the American empire of debt rests on 10 delusions. Why is it that people believe things that history has proven are not worthy of belief? Do you believe that these delusions are dangerous?

Bill Bonner: People cling to delusions because life can be extremely complicated, and delusions can be a source of comfort. Since the book came out, I've done a lot more thinking about why people do what they do. People prefer delusions because the truth itself is just too complicated. That's true when you're talking about economic truth; for example, if you ask why the price of gold is going up or down, the answer is infinitely complicated. You can't reduce it to a formula or a simple logical expression. All of life is that way. When you have a political campaign, for example, the most complex issues get reduced to a single phrase, like "protect freedom." People need those kinds of things in order to be able to operate. Otherwise it's just much, much too complicated to try to figure out how things actually work. And so they end up believing what they want to believe, but what they believe is so far removed from the facts that it's a delusion.

Q: What are some of these delusions?

Bill Bonner: People always want to believe that their houses are always going up in price. They want to believe that they're going to earn more money next year. They want to believe that their investments will go up. And they want to believe that they can get away with spending more money than they actually earn, and they do that in America now because credit is readily available.

These delusions don't all happen in the same way. They're episodic and cyclical. In one generation, over a period of time, a delusion builds up; it builds up like debt, in fact, until it's crushed by events. The way our parents and grandparents looked at things is very different from the way we look at them. They had delusions of their own, of course, but their delusions were very, very different. Our parents did not think that they could live on credit and borrow their way to prosperity; they believed that if they borrowed some money they'd have to pay it back. I remember how happy my own parents were when they paid off the mortgage. The mortgage they had taken out on our house in the late '50s was something like $5,000, with a 5 percent interest rate. And when they paid that mortgage off, they were delighted. But today, people would be delighted to have that mortgage. My parents were children of the Great Depression and didn't have the delusion that you can get away with spending more money than you earn. They thought that not spending too much was the way to go, and they thought that savings were important. The delusion of debt had been crushed out of people in the United States in the Great Depression, but gradually it took hold again. And we who grew up after the '50s and '60s never had that experience. So here we are in the twenty-first century. We've never suffered from a real debt deflation and we don't know what it's like. I think we're going to find out, but it's not going to be pretty.

Q: What do you think lies ahead, given the lifestyle that we live today in our country?

Bill Bonner: We had an expression in the book that basically said that there are not many people who can afford to live like Americans today, and too bad Americans can't either. The fact is that Americans live beyond their means. This is a very, very old concept, but today people don't even think about it because they don't know what their means are. You know, when you start down this path where you're introducing so much credit and monetary inflation, which just means that there are more and more dollars floating around, then people don't know what a dollar is worth. For example, when you get a credit card in the mail with a credit line of $2,500, does that mean that you can spend $2,500? As Warren Buffett has explained many times, you can't live beyond your means forever; eventually it catches up with you. What's happening in America today is that people are taking their credit cards, spending money they don't have, and believing that they'll never have to pay that money. But they will, somehow, sooner or later. That mathematics has to catch up to them, and they'll have to spend less money, because they're right now spending more than they can afford.

Q: If the current generation is getting into a position where it can't pay off its debts, who is going to pay those debts? Is it moral; is it fair what's happening? With both a family that has large debts and a country that carries large debts, what happens to the next generations?

Bill Bonner: Jefferson went on record saying that it was immoral for one generation to load up the next generation with debt. And in private life we don't do that. A person goes to his grave and his debts go with him, more or less. In public we have this system whereby one generation can spend money before it's been earned. Then somebody's got to pay that money in the future, and that somebody is the next generation. To me, that is an immoral situation, and it's not just immoral, it's fundamentally wrong—and mean—for one generation to spend the next generation's money.

During the Depression, people didn't have any money, but at least they came into the world without money. They didn't have any debts either, so they came in as free people and they could create whatever lives they could for themselves. But now, when a person comes into the world and into the United States of America, he carries with him this enormous public debt. It's like part of his time and money has already been spent and now he will have to spend time earning money to pay for things that people enjoy today. The official public debt is $9 trillion, but the financial gap is something like $60 trillion. If you divide that up among all of these babies being born, each one has a lot of money to pay out over his lifetime. When a person goes to the drugstore and gets some pills on Medicaid, where does the money come from for that? His children and his grandchildren will have to work to pay for those pills that he took in 2007, or roughly speaking.

Our whole society is in a trap where it is spending more than it can afford and is transferring its assets. Foreigners end up with our money and they use the money to buy U.S. assets, and so Americans become less and less likely to own their own property. And we've seen this, of course, in a very fundamental and simple way in the housing market. People used to own 70 percent of their homes; 30 percent was mortgage, 70 percent was owner equity. And now that figure is down to 52 percent, meaning that the average American barely owns half of his house. Who owns the other half? Is it the neighborhood bank? No. The neighborhood bank has sold the mortgage to a financial company, which probably sold it to a hedge fund. Now it's floating somewhere in the great wide world. It may be in the hands of the Chinese financiers or London speculators. Who knows? But it's just not the world that it once was, and it doesn't seem fair to me that these poor children coming into the world should come in with so much debt on their shoulders.

Q: **But if we understand that that's such a despicable concept, to give your children a pile of debt, how is it that we as a country have bought into this? Is it happening on an individual** level or is it happening in Washington or is it happening in both places?

Bill Bonner: Things that people will not do to themselves and their own children, they will do collectively. We see episodes of collective madness all the time. As a recipient of government money, such as Medicaid or an agricultural subsidy, you think that somebody else's children are going to pay for it. The debt is in the hands of the public and it becomes so lost in generalities that you're not really worried about your own children having to pay off that debt. You know that you've got money in the present. You're not going to worry that most likely someone else's children are going to be paying. Institutions have a tendency to work this way. If a politician wants to get reelected, he'll get reelected by giving people something. And if you have to take it from them first, it's not a very good deal. So the voter will say, "Wait a minute, you took $10 in taxes from me, and now you're giving me back $10? That's not a very good deal." The politician gets the vote when he gives the person $11. And where does the politician get that other dollar? He has to borrow it from somewhere. That's a good deal for the taxpayer. But that one dollar is now hanging over the heads of the whole society. Over time, this system of buying power and buying votes becomes institutionalized and entrenched. And you gradually get a more and more corrupt system where you have to spend more and more money in order to keep voters voting for you. Finally, the system collapses, but that's sometime in the future and we haven't seen that in America yet.

Q: **Warren Buffett says that people should understand economics, because if they don't, they're going to be subject to a lot of demagoguery. If they don't understand what's going on financially around them, they can buy into a lot of really bad reasoning and bad logic from their leaders that may want to take them off to war. And that to me seemed to echo your "As We Go Marching" section in your book. Can you explain to me why that becomes the option?**

Bill Bonner: Hemingway said the first panacea of a mismanaged government is the inflation of the currency, and the second is war.

Both bring a temporary prosperity, but both bring permanent ruin. When you start spending more money than you have in a government, first you get the support of the masses and that's how you get reelected. But eventually it becomes harder and harder to do that; you run out of money, and you begin to get a backlash from people when they see that the programs don't work. They see their money squandered, they see inflation, they see debt, and you get resistance, primarily from the most conservative citizens or people who are afraid of those kinds of things. And the way to overcome that is to go to war, because nobody, apparently, can resist the call to arms. You know, if you have a real war, everybody tends to get behind it. We've seen that recently in America. Almost any war, for almost any circumstance or any pretext, is a way of unifying the population behind its leaders. That's why George W. Bush wanted to be a war president, because all of the great presidents in American history were either war heroes or served as presidents during war: Lincoln, Wilson, and Washington—after the war, but he was a military hero; Eisenhower was a military hero. People get behind you when you're going to war. So when the rascals and scoundrels in public office can no longer spend their way to popularity, then they typically choose to go to war.

We've seen that a lot. Of course that was the story of the whole Roman Empire—they handed out the bread and circuses and they kept fighting. They fought all around the Empire. They always had a war going on. That's what empires do, and that's why our book is called *Empire of Debt*, because it is an empire. It's an empire founded on debt but it's an empire that acts like an empire, and an empire is a military thing. It's a thing that provides order or establishes order, and it's always at war one way or another—that's the kind of business that it's in.

Q: Can you talk a little bit about bread and circuses?

Bill Bonner: Bread and circuses was a system whereby Roman politicians were able to keep control of the population of Rome. The population of Rome was very important because it was a big city, and if Roman politicians lost control of the population of

Rome, they lost control of the Roman Empire. So they were very careful to keep the people of Rome happy, and they did it by giving them something for nothing. They gave them bread and circuses, just what the mob wants. Rome seized Egypt and took a lot of grain from Egypt every year, and the grain was distributed as bread to the people of Rome. Likewise, they held games in the Colosseum. And so bread and circuses allowed the Roman Empire to maintain popularity with the people at home and effectively got the Roman people to support their political leaders, and allowed the Roman Empire to continue going for a long, long time. But it began to cost more and more to keep the Empire in business. So the politicians spent more and more and went further and further into debt in order to get the money. In the case of the Roman Empire, they didn't have paper money, they didn't have the dollar. They had to send more slaves to Spain where they had silver and gold mines, and they worked around the clock. That was what we call monetary inflation. They produced more money by mining it out of the ground in order to buy the things they needed to control the population and pay the soldiers. But none of these things will work forever. All institutions have a way of growing older and becoming corrupt and then falling apart. And that's what happened in Rome. They spent too much money and kept going into debt, and finally the whole Empire became corrupt and it fell apart.

Q: Can you talk a little bit about what happened in the early part of the twentieth century, with Mussolini and Hitler?

Bill Bonner: After the reorganization in the mid-nineteenth century, Italy had a government that tended toward debt, and it always had some terrible crisis. And each time, Roman politicians tended to want to go to war. I don't know where they get this; maybe it's in their genes or maybe they've just read a lot of history. And Mussolini was no exception. In his election campaign, he railed against debt. He said that the Italian state was spending too much money, and he was going to bring the debt under control. But once he got into office he realized that bringing the debt under control was no way to run a country or to get popular support. And he couldn't spend more money because they were already deeply in debt, so he conjured up a war. We saw that in Argentina, too. Those generals were in a bind so they decided to divert the public's attention by starting a war with England, and so they seized the Falklands. England didn't put up with it, and sent a fleet and took it back. This is not a new theme. We've seen it many times in history and probably will see it more.

Q: How did it work out for Mussolini?

Bill Bonner: It didn't work out well. They hung him, and his mistress, upside down.

Q: I want to talk about the idea of what America was when it started, a long time ago. What was the dream of what America could be and what was it that the settlers were trying to break away from? And do you feel that perhaps this idea of independence has been lost? Clearly we're not an independent nation if we rely so heavily on other nations lending us money.

Bill Bonner: John Milton said, in the beginning all the Earth was America. What he meant was it was just open, and it was free, and it was available. When people came to America originally, they came for a lot of personal reasons, but they came with nothing, generally, and they came expecting to find a place where they could build the life that they wanted for themselves. They didn't ask for a government handout, or a subsidy, or a license. They didn't ask for anything; they just wanted to be left alone to do their own thing. Some were religious people who wanted to set up a City of God, which they did in New England. Others wanted to farm in the south. What they shared was a common idea about what America was. It wasn't exactly a place because it had no boundaries. They were pushing back the boundaries of America all the time. As far as they knew, America was almost infinite; they didn't know how far it went. So it wasn't a place and it wasn't a government. They were colonies of Britain, each one governed its own way. Later they set up their own government and declared that they had the right to decide for themselves how they would be governed. But it was a place where people could come and live freely. And it meant that they were free from the burdens of centralized government.

But now, America is not really very much different from any other country. Generally America's not particularly more free than Britain or France or practically any other country we can find. They all have their different cultures, a different style of food and dress. But the fundamental difference that used to separate America from the rest of the world no longer exists, and that difference was that America was a free country. The rest all had their governments, they had their aristocracies, they had their special classes, they had rigidity, structure, establishments, institutions, and these required people to be a certain way. If you were in a certain segment of society you had to play that role, but in America you could be anything you wanted. So it was a very, very different place. And now America's not such a different place. Now America's acting like an empire. It's spending more money than it has and it's throwing its weight around, as empires traditionally do.

Q: Can you go a little bit further with that?

Bill Bonner: One of the great delusions that Americans live with now is the delusion that they are a freer people than others in the world. This is something that animates the Bush administration; they believe that they've got something that everybody else would like to have and so they're going to force them to have it. But America really isn't that much freer or any different than anyplace else now. You need a permit for anything you try to do. There's a regulation for it or there's a tax.

Q: We choose not to listen to advice that was given a long time ago. Is that part of our culture, is that something that's just human nature, or is that particularly present in American human nature?

Bill Bonner: I think Americans particularly are susceptible to what I call the tyranny of the here and now. Americans have no history. That's not always a bad thing, because it makes Americans a very inventive culture. Jefferson and the Founding Fathers were scholars. They read the history of Rome and read it very carefully. They tried to build into the U.S. Constitution certain checks and balances. These were designed intentionally to avoid the kinds of problems that they had seen occurring in history over many, many generations. And that sort of ignoring dead people is a risky proposition. But dead people don't vote; it's only the living who vote. And what do they vote for? They vote to give themselves more money. Where do they get the money? They get it partially from the dead by stealing the treasures that have been built up over many, many years, and they get it partially from children who haven't been born yet. They say, okay, well we're going to borrow money and we're going to pay it back 50 years from now—or never, actually, because the debt keeps rolling over and over and over. And so, effectively, they're stealing from the past and stealing from the future, and they get away with it.

Q: **Do you think they will get away with it forever?**

Bill Bonner: Eventually what happens is that people don't take their IOUs anymore. When people spend too much money, for a while they'd get away with it, but eventually people would begin to wonder what their IOUs were worth. They'd begin to ask themselves whether you were actually going to pay off that debt, and pretty soon they'd begin to be wary of lending you any more money and begin to say, "Those aren't worth what we thought they were worth." Then the whole system falls apart, and you then have to earn a living and pay people off and save money. That's one of these lessons that dead people have learned, and we haven't.

Q: **What can we learn from Bretton Woods and the Nixon shock of 1971 and 1972?**

Bill Bonner: As I was saying, people can learn a lot from dead people, and what they had learned in the eighteenth century was that paper money doesn't work. John Law had famously created a big scandal in France and practically bankrupted the French government. But in the nineteenth century, starting with Napoleon, all of the major money systems of Europe were anchored by gold. When countries traded with one another, they traded with gold; and when you had a pound or a franc, it was backed by gold. That system was very, very successful; the prosperity of the nineteenth century was amazing. But that system broke down in World War I; you know, the governments, as they always do, spent too much money. Britain borrowed too much, France borrowed too much, and then they couldn't pay it back because they didn't have enough gold to pay that kind of expense.

That gold-backed system lingered on through a lot of the twentieth century. Governments would still trade gold, and currencies were still backed by gold—not perfectly, but still that system existed. The last stage of it was called Bretton Woods, and that lasted up until 1971. Prior to 1971, we had the Johnson Administration, we had the Great Society and the Vietnam War, and those things were very, very expensive. And somebody told Johnson, "Wait a minute, you can't have both guns and butter. You can't have a huge domestic spending program, the Great Society, at the same time that you have a huge war going in Asia. That won't work; we can't afford that." At the time, the Democrats, led by Johnson, said, "Oh, yes we can. We're a big rich country, we can afford both guns and butter." But they couldn't afford that much without raising taxes, and they didn't want to raise taxes because then they wouldn't be reelected.

What resulted from that was a run on America's money, because people, especially the French, led by de Gaulle, saw that the dollar was weakening. France came to the U.S. Treasury building in Washington and said, "Look, I've got all these dollars, I want gold." Richard Nixon looked at the situation and said, "Boy, if they take all that gold, we're not going to have much gold left." He *closed the gold window*—a phrase said by the Treasury Department—on August 15, 1971, and henceforth no foreign government could trade its paper for gold—trade dollars for gold.

After August 15, 1971, the worldwide financial system no longer rested on gold. From then forth you could just trade paper. The dollar is a faith-based currency now; it's not based on gold, but on the faith that people have that it's worth something. This system we have today is a very funny system, because at the bottom of it there's nothing but air. And we have dollars floating all over the world.

Nobody wants to really pay any attention to the international money system, but it's important to understand how it works. In the 19th Century, and up until 1971, gold was beneath the paper money floating around the world. You can't create gold. You have to dig it out of the ground; it's hard to get; and there's not very much of it. But paper money is different. Since 1971, with no gold to back up the paper, all we have is paper. That means that you can create a lot of paper and you don't have to connect it to gold. They've been creating United States dollars like crazy for the last 20 years, and now they're creating them even faster. They're not down in the Treasury Building, with a little-bitty glazier printing press, printing out bills; they're created by electronic transaction. They can just credit a bank with money and then the bank lends out money. The whole thing now has gotten so out of control. Money is created all over the world by financial intermediaries, including, hedge funds and investment banks and so on. You have this explosion in what people call money. Is it real money? It's not backed by gold. They're simply pieces of paper and little electronic zeros and ones.

Now our whole society has something like $500 trillion nominal value, or face value, of derivative contracts. What is that? Nobody quite knows, because there's nothing real in the system. It's all based on faith that somehow it'll work out and that those mathematicians who created all those derivative contracts know exactly what they're doing. We know from history that it doesn't work out that way. There are booms and there are busts, and when you have a boom, people forget the lessons of the past and start spending too much money. They spend too much money when they buy assets—stocks and bonds and apartment buildings and Monet paintings. And they forget about it when they buy ordinary things too, like when they want to take a vacation or when they go to the store and take out a credit card representing a kind of money.

Money—the money that we keep score in, the money that everybody talks about, the money that everybody cares about—is kind of a fishy thing. Without gold, or something solid beneath it, we don't know what it is. Since governments don't need gold in the system anymore, they can create as much of this money as they want. This is what has created this big, huge, worldwide boom that we either enjoy or curse today, depending upon your point of view. This boom is making a lot of people rich. It's raising living standards in places like China, India, and even America. But there's a big difference. In America we're spending debt—you know, we're taking this paper, we're sending it out, off overseas, in a kind of IOU, to foreigners in exchange for goods and services. In foreign countries they're creating goods and services, building economies, and building factories. They are creating real wealth in China and in India, but in America it's a phony wealth we get by spending money we don't really have for things we don't need. It's putting us in the hole, rather than putting us ahead of things.

Q: Can you tell me the difference between the gold standard and fiat currency?

Bill Bonner: The gold standard is a standard in which money itself is defined as a unit of gold. Because gold is very, very limited and rare and hard to get, it limits the amount of money in circulation. There's no magic to gold. It just happens to be provided by Nature herself, and it never goes away. It doesn't melt or corrode or flake away. Gold endures. Gold mining traditionally has produced new gold at about 3 percent more new gold per year, and now it's producing 2 percent more. And that happens to be about the rate of GDP growth in the world. So gold is a near-perfect money, because it increases in supply at about the same rate as the goods and services that it would be used to buy. That's the gold standard.

Then there's the other standard, the fiat paper standard or the faith-based standard, which we have today. This is entirely different because there's nothing solid in it; there is no gold in it. Governments create money out of thin air. They create it by spinning the printing press or by just crediting their member banks with a few billion dollars more. This type of money is fishy, and the boom that this money creates is also fishy, because it's created from nothing. There are no savings and there's no real money in it. Consequently you get a lot of spending but not much real wealth creation—not in America, anyway.

Q: Can you talk about the fact that Alan Greenspan, who had a very long and prestigious run at the Fed, was a gold bug at one point, and that he later embodied the opposite of what the gold currency was set up to try to do? Is Greenspan a paradox in some way?

Bill Bonner: Well, I wouldn't say Greenspan is a paradox. Certainly, Alan Greenspan appears to us as a paradox, but to me it's not much of a paradox. When he was young, before he had a dog in the fight, he was a very keen and smart observer, and he observed that gold was very important to an economic system. He said that if you take gold out of the system, governments are able to inflate the currency much more easily. It's kind of a fraud on people who save, because they've been saving something that they thought was valuable, and when the government just spins up some more of it, all of a sudden it's not worth so much. Greenspan wrote that it was a fraud: that it was a theft to take that money from them.

But he was a human too, and human beings have their weaknesses. One weakness is that they want power. When Greenspan got power, he realized that his hard money views— it's called *hard money* when you believe in gold as a basis for currency—don't square with the lust for power. When given the choice between his hard money views and his role with the Fed, he chose the role with the Fed. He always says that he still believes in what he wrote many, many years ago, but he certainly doesn't practice it. During his time at the Fed, more new money was created than under all of the Fed directors and secretaries of the Treasury in American history. And again, this money was created out of thin air. This is just the thing that he argued was a kind of theft, when he was a young man.

Q: Why was Wilson's presidency and the Federal Reserve Act important? Was that a watershed moment in economics, and in the ability for the American soon-to-be empire, to be able to create money?

Bill Bonner: When we look at real economics, what we're really talking about is real human beings and what they do. And when you look at real human beings, you find that they have good points and bad points. One of the points about human nature is that they do like power. And the way people get power—this was true in Rome, and it's true in America today—is by giving people something for nothing. Of course it isn't really something for nothing; either they have to steal something from somebody else in order to give it to them, or it really turns out to be nothing at all. But this giving something for nothing is the basis of government debt and is also the basis of a lot of the mischief in foreign affairs. People get the idea that they're going to pull off something really great and it never happens.

We see that over and over again in history. Read the history of Rome, of course, and it's full of blood and guts and gore. But in American history you see it too, and we saw it with Wilson. Wilson was a professor of government at Princeton. When he got into government, you could just watch his character evolve, and he gradually took on the role of a power broker. When World War I came along, Americans wanted to stay out of that war. It was a European war and they didn't see any point in going to war in Europe. But Wilson managed the public opinion, with the help of the British, to stir up a kind of war fever. Why did he want to do that? Why would America want to get into Europe's war? It was because Wilson himself wanted to be a power broker. If he could get into and be decisive in that war, then he could set the terms by which the war was settled. Sure enough, he went over to France. And as soon as he got there, of course, all the Europeans, who were as cynical as hell, stabbed him in the back. The poor man had a stroke and never actually recovered. But he set the stage for this next phase of American military and political development. After World War I, America was ready to play a role on the global stage, because America at that stage was the world's number one military and economic power. It also set the stage for the financial development of America, because by setting up the Federal Reserve, by setting up the institutions which allowed America to go to war, it allowed America to begin social programs. These programs were not invented by America. They were invented by Germany, by Bismarck. But these things created the foundation of the next stage of American growth, which was going from the simple republic of the Founding Fathers to the megalomaniacal kind of empire that we have today.

Robert Rubin

Robert Rubin, the 70th secretary of the U.S. Treasury (1995–1999), was one of the key players in the Clinton administration's balanced budget. In 1999, he, along with Alan Greenspan and Larry Summers, was dubbed by *Time* magazine as "The Committee to Save the World" after their work with the IMF and others to combat the financial crises in Russia, Asia, and Latin America. He is currently a director and chairman of the Executive Committee at Citigroup.

Q: Can you tell me about Little Rock, Arkansas, in January 1993?

Robert Rubin: What happened is that the president-elect got us all [everyone involved in economic policy] together in the Governor's Mansion and we had prepared a presentation with respect to what we at least thought an economic policy ought to look like going forward. And we started that discussion with President-elect Clinton, and very shortly into the discussion, President Clinton said, "Look, I understand. Our threshold issue has to be to restore physical discipline if we're going to have sustained recovery. And then on top of that, we can build everything else that we want to do." And that really was the beginning of the formulation of his economic policy, and all that we did for the next eight years.

Q: Was there a sense at that time that a recovery for the United States was necessary?

Robert Rubin: Well, the country, as you may remember, in the very end of 1989, started to have a decline in economic conditions, in what's called gross domestic product. And by the time you got into 1990, unemployment was increasing, and at some point we had a recession. The presidential campaign of 1992 was run in fair measure on economic issues because the country had had by that time, roughly speaking, three years of relatively difficult economic conditions with relatively high levels of unemployment. By the time you got to the end of 1992, unemployment was over 7 percent, and President Clinton had been elected on a platform of putting in place economic policy to create sustained recovery, increase jobs, and increase standards of living. And that was a very important part of what he focused on in the early part of his administration.

Q: Were some other people arguing for a middle-class tax cut?

Robert Rubin: Well, President Clinton never wanted to have a middle-class tax cut, and I think he was right in many ways. But the problem was that by the time you got to the point where we were actually formulating a policy for the new administration, the deficit projections that had come out of the prior administration were so substantial that we had to make a different set of choices or trade-offs than we thought we were going to have to face during the campaign. And in the context of that substantially worsened prospective fiscal picture, the conditions didn't allow for a middle-class tax cut and the other purposes that the president wanted to accomplish. So what President Clinton decided to do was to put in place a program that would begin the process of deficit reduction, which turned out to be very successful, and at the same time, to make room for public investment in areas that he thought were critical economically or socially. For example, a very large increase in the earned income tax credit, a program that most people know nothing about in our country, but which is really an outstandingly successful program to help low-income working people have increased incomes.

Q: Speaking of deficits, do you think deficits matter?

Robert Rubin: Well, I don't think there's any question that deficits matter, and I think there is probably virtually no mainstream economist who doesn't believe that deficits matter. Deficits over time—and we're talking about deficits over a period of time, not just for a little while—lead to higher interest rates, they can create the risks of market disruption, and they undermine the ability of government to engage in public investment, which is so critical economically and socially. They reduce our leverage abroad when we try to negotiate on international economic policy issues that are important to our country.

What we found in the early 1990s, when President Clinton put in place a powerful deficit reduction program, is that deficits also undermine business and consumer confidence more generally. So I don't think there's any question that deficits matter. And I think it's a broadly accepted view that sustained deficits over time can have significant adverse impact on jobs, on standards of living in our economy more generally.

Q: Can you explain to me what would life look like in America and our economy if the dollar declined, if people didn't have the confidence that they have now or once had?

Robert Rubin: Well, all during the Clinton years, one of the points that we made in the public discussion of economic issues was that a strong dollar is very much in our country's interest. Now, that concept was the concept of a strong dollar based on strong policy. Remember, the dollar exchange rate, the exchange rate between the dollar and foreign currencies, represents the rate at which we take the goods and services that we produce and exchange them for the goods and services that others produce and that we import. So the stronger the dollar, the more goods and services we get from foreign countries in exchange for the goods and services we give them, and that obviously improves our standard of living. Conversely, the lower the dollar, the less we'll get in return for the goods and services we produce, and therefore the lower our standard of living. So having a strong dollar based on strong policy is very much in the economic interest of our country.

Q: Can you imagine for a moment that it's 1999 and you are about to leave the White House and leave the Treasury? Would you be surprised if someone told you on that day that we would have the debt levels and the deficit spending that we have these days?

Robert Rubin: I left Treasury in July 1999. In 1998, the federal government of the United States had a fiscal surplus for the first time in, roughly speaking, 30 years. And the projections forward based on the fiscal policies then in place were for continued surpluses for long, long into the future. And I thought that what had happened—well actually, I'm not going to say what I thought. What *had* happened was that a political coalescence had occurred or developed around maintaining fiscal discipline, which is a very difficult thing to do politically because it requires spending constraint and adequate revenues. And I thought we were on that track.

Unfortunately, what happened early in the next decade is that that coalescence fell apart and we got on a very different fiscal track so that we now have substantial deficits, and very substantial deficits are projected into the future. And I think it's imperative that we reestablish that politically very difficult, but economically imperative coalescence around sound fiscal conditions.

Q: I'd like to explore further something you just said, and maybe this speaks to your experience at Treasury: How difficult is it to balance the budget?

Robert Rubin: The politics of sound fiscal conditions, which ultimately should result in a balanced budget, are very difficult because the natural inertia in the political system is toward federal programs, most of which are very useful. And therefore the inertia is toward spending on the one hand and tax cuts on the other hand. But if you're going to have sound fiscal conditions, you have got to constrain your spending and you also have to provide for adequate revenues. And what ultimately is involved are very difficult trade-off decisions involving federal programs and what the American people want their government to do, and then providing the means to pay for it. I think what we've got to do right now is get back on a long-term path, taking into account entitlements and all else, which brings our deficit down over time, to the point where we have a balanced budget. But at the same time, we need to provide the room for public investment in critical areas like education, health care, infrastructure, basic research, and so much else, which is a requisite if we're going to have the kind of very successful economy I believe we can have if we meet these challenges.

Q: If we aren't able to get fiscal issues a priority in the next presidential campaign, what are the chances that the rising debt and the rising deficits would threaten the status of the reserve currency? What would be the impact on the American family?

Robert Rubin: At the present time, the United States has significant fiscal deficits, and they'll fluctuate depending on short-term circumstances, but in the long-term sense, we have significant deficits—they get substantially worse over time because of entitlements. And at the same time, we have very large trade deficits. At some point, these become a deep threat to our economy and to the global economy. Our political system is going to have to address this predominantly through putting in place a sound, long-term fiscal regime.

One of the risks, and there are many risks in this combination of imbalances, is that at some point people can lose confidence in the dollar. And if the global community lost confidence in the dollar, it's conceivable that we would no longer be a favored reserve currency. That's a very technical matter, but it could have enormous significance for our country. I don't believe that will happen, for a whole host of reasons. I believe we'll remain a reserve currency, and I believe at some point our political system is simply going to have to address these long-term fiscal issues. But it's going to be very difficult to do it, and it's enormously in the interest of the American people that our political system address these issues before they're a substantial difficulty, rather than in response to substantial difficulty. But our political system has a tendency to respond more in response to difficulty than in anticipation of difficulty. The United States has many great strengths, which put us in the position to thrive over time economically, but in order to thrive we have to address these issues, and if we don't, then I think we could have serious difficulty.

Q: What does life look like for your kids or grandkids if the financial road that we're on is not changed or altered?

Robert Rubin: If the financial road that we're on—which consists of substantial fiscal deficits that get far worse as time goes on, in large measure, but not totally because of entitlements and because of inadequate revenues and large trade deficits and a very low savings rate—if we stay on that financial road, that could very seriously threaten our economy, job creation, and standard of living in this country.

On the other hand, we have enormous strengths. The United States economy has enormous strengths and we could have very good economic conditions in this country for a long, long time to come. But we have got to change, dramatically change, the path we are on with respect to financial conditions. This includes addressing our long-term fiscal deficits, which is a question of government spending, including entitlements—plus having adequate revenues, and you're going to have to act on both sides. We're going to have to have public investment, we're going to have to address our large trade imbalances, and in some fair measure, I think you can do that through addressing your fiscal issues. We are also going to have to aim toward a higher savings rate which, once again, in part can be addressed through having the kinds of surpluses we should have had during a period of good growth, and having sound fiscal conditions over time instead of having large deficits.

Q: It seems very difficult for a politician, especially a presidential candidate, to run on that ticket. Do you have any comments about that?

Robert Rubin: The politics of this are extremely difficult because basically, in order to accomplish sound fiscal conditions, you have to both constrain spending and also have adequate revenues. And the whole thrust of the political system is to want to spend on federal programs—most of which may be very good on their own merits, you just have to be able to afford them—and to have tax cuts. One of the political problems is that it is very difficult to explain all this in ways that people can relate to and that has political resonance.

In 1992, during the presidential campaign, one reason I believe that the restoration of the fiscal discipline became such an important and powerful political issue was because by that time we'd had, roughly speaking, 3 years of political difficulty; we'd had 12 years of unsound fiscal conditions, and the American people associated the economic difficulties of those roughly 3 years with the unsound fiscal conditions, with the deficits, and I think rightly associated the two. In a very real political way, I think the deficit became the symbol for all of their concerns about our economy at that time, and so the major candidates were all focused in varying degrees. Particularly President Clinton was very much focused, but as you may remember, Paul Tsongas had run at that point in the primaries, Perot had run at that point as an independent, and they had all talked a great deal about restoring fiscal discipline.

Q: Do you see that the economic environment now or the fiscal condition is similar now to 1992? Do you see similarities between 1993 and possibly '09, or '92 and '08?

Robert Rubin: With respect to reestablishing fiscal discipline and putting in place sound fiscal policy, you have a very different environment today than President Clinton faced—or then Governor Clinton faced in the 1992 presidential election because we've had strong GDP growth. That's on the one hand. On the other hand, we've had, roughly speaking, stagnant median real wages; we've had large increases in inequality; and we've had a seeming increase in economic dislocation. Most Americans do not feel comfortable or are very concerned, economically. But it is not a similar kind of economic circumstance to those we had in the three years leading into the '92 election. And as a consequence, I think fiscal issues will not play a large role in the '08 campaign. I think they should, if the judgments were made with respect to the importance of the issue, but I think the politics probably will tend not to create the imperative and same kind of environment around fiscal issues that we had in 1992.

However, I think that there will be a manifest imperative that the political system and whoever is president at that time will face these issues at some point, because I think if we don't face these issues at some point, they will begin to create the kinds of difficulties that are going to force the political system to address them. Now, when that might be in time is impossible to predict.

Q: What is it that you enjoy about the career that you've had and your role? What is it about economics for you that made it not the "dismal science"?

Robert Rubin: I remember a few years ago, I was speaking at a venture capital conference and I started talking about fiscal policy. And I began to express my views about the absolute imperative that we address our fiscal issues, that we address our trade imbalances and all the rest. Afterwards, somebody said to me that I was the only person they'd ever met who could get passionate about the federal budget. But I think it is an imperatively important issue, and every once in a while, in the course of our economic history, the importance of that issue has imposed itself on us because of the adverse effects that can occur from unsound macroeconomic policy.

More generally, I've been lucky or fortunate in my life in having the opportunity, even though I was involved in a business career, to be engaged pretty much throughout that career in another dimension of life, at least for me, which was political and policy activity and the intersection between the two. And I think it is both enormously important and also endlessly fascinating. Not only is the economic policy itself endlessly fascinating, at least for me, but I think the intersection between economic policy and politics, how to deal with very complicated economic issues of enormous consequence in the political environment, to me is an endlessly fascinating subject.

Q: What would you say to somebody who said, "I'll never understand that stuff—it's too complicated"?

Robert Rubin: It's actually not that complicated. I think you can bring it down to some pretty understandable terms. You know, there's this old saying, there's no free lunch, and I think that almost captures the whole thing. Just as for an individual, in the final analysis there is no free lunch, there's no free lunch for a national economy. I heard someone say not long ago, and I think this is right, that what we've got to do is to pay our way now, we've got to be on a road to paying our way for the years and decades ahead, and we've got to invest in our future. And at the present time, we're not doing any one of those three. If we do them, we can have an enormously successful economy over time, and if we don't, then I think we run the risk of having very serious difficulty.

Q: Can you talk a little about foreign ownership of debt and its impact on interest rates in this country?

Robert Rubin: If you look at where we are today, debt as a percentage of GDP is not at unreasonable levels, although it should have been much lower because we should have had surpluses during this period of growth, given that we started this decade with surpluses. . . and we've had some very good fortune with respect to revenues being much higher for all kinds of reasons. I think relatively temporary revenue's been much higher than had been expected. And had we had the surplus, we could have had a much lower level of debt relative to our total economy. But the problem is that if we stay on our current fiscal path, the ratio of debt to our total economy will grow and grow and grow over time, and as time goes on, the rate of growth is going to increase because we have these very large, unfunded liabilities.

A lot of people, and I think the markets, for that matter, don't tend to worry about this too much because they think that at some point the political system will fix this before it becomes a serious problem. Somebody described that to me the other day as believing in "just-in-time politics"—that we won't deal with it until we come up right against the serious difficulty that this could lead to, and then on a just-in-time basis, we'll fix it. I think that's a relatively unrealistic view of how our political system works. And I think that if we don't address this in some reasonable fashion, then the likelihood that we will do it before we have trouble is probably not as great as we would like to believe, and the likelihood that we'll only do it in response to trouble is higher than we'd like to believe.

So I think that this belief in just-in-time politics is a comforting thought, but I suspect it may be a relatively unrealistic thought. I think there is a tremendous opportunity for whoever is the next president to really make a very big and important difference for this country by providing serious leadership on this very difficult set of issues.

Something else to look at is that more and more of the debt of the federal government is owned abroad because we have a combination of very large fiscal deficits that have to be funded someplace, on top of a very low *de minimis* national savings rate and a large trade deficit. And the consequence of all this is that a larger and larger percentage of the debt of the federal government is owned abroad. But does that matter? I think it probably does matter, because there's a higher probability that a continuation of the current set of financial conditions that we have—a low savings rate, fiscal deficits, and large trade deficits—will create unease abroad and in foreign capital markets, which would then translate back into higher interest rates in this country and a lower currency than would be the case if we were dealing only with our own domestic markets. But that's a very complicated subject. The bottom line is I think probably foreign ownership of debt creates a somewhat greater risk of adverse interest rate effects and currency effects than if the debt was domestically held. But it is an inevitable consequence of today's fiscal conditions, savings rate, and trade deficit, and the way to get at this is to put in place sound, long-term fiscal policy.

Q: What happens to the first person who raises their voice about these fiscal imbalances and the overall financial situation?

Robert Rubin: I think it is absolutely imperative that our political system address what is now a very unsound, long-term fiscal situation, and I think it's going to have to act both with respect to spending, including entitlements, and we're going to have to have increased revenues. If we do all that, I think we can have a very successful economy for a long time.

The problem politically, however, is that putting forth a specific proposal, given the very deep, long-term fiscal hole we're in, putting forth a specific proposal is more likely to generate antagonistic response and a moving away from that, a criticism of that proposal, than it is any kind of constructive reaction. And in a sense, it can lead toward that proposal being, as a consequence, taken off the table politically. Somebody described it as being like a turkey shoot. If you're a bunch of turkeys, the turkey that puts its head up gets shot off. And so there is actually a nonconstructive dimension to putting forth specific proposals. Therefore, what I think we have to do is have some kind of special political process outside of our normal processes, involving the president, the leaders of both Houses, and the leaders of both parties coming together to take joint political accountability for the very, very difficult decisions that are going to have to be made about spending and about revenues and the trade-offs amongst them.

Q: Can you explain to me, what is the *American economy* and what role does that play in this country and in the world?

Robert Rubin: The term *American economy* is simply a phrase that captures the full output in our country of goods and services. So in a sense, it's the aggregate standard of living of all of us. Even with the growth that has occurred around the globe over the past several decades, the United States is still the engine of economic growth for the global economy. When we do well, that helps fuel growth around the world; and conversely, when we do badly or when we have difficulty, that creates or can create economic difficulty around the world. As a consequence, the fiscal issues, our unsound fiscal conditions, our low savings rate, and our large trade imbalance, which are a threat to our own economy, are also a threat to the global economy. For that reason, there is enormous focus around the world on our unsound, long-term fiscal prospects and an enormous focus on the importance of our reestablishing sound fiscal policy, not just for our sake, but for the sake of the entire global economy.

One of the political problems with the fiscal debate is it does crosscut with ideology, so that some who believe that fiscal conditions are very important say that we have to solve it solely on the spending side and that we should not do anything to increase revenues; in fact, we should even reduce tax rates. And others will look at the same set of facts and say that we shouldn't reduce government expenditure; in fact, we should increase government programs and government expenditure and increase revenues to pay for that. I don't think there's any question that the reality lies in putting aside all ideology and making very practical trade-off judgments based on fact and analysis about the government programs—most of which are very important to our economy, national security, and all the rest—and also about the revenues to pay for them. And I think when you're all finished, the conclusion that you're going to reach is that you have to have serious spending discipline, you also have to make room for critical public investment, and we're going to have to have increased revenues. And if we do all that, I think we can thrive for a long, long time economically and socially.

Peter G. Peterson

Peter G. Peterson, a fiscal conservative with 60 years of experience in top government and industry positions, co-founded the Concord Coalition with the late Sen. Paul Tsongas (D-MA) and former Sen. Warren Rudman (R-NH) in 1992. More recently, the former secretary of commerce founded the Peter G. Peterson Foundation and endowed it with $1 billion to tackle some of the critical challenges threatening the nation's well-being. Among them: large and growing budget deficits, dismal national and personal savings rates, and a ballooning national debt that endangers the viability of Social Security, Medicare, and our economy itself.

Q: Tell me about these things that people in Washington refer to as the *trust funds*. What are they, and are they appropriately named?

Peter Peterson: Social Security trust funds are a misnomer, and in fact they're an oxymoron. They shouldn't be trusted and they're not funded. They were intended originally for the surpluses that were building up as the boomers were working, to be set aside and saved for Social Security. Instead, they were spent for other purposes. As a result, all we have in there is a bunch of liabilities.

Q: Those surpluses have been running now for 20 or 25 years. What does the future look like for those surpluses?

Peter Peterson: For the next seven or eight or nine years, they'll continue to approach a trillion dollars in total, but in 2017 the boomers will retire in force and at that point the deficits grow at an extraordinary rate. In other words, we've got to learn to think in terms of the cash in, cash out, pay-as-you-go system, not a trust fund at all. And when we're told by the politicians that the Social Security trust fund will be solvent for another 40 years, that is totally disingenuous and not true.

Q: Why aren't we fixing it? Why don't people like to talk about this in Washington? Nobody disagrees with what you're saying.

Peter Peterson: I call these long-term challenges undeniable and unsustainable but politically untouchable. When I speak privately to our senators and congressmen, they all agree these long-term challenges are unsustainable, and no one is denying them. They're just saying that politically we have gotten so used to getting it all, to all of us being entitled, to never giving up anything or paying for anything, that it's become politically incorrect to ask the American people to make any sacrifice. In fact, many of our politicians believe it would be politically terminal if they were to do that.

Q: What would you say to somebody who may not know this story as well as you do, but characterizes fixing entitlements or reforming entitlements as something that the right wants, but that the left side can figure out just through tax reform? Does that make sense? Is there any truth to that?

Peter Peterson: Well, let me give you an idea of the magnitude of the problem. If you look at the projected spending for Social Security and Medicare, it's stunning. Just the increase is 9 percent of the GDP, but roughly three times what we spend on defense. Now the left is inclined to say, "Well, let's just get rid of the Bush tax cuts," even though most Democrats are only talking about getting rid of the tax cuts on fat cats like myself. If we were to do that, we would increase revenues by 1 percent of the GDP, so it's only one-ninth of the total increase in spending. If you tried to solve this problem with tax increases, you would end up having to more than double our income taxes and double our payroll taxes. The payroll taxes are already the biggest tax, which 80 percent of people pay, and it falls on the middle class, whom everybody says deserves a tax cut, not a tax increase. Now I'm the first to say that the solution to this problem will undoubtedly involve some increase in taxes, particularly on us fat cats, but there is no way you can solve this problem just through tax increases. It's going to require benefit reforms, and if we start early enough we can do these in a way that is fair and protects the safety net for the truly needy. But if we wait, it's going to be more and more difficult to solve this problem.

Q: Who was Wilbur Mills and what was his great idea?

Peter Peterson: I'm a little chagrined to tell you, because I was on the Nixon White House, first as an economic adviser to President Nixon and then as secretary of commerce. Wilbur Mills was a Democratic Arkansas congressman who decided one day that he wanted to be president of the United States. And his opening bid was that we were going to 100 percent index Social Security benefits to inflation, something that is very rarely done in the corporate sector. Not only that, but we'd increase the benefits by 20 percent. Now obviously the Democrats before us, LBJ, had been criticized for big spending. You'll recall guns and butter. But what I'm chagrined about is that we were supposed to be the fiscal conservatives, and we lost our fiscal mooring. The next administration caved in to Wilbur Mills and, without doing a serious systematic study of the long-term costs, which will have amounted to hundreds and hundreds of billions of dollars, they caved in and went along with it. These benefits have been going up ever since, up and up, in only one direction.

Q: How would you characterize or grade the fiscal record of the current administration?

Peter Peterson: I guess you'd call me a moderate Republican, maybe a Rockefeller Republican. I have a feeling that if that's the case, there are only two of us left, David Rockefeller and myself. I am a moderate on social issues but a true fiscal conservative. I would be the first to say that I applauded what happened in the 1990s when, between the Congress, Bill Clinton, and Bob Rubin, Treasury secretary, they put in spending caps, they put in pay-as-you-go rules, and you know what happened. We had budget surpluses. Alas, for reasons I do not fully understand, in a Republican administration we've ended up with not just guns and butter but guns, butter, and big tax cuts, and we've gone from having a budget surplus to having very, very large deficits. Now the president could have vetoed some of these spending bills, but until very, very recently he didn't veto any of them. So we have this phenomenon that not only have defense expenditures gone up, not only have we had big tax cuts, but so-called discretionary spending has gone up at record levels. And don't ask me to explain what has happened here, because this administration and Congress has truly lost its conservative moorings.

Q: As a moderate Republican, do you feel that the party has left you, or something along those lines?

Peter Peterson: I do think the party has left its basic conservative principles. The reasons are not clear. We even have books being written by Secretary of the Treasury O'Neill in which very senior officers of the administration are saying deficits don't matter. So there is no question that we've lost our moorings and we've got to regain them.

Q: You had a front-row seat to what happened in the '60s and the '70s. Can you explain what the many key factors were that made inflation go like this and pave the road for the work that Paul Volcker had to do?

Mr. Peterson: Remember, we had the oil embargo in 1973, and oil prices suddenly went up several times. We had big increases in food costs. This was a period when there were big wage increases, big increases in benefits. Remember, the '60s saw the launching of Medicare, which is a problem today that is five times bigger than Social Security. So the money supply, I'm sorry to say, went up very dramatically during that period of time. Paul Volcker absorbed what you might call a triple or a quadruple whammy, and in my view, handled it brilliantly and courageously.

Q: Did the Federal Reserve at that time do anything to make the situation better or did they do anything, possibly, to make the situation worse?

Peter Peterson: I think history will record that the Federal Reserve was part of the problem. They let money supply get out of control. When Paul Volcker took over, he realized the need for tough action, but it's hard for many people to believe that interest rates were, as I recall, at the extraordinary level of 15 to 20 percent annually. He had to take truly courageous action, and he did.

Q: When inflation does rear its ugly head, is it true to say that inflation affects some people in our society differently than others, and if so, how is that?

Peter Peterson: In a curious way, having 100 percent inflation indexing protects the elderly on their Social Security benefits, but very, very few other people have inflation protection on their pension plans. So we have the anomalous situation where those in the private sector don't get the advantage of inflation indexing and the government retirees do, so that's one of the differences.

Q: What about someone who is in a minimum wage job or someone who has lived very far down on the income ladder? Is it difficult for people like that when prices start to run away from them?

Peter Peterson: Things become very difficult for them for other reasons besides inflation. What accompanies inflation often is a rapid rise in interest rates and a slowdown in the economy and a recession. When we have a recession, the people that tend to be hurt the most are those at the bottom end or the poor end of the scale, so it affects them doubly. Not only do their costs go way up for food and essentials, but they are less likely to keep their jobs.

Q: What factors led to inflation?

Peter Peterson: In 1971, I joined the White House staff as an economic adviser to President Nixon and I became secretary of commerce. Inflation became an issue. Recall that the energy problem got much worse with the embargo in 1973. Recall that food costs were going up. Recall that wages, particularly in manufacturing, were going up, and recall that during the '70s the money supply created by the Federal Reserve had gone up very dramatically, so we were confronted with a significant inflation problem. Now the president chose to do something that shocked a number of us on his staff. You may recall that they put in wage and price controls. That's how concerned they were about inflation. The Republican Party was not only supposed to believe in fiscal conservatism, but in allowing the market to make these adjustments. Wage and price controls were normally something that one thought of in socialist or state-controlled economies, and a number of us were utterly shocked by the decision to set up wage and price controls, but it was some indication of how concerned the president was about inflation.

Q: **When runaway inflation occurs, what does it feel like for the country as a whole?**

Peter Peterson: Runaway inflation tends to hurt fat cats like myself considerably less, because we have a lot of reserves. But if you're a poor or a middle-class family, and you spend a lot of what you make on necessities, on food, on clothing, on rent and mortgages and so forth, all of those things go up very substantially in an inflation period and interest costs go very high. As a result of that, inflation is often accompanied by recession, so that the less fortunate in our country end up not only having to pay much more for necessities, but lose their jobs because the economy is slowing down.

Q: **It sounds like you know a little bit about growing up in a family that didn't have a lot of money. Can you tell me what it was like growing up in Nebraska?**

Peter Peterson: Yes. I'm the very fortunate recipient of the American Dream. My parents were Greek immigrants who came to this country at age 17. They came without a penny and without a word of English. My father took a job that no one else wanted, washing dishes in a caboose with no air-conditioning in the middle of the Nebraska plains, and he saved his money and saved it and worked and worked. His restaurant was open 24 hours a day, seven days a week, for 25 years. When it came time to close the restaurant he didn't even have a key to lock the door because the place had never closed before, but during that period unemployment was 25 percent of the work force. We were in a true, true depression and all of us learned to live on a very, very, very low budget.

Q: **It sounds to me that, as you talk about finding a solution to this big problem that we have, you are thinking about people that are in that position. Are you not?**

Peter Peterson: Yes. Call me a moderate. Call me whatever you will. I think that, whatever we do with our entitlement programs, we have to do everything we can to preserve the safety net for the people that really need them. We've gotten into some very bad habits in this country called entitlements for all, whether we need the benefits or don't need the benefits. I have arguments with my Democratic friends in which I suggest that perhaps some of us who are well off should be willing to give up a lot of our benefits, and they say, "Oh, no. You can't do that because programs for the poor are poor programs and they don't survive." And my question to them is, "If you have to bribe the rich to pay the poor, and if everybody is entitled to be on the wagon, who's going to pull it?"

Now I would say something else about all this. It's easy to get very gloomy about these things, but I remind you that this marvelous country has always been among the most resilient of countries. Look at what the Greatest Generation did. They confronted problems at least as serious as these: the most costly war in the history of this country, in every sense of that word, *costly.* They not only paid down that debt with years of surpluses, but they launched an infrastructure highway program, they launched the GI bill, which was such a wonderful program for the veterans coming back. They did all of those things, but they learned that fairly shared sacrifice is sometimes essential. And that's essentially what we need now, too.

Q: **Would you characterize yourself as a big, easy target for critics from the left?**

Peter Peterson: I don't have any trouble understanding why fat cats are an easy target. Looked at from the standpoint of the lower and middle classes, we've had a situation where their incomes have been flat, and perhaps even down a bit, when you consider the costs of energy and health care costs and so forth. So I can understand why they look at the big fortunes of people like myself and say it's unfair. I would be the last to deny—and this doesn't make me terribly popular with some people in my party—that people in our categories are going to have to pay more taxes. But the point I keep making is that isn't going to be nearly enough to solve the problems of this country. We all have to participate in this, except perhaps the truly needy of this country.

At bottom, I would like to suggest that this is really a moral issue. I remind you of what a German theologian named Bonhoeffer said: The ultimate test of a moral society is the kind of world that we are leaving to our children. Think of the taxes that are implied, which would have to be inflicted on our own kids and grandkids. Think of the debts that we are piling on them and the costs to them of paying back those debts. The idea that we're slipping this check to those kids for our free lunch is essentially a very immoral proposition, in my view.

Ron Paul

Rep. Ron Paul (R-TX) has been shaking up the political arena since 1976, when he first ran for Congress as a proponent of free market economics and started railing against the Federal Reserve system. In 2007, Dr. Paul turned heads once again with his grassroots presidential campaign by breaking two fund-raising records: one for the largest single-day donation total among Republican candidates, and twice receiving the most money received via the Internet in a single day by any presidential candidate in history.

Q: How did a very well-liked doctor find his way to Washington?

Ron Paul: In the early '70s, the breakdown of the monetary system excited me enough to want to speak out because I had been studying Austrian economics for a good many years, and there were a lot of predictions made about the inevitability of the breakdown of the Bretton Woods Agreement. When that happened in 1971, it confirmed my beliefs in what I had been reading, and in 1974, on a lark, I ran for Congress—and the following year I was elected in a special election. My main motivation in the early 1970s was to talk about economic policy from an Austrian viewpoint, and from the viewpoint of sound money and a Constitution that rejects the whole notion of the paper money system and the Federal Reserve System that we have today.

Q: In a nutshell, what is the Austrian school of thought?

Ron Paul: Well, an easier term to use is the *free market score*. A lot of people in this country are for free enterprise and they talk about it, but they don't really understand it or believe it. It's called Austrian economics because some of the founders of that school of thought came from Austria; in particular, [Ludwig von] Mises and [Friedrich A.] Hayek. They are the ones who in the twentieth century kept alive classical liberalism when it came to free market economics and sound money. So we refer to it as Austrian economics but the best way to refer to it is *free market economics*, in contrast to Keynesian economics or socialism.

Austrian economics is different than the economics courses you would take in college because it takes into account the action of each and every individual. And of course the great book of Mises was called *Human Action* [1949; 4th rev. ed. Laissez Faires Books, 2008], so there's a subjective element to economics so it's really fascinating and much easier to understand. The reason why everybody has to be interested in this subject is out of their own self-interest, because if it's monetary policy or economic policy it affects us. If you have socialism and it produces poverty then you don't want it. If paper money eventually leads to runaway inflation and destruction of the financial system as well as the political system, you have to know about that. But a lot of people duck economic interest because what is taught in our colleges is so often very boring—and, quite frankly, often wrong. But free market economics explains how freedom and liberty generates free markets and free choices and essentially the only way you can have prosperity. So everybody, out of their own self-interest, should investigate and understand why free market economics is so important.

Q: Why is it that a family or a company has to stay on budget? They can't run deficits forever, otherwise they're going to end up in jail or living at home with their parents or something. Why is it that the government gets away with running deficits?

Ron Paul: Well, they do it because they have power, more power than they should have and certainly more power than the Constitution gives them. Our country was supposed to be designed not to have this type of authority, and we didn't have the authority to tax before 1913. But they spend too much because they have taxing authority, and it seems to be part of human nature that politicians like more authority. And a lot of them are motivated by good intentions; they always want to take care of people and manage their lives. Most politicians enjoy being somebody important, and the best way to do that is promise people something for nothing and not have to worry about really paying for it. Today, if we had to pay for fighting this war and financing our welfare state, there would be a tax revolt in this country because it would cost so much.

But they can delay this by borrowing, by inflating. That is literally just creating money out of thin air to pay the bills and delaying the payment. So the whole idea of these deficits we run up and the fact that we have a financial monetary system that helps encourage politicians to do exactly the wrong thing instead of working to limit the size of government and maximize individual liberty and maximize the marketplace . . . Politicians end up doing the opposite because they get rewarded. Most incumbents win by being errand boys, coming to Washington and delivering the goods. But my point over the years has been that eventually that system breaks down, and it's very, very dangerous and very harmful to everybody concerned.

Q: Have you ever met a parent or grandparent who has admitted to you that they wanted a better life for themselves than they wanted for their children? If not, then why are we doing that?

Ron Paul: Well, the children are starting to recognize that there's a tremendous burden placed on them and they will be taking care of those in retirement years. The old saying used to be that we always wanted a better life for our children, yet literally in the last 60, 70 years it's been reversed: that the young people finance those in retirement. And it's a mixed bag because a lot of people have paid into Social Security, and they make token payments for their medical care and they think that they're getting their own money back, but their money has already been spent. I've been finding out lately that a lot of young people are coming to the realization that they're getting stuck with the bill.

Q: Can you characterize what happened in the last six or seven years here in Washington? What would be the grade that you

would give our current administration and current group of leaders in Washington?

Ron Paul: Financially, we're doing a lot worse than we were in 1999 or 2000. The deficits have exploded and we got involved in a war that has drained us because we're spending so much, and although Republican conservatives were in power, they never held back on passing more entitlements—whether they were education or medical entitlements.

But quite frankly, there was a lot of deception in 1999 and in the 1990s. Yes, the deficit during that decade was lower; we were never in the black, as they said, because we kept borrowing from our trust funds. So, although it looked a lot better, it really didn't solve the problem because government kept growing. It was almost deceptive in the sense that "uh-oh we're managing this, maybe the supply siders are right, maybe cutting taxes raises revenues and if we hold back a little bit, everything is gonna be okay." But I don't like that approach because even if you could make a tax rate at 10 percent and it increased the revenues to the government because the economy blossomed, I wouldn't be happy with that because I don't want the government to grow. Because eventually it'll get out of control, and when government gets big, individuals get minimized—they have less freedom. So I don't want to make it look easy for the government to spend money.

In those years where it looked like the deficit wasn't so big, it more or less lulled us to sleep and we said "Oh yeah, we can do these things." But it is true in the '90s we weren't quite as abusive with the budget because we didn't have a major war going on and the number of entitlements weren't being passed as they have been in this past six or seven years.

Q: Has it been hard to be here in Washington and watch what's happened financially to our country?

Ron Paul: Well I don't know whether *hard* is the right word, but it is aggravating. I never consider myself frustrated, because I came to Washington with full knowledge of how the system works. I know the system is bad, and I vote a certain way, I try to make the points on what's wrong. Everything that is happening, I've sort of expected, but it's still pretty annoying to find out that people don't respond to common sense, but hopefully they do before we have a tragic outcome like a financial or a dollar crisis. After that, the conditions are much tougher to come back with reforms, which we need, and we also need a different attitude about the role of government. We need an attitude that's different about what we are supposed to be doing overseas, as well as how we run this welfare state. And if we don't change our attitude then we're going to have an economic crisis, which surely could lead to a political crisis.

Q: Explain to me, what is inflation and why is that something that should be avoided at all costs?

Ron Paul: Well, inflation is very simple. When government arbitrarily, out of thin air, prints money—creates money and credit out of thin air. When I talk to many teenagers and grade schoolers, they seem to have no problem comprehending the fact that if you just create a lot of money it'll be like Monopoly money and it won't have value. Governments do that for all kinds of reasons, especially to enhance political power to fight wars we shouldn't be fighting or to be passing welfare programs that aren't deserved. When you print that money, the value of that dollar has to go down and then one of the consequences of inflating the money will be higher prices. But there are a lot of other problems, too, with inflating. It causes a business cycle, it causes financial bubbles, and it causes a lot of economic distortions and unemployment. But, in a nutshell, inflation is very simple. When governments create new money out of thin air you have inflation.

Q: I've heard other people say inflation is immoral. Do you feel that way?

Ron Paul: Inflation is immoral because it's theft. Think about it this way: If you or I had a printing press and we could print the money just like the government does, we would be arrested and put in jail for a long, long time because we've stolen value—we're pretending these pieces of paper are worth something. The founders understood this very clearly and that's why they said in the Constitution that you can't emit mills of credit, which is paper money, because they knew what runaway inflation is like.

Inflating is immoral in the sense because it steals value. If you double the money supply and your prices go up twice as much, it's an invisible hidden tax. But the real immorality here is that some people pay higher prices than others. So if you're in a middle class, or especially in low middle income, your prices might be going up 15 percent a year. Somebody on Wall Street might be working leveraged buyouts and making billions of dollars and they don't have to worry about the rising costs of living. This to me is an immoral act that is prohibited by the Constitution, and the outcome is always tragic.

Q: You and former Fed Chairman Alan Greenspan have famously knocked heads over the years. Can you tell me a little about that? Why it is that you seemed to be at times the only person that seemed to be keeping a very close eye on the goings-on at the Federal Reserve?

Ron Paul: Alan Greenspan from '87 up to over a year ago was the Chairman of the Federal Reserve Board, the U.S. central bank. I see the central bank and the Federal Reserve System as unconstitutional in that they have this tremendous power and a monopoly control over money and credit, which is an ominous power. Greenspan, or any chairman of the Federal Reserve, is more powerful than even our president because he has so much control over the economy. But the interesting thing about Alan Greenspan was that he was a true believer in Austrian economics and in the gold standard. So in a private conversation I had with him I told him that I followed what he taught. In the 1960s he was very clear on his position on gold, that he liked gold and rejected the fiat monetary system, because if you have fiat money it leads to deficits and to the expansion of government—all of which he opposed.

So it's rather ironic that now that Dr. Greenspan accepts the paper monetary system (which is a fiat system). He literally was the participant in these deficits, and I would bring this up to him in the committee because the Federal Reserve Board's chairman always condemn deficits; it's always Congress's fault. But my point was Congress couldn't do it if they weren't complicit: If we don't want a tax and we can't borrow and then they have to print the money in order to accommodate the big spenders. If the Federal Reserve couldn't do that, interest rates would go up and there would be restrain on spending. So he literally became one who once believed in the restraints of the gold standard to one who was converted into becoming the Federal Reserve Board Chairman—the one that ran this whole system of fiat money and central economic control. I would chastise him quite frequently about how can he be for a free market when he endorses a system of central economic planning by controlling the money? And when you think about it, the monetary unit is used in every single transaction, so if you can control one half of every single transaction you have a lot of power, and a lot of control.

Q: There is a story you are asked to tell often, about having Alan Greenspan sign a copy of a book called *Gold and Economic Freedom*. What happened there?

Ron Paul: In the 1960s, I was studying and reading Austrian economics and I received the *Objectivist* newsletter that Ayn Rand put out. Alan Greenspan had a piece in the newsletter and it was a delightful article—it said all the things I believed in.

One day, we had a personal meeting with Greenspan just to get our pictures taken and chat for a few minutes, and we knew that was coming up. So I dug out my original copy, and I took that with me, so when we were getting ready to get our picture, I flipped it open to his article and said, "Do you remember this?" and he said he did. Then I asked him to autograph it, so he got out his pen and he was signing it, and I said, "Do you want to write a disclaimer on this article?" He said, "No, I wouldn't do that. I just read this recently and I fully support everything I wrote."

Which is interesting because you don't know exactly what he means. If he fully supports what he wrote, why was he managing a monetary system that was exactly opposite of what he wrote in 1966?

Q: David Walker says in his talks that he thinks we've lost our way, that the idea of what America was a long time ago and what it could be is somehow getting away from us. Is this something that rings true to you?

Ron Paul: Oh yeah, we've lost our way because the majority of people—certainly in Washington—really don't care about the Constitution. The Constitution restrains government power and enhances personal liberty. We've lost our way because we've given up on our faith and our conviction and our understanding how freedom works. We don't believe free markets will take care of people. Everybody has to have a safety net. Big businesses have a safety net, small businesses have a safety net, and poor people have safety nets. Medical care can't be delivered by the marketplace and housing has to be delivered by government, and they never look at the problems: whether there's going to be a housing bubble and whether medical care is not only getting too costly but it's not improving, and whether the military industrial complex takes over the system.

Now we've lost our way; we don't believe in what made America great, and that was individual liberty. We've become too dependent on government, and yet, in spite of all those negative things I've just said and how bad Washington is and how bad the financial system is, in my travels around the country I'm really encouraged. Because so many young people today understand this and they're getting information off the Internet and different sources. A lot of them get bored with this silly Keynesian economics, which is very hard to understand and impossible to get fascinated with for the average college student. So the fact that there's so much information on the Internet is remarkable, to stimulate and arouse a whole new generation. In the '50s, when I was interested in finding this information, there was one group in the whole country and that was the Foundation for Economic Education in New York. They produced literature and you had to search for a book. There was no Internet, nothing on television that your schools didn't produce. Today everything is so much better.

So I think the undercurrent is very, very favorable and I think the next generation is not as tolerant for this acceptance of big government, and there's probably two reasons for that. I think they're attracted to the ideas and the principles of liberty, but also I think they sense that we have problems and they don't know how they're going to pay these huge debts and these entitlement burdens that are coming. They're sick and tired of the foreign policy, so in some way the problems are arousing a lot of people. As long as we do our job in spreading the ideas of freedom and emphasizing the rule of law and the restraint of government, there's reason to be hopeful.

Q: How would you characterize a generation of people who live beyond their means and pass that debt along to their children?

Ron Paul: I don't think people do it thinking, "Let's see, how many benefits can we get from government and stick it to the kid's tab?" But in a way, financially, it looks like that. But they can rationalize and say, "Well, I paid into these systems, I've been paying taxes, I just want to get some of my money back," not admitting the truth to themselves that all their money's been spent. I think it all came out of bad economic teaching of the Depression. In the early '30s when we had our Depression it was taught that capitalism and the gold standard caused all the problems, and therefore, you had to have government bailout programs and safety nets and they ushered in the whole age of welfarism, Social Security, and the government had to take care of us. At the same time, they had been taught ever since World War I that it is our obligation and responsibility morally to spread our values around the world. We have to have a war to spread democracy throughout. This whole generation accepted this but it was fallacious. It's based not on principles of liberty and self-reliance. It's based on the fact that, "well, we do need government to take care of us," and they never ask the question, you know, "Who's going to pay for it?"

We have dropped this moral constitutional approach to what we do, and yet a whole generation if not two or three have accepted this idea because we've been so wealthy and we're still doing pretty well on the surface. People seem to be doing pretty well. The tragedy is, it is all on borrowed money now. The finances are in such disastrous shape because we can't survive without borrowing $2.5 billion every day from overseas because of the current account deficit, and a country can't continue to do that. They can't continue to borrow from overseas and print money. They will come up short, and they can't just print the money—it just won't work. Eventually that ends up in big economic problems.

Q: Back in the mid- to late '90s, you were one of the only people who was blowing the whistle and speaking up against Dr. Greenspan and the Fed. What does it feel like personally to be out there on your own? Do you ever feel that you wish you weren't sometimes the only person in Washington to vote against the bill of "Let's save"?

Ron Paul: It is a lonely position, but I came with full knowledge that I expected to be in that situation, and I guess I looked always to the positive if I'm lonely here in Washington. When I leave Washington, I'm not quite so lonely. When I'm back in my district or talking around the country, all of a sudden there's a lot of support. There's a lot of grassroots support for my position about getting rid of the income tax and privatizing Social Security and letting the young people get out of it. There's a lot of support by a lot of people that understand the danger of a central bank, and they understand it when I say, "Let's just get rid of the central bank. We didn't have it before 1913, we don't have to have one."

I make up for it by looking for allies outside of Washington, but I also have a nucleus of people here in the Congress who would, behind the scenes, agree with me, and a lot of times they'll say, "Well, I would vote with you more often, except I'd have more trouble explaining it back home." They are afraid that the conventional wisdom at home is such that it might hinder their reelection. But I have found that it's a political benefit to try to talk about these difficult issues.

Q: **Can you talk for a moment about your candidacy for president? How would you define a successful campaign? Would it be winning the election, would it be winning a nomination, or would it perhaps be that your ideas that you're fighting for win and take hold and take place?**

Ron Paul: If you enter a race and say, "Well I'm not in it to win, and I'm just going to go out and make a couple points," it's not a very good campaign, either for yourself or for your supporters. So you have to set a goal of getting the maximum number of votes and setting the goals should be to win. However, the first time I ran for Congress I didn't think much would happen—and not too much happened, but something came of it. I'm issue driven and I would think that others lose a lot when they lose a race; they lose everything, because all they want is political power, and that's the least of my goals. So if I win a political race, win a Congressional seat, or win in another office, that's a plus, but I still end up with the satisfaction that I've introduced a lot of ideas to a group of people.

Q: **On a personal level, how is that you came to be a public servant? Was there something that happened in your life?**

Ron Paul: It was mainly that I wanted to talk about economic policy. And I thought that after my study in hard money economics and free market economics in the '60s, and the confirmation of the breakdown of the monetary system in 1971, that I just was motivated to talk about economic policy without much plans or expectations. A lot more has happened than I ever thought would.

Q: **If we don't right this course that we're on, reel in the deficits, and address this ever-expanding spending, what do you fear could happen?**

Ron Paul: Well, the worst thing is that the dollar's value is being eroded systematically every day, and that is since 1913. Since we've had the Federal Reserve, we have lost about 96 percent of the value of the dollar. If we don't course-correct, we're going to have a crash in the remaining value of the dollar, and you could lose it quickly. When a currency gets up to end stages, it goes quickly. A lot of people remember what happened in Germany when the German mark lost all its value. When that happens, there's runaway inflation, no controls, and economic breakdown. This usually invites a dictator—that's what helped usher Hitler into power. So many countries have bitten the dust through inflation, even in ancient times. They didn't have printing presses, but they would dilute the metal or clip the coins and deceive and steal from the people—things the government shouldn't be doing. This is a very serious problem and the biggest reality that we have to come to grips with is that we can't afford to pay all these bills, and if we just pay for these bills by printing money, then we'll destroy the currency. And that will be a much, much more painful reaction than us just tightening our belts and living within our means.

Q: Would you say that monetary policy is largely a disincentive to save?

Ron Paul: This system discourages people from saving, because if the money loses value they can't keep up. So it's better they spend the money and get something of value, and borrow the money, and this is what has happened. Too many people depend on borrowing instead of savings. But if you didn't have a Federal Reserve System, it wouldn't work that way because somebody has to produce the credit and the funds in order for people to borrow, and for businesses to borrow—and they create that out of thin air.

But a negative savings rate is very, very detrimental. True capital comes from savings. You should have what you can earn over and above what you have to use to run your business or live on. This should be savings and that should be used to be loaned out to create more jobs and more wealth. But today, because the dollar loses its value, and then it if earns a little interest then we go ahead and tax people for the interest they've earned. So if in order to regenerate savings, you should have sound money, get rid of the devaluation of the currency and get rid of all taxes on savings, and then people would go back to savings again. At the same time, we should prohibit the Fed from creating money out of thin air.

Q: In the '30s one of the ideas that came out of the Roosevelt administration was that our federal debt is a public debt, and therefore we don't ever have to pay it back. But now we're seeing an ever-larger amount of that debt held by foreign investors. Do you see that as a threat?

Ron Paul: Some people argue the case that debt doesn't matter because we owe it to ourselves. There's not much truth to that, because you have to look at the reason the debt occurred, and it usually occurred for a bad reason, say, because they were promoting a program they shouldn't have been promoting. Even if you looked at that argument today, we're owing our money overseas, so that contributes to our current account deficit when we pay interest to those holding securities, say, in China or Japan or Saudi Arabia, and that's a drain on us. That means we don't even literally pay it to ourselves anymore and therefore it just compounds. The more debt we accumulate overseas, the more interest we pay to overseas creditors, which makes our current account deficit even worse.

Q: Do you see the housing bubble as somehow being tied to the lack of savings today?

Ron Paul: Alan Greenspan and I got into a little debate when I was complaining about no savings rate, and he says, "Yeah, but housing prices are going up, and therefore people have savings." I told him that he was getting savings confused with inflation, because as a consequence of inflation the nominal price of houses was going up, but that really isn't savings because as something like that can go up in price, it can also go down. And that's exactly what has happened. In the old days, when I bought my first house, I went to a savings and loan, and somebody put money in that bank and I borrowed it and I had to pay it back. That's basically the way a market should work: Somebody should put money in the bank and you should borrow it out.

Today, because we don't have any savings, we depend on the Fed, and the Fed creates too much money, lowers interest rates too much and then they create a bubble. How long has it been that many, many good economists have been predicting that the consequence that we're facing is the collapse of the housing bubble. When the markets finally realize how damaging this is and how pervasive it is and how it's going to affect all of our other markets, we're going to have a lot more unwinding to do and it's going to affect our whole economy, because housing is a significant part. I'm probably impressed that it hasn't stirred the markets up that much yet but I think in time this is going to be much more of an issue in the economy and on the financial markets than it is today.

Paul A. Volcker

Paul A. Volcker has had a long and successful career in monetary affairs but is best known as the chairman of the Federal Reserve from 1979 to 1987. Dr. Volcker is lauded for battling inflation during a time of major economic imbalances in the United States. However, to do so, he had to raise interest rates to an all-time high: 19 percent.

Q: What do you find interesting about economics, and what drew you into the profession?

Paul Volcker: Well, I'm not sure it's easy to say what interested me in economics. After I completed university, I debated about what I should do next. I was torn between going to law school, becoming an economist, or becoming a government official. I ended up not becoming a lawyer, but becoming a combination of an economist and a government official. I'm not sure I'd call myself an economist anymore. It's a long time since I've been in graduate school.

Q: In the film, we talk a great deal about the dollar and its value. Since the dollar is the medium by which people save money and right now we're running out of it, our country is faced with a savings deficit. What is a fiat currency and what is the importance of gold in the monetary system?

Paul Volcker: Throughout my career, I have worked in finance, particularly in the Federal Reserve and the Treasury. I've also been concerned with the management and the stability of the dollar. Although the dollar had its ups and downs during my career, it has been an interesting period, to say the least. After World War II, we started out with a bright new monetary system, the so-called Bretton Woods system, which IMF created. The basic fulcrum of the Bretton Woods system was the stability of the dollar and its conversion into gold. It was assumed that exchange rates would be fixed and not change very much. And that's the way it was for about 20 years. In the 1960s, the system came under increasing pressure when the United States had a small amount of inflation. At that time, this small inflation was actually considered rather large, particularly against the growth of other countries whose economies were becoming stronger. While other countries got more dollars and exchanged some for gold, we began running balance-of-payment deficits. That put pressure on the Bretton Woods system. In 1971, we broke away from it. At that time, I was the secretary of the Treasury for monetary affairs, so I was right in the middle of that decision making.

Q: How did you feel about the decision at the time?

Paul Volcker: Well, I was in favor of the decision. I was one of the proponents of the decision, but I had very mixed feelings about it because I was brought up in defense of the system. I believed that the dollar should be supported at the center of that system and that a stable monetary system was important to the prosperity of the world. The system was set up in reaction to the turmoil in the 1930s—in the Great Depression of the 1930s—which had a lot of currency instability and antagonism between countries. So to see that system potentially undercut was a rather traumatic experience for me, especially since I was hoping for it to be restored at the time.

Q: Once the Bretton Woods exchange rate system was abandoned, did the Federal Reserve became the proponent of a sound currency?

Paul Volcker: Once we moved off gold, which was kind of the last vestige of a gold-based system, we entered a world of so-called fiat currencies. In that world, there's nothing behind money except the credibility of the government and of the central banks. They have the responsibility of maintaining the stability of the currency. Yet this country and other countries did not always honor this responsibility because of the ever-present tension between maintaining stability of the currency and maintaining full employment or economic growth. I think maintaining full employment is a false economy. Most central bankers and most economists now understand that you shouldn't set up full employment in opposition to stable currency, but the stable currency domestically is important to building a base for prosperity over the long run.

Q: **Following the end of the Bretton Woods era, the United States entered an era of rapid inflation. Were you surprised at the high rate of inflation? What do you think were the root causes of the '70s inflation that led to you taking over the Fed?**

Paul Volcker: Well, I don't know whether it's fair to say I was surprised. I was disheartened, I suppose. It is difficult to sustain the domestic price stability. But there was a combination of problems that led up to this high level of inflation. The 1970s was also a period of great instability in exchange rates, which led to some difficulties for the economy and for relations with other countries. People had become rather inured to a small amount of inflation. And as I indicated earlier, there was this feeling of a trade-off between maintaining price stability or maintaining economic growth. I think that this false trade-off made people more relaxed than they should have been. When these inflationary forces began getting stronger, it affected wage demands and pricing policies, and had a certain built-in momentum. And that whole process was aided and abetted by the big increases in oil prices and was something of a chicken-and-egg situation. For instance, you can argue that the inflationary pressure has encouraged OPEC to increase the oil price, and the increase in oil prices led to inflation, or more inflation. So we got into a discouraging passivity and cycle of poor economic performance and inflation. And I think they were related.

Q: **The popular press also tells the story of how you came in and raised interest rates in order to slay inflation. I even noticed you have the famous painting out in the hallway of you with a shield, fighting off inflation. Can you just tell us how it felt to be in that position, and also describe what was**

really happening rather than the popular portrayal expressed in that painting?

Paul Volcker: When I became chairman of the Federal Reserve, I think there was a general feeling in this country that economic affairs, and inflation in particular, had reached a kind of crisis point. Things were not going very well. There was a feeling of uncertainty. There was a lot of speculation in commodities and the gold price, which was then free to fluctuate up to $800 an ounce. In an odd kind of way, that's a good time to step into a job because people thought that something needed to be done. I also think the mood of the country was willing to accept action, which 10 years earlier they wouldn't have been willing to accept. And once we got caught up and I got caught up—or the Federal Reserve Board got caught up, for that matter the country got caught up—in an anti-inflationary effort, there was a certain willingness to take very high interest rates and eventually a rather severe recession, with the hope and expectations—certainly, the expectation that I had—that things would get better. And if we could restore any sense of stability in the currency, the country would be better off as long as we sustained that phase.

Q: Would it be fair to say that in that era the high interest rate was the tough medicine?

Paul Volcker: No. There was a lot of opposition and concern, understandably. It was a bad recession, but I think there was this underlying core that the country had not been on the right path economically and that it needed to be shaken up in order to restore stability. And that faith not only sustained me, it sustained the country.

Q: What do you feel were your proudest achievements? If you were able to restore stability, how did that come about?

Paul Volcker: Well, it's not a question, of course, of me achieving stability and sustaining stability. It was a situation in the country as a whole that a stronger approach was acceptable and that we have a Federal Reserve Board and a government who's all in. Although it was controversial—I don't want to minimize the controversy—there was a basic core of support and willingness to do it. And I think one of the lessons of the early '80s is don't let inflation get started, because once it gets some momentum it's very difficult to deal with, but it's also destructive for economic growth and prosperity. That lesson is also important today. I repeat it all the time ad nauseam: Don't let inflation get out of control and build a kind of momentum that's inevitable. If that happens—and right now it seems like there is a little flavor of it—we will all find ourselves back in the days of stagflation and unacceptable economic performance.

Q: Do you feel like that the policies that are in place are reactive enough now?

Paul Volcker: Well, right now we are in a very difficult circumstance. We are in a financial world with lot of excess spending and lending, particularly in the infamous subprime mortgages. These many excesses put a lot of pressure on economic institutions. The question becomes, how much pressure will they put on the economy as a whole? In the past 20 years, we have had a very good run of economic activity and a lot of success in the financial world. But now we have reached a point of excess, maladjustments, and tensions. Correcting them is going to be a little bit painful.

Q: When we spoke to Dr. Laffer yesterday, he credited you and the policies that he was involved with during the Reagan years as laying the groundwork for those 20 years of economic expansion. Do you agree? He also credits Clinton and then even George Bush with responding to crises in the 1990s and early 2000s. Since you believe we may be heading down that path again, how do you feel about this comment?

Paul Volcker: The period beginning in the mid-early 1990s has been one of remarkable succession and leadership in the world economy by the United States. But a lot of things have contributed to it. As mentioned earlier, price stability, which has been characterized with higher stock prices or lower interest rates, is one factor that has contributed to that success. Following a period of low-productivity growth in the United States, the explosion of high-tech industries and high productivity in the 1990s also led to broader economic policies. One crucial occurrence was during the Clinton administration. The movement toward a balanced budget was something that this country had not seen for a long time, and there was this worry that we would be so successful in running budget surpluses that the national debt would disappear in a few years. I thought the political system would make sure that that didn't happen, but it was an indication of a sense of financial discipline that hadn't existed earlier.

Now that has been eroded. In recent years, we had a small recession, which grew out of the excesses of the high-tech era and the extremely high stock prices for Silicon Valley–type firms. I'm afraid budget deficits, which to some degree are certainly tolerable and manageable in the light of the economic situation, will get us back in the habit of running deficits as a matter of course. And of course the big problem for this country fiscally is a need for more spending—an inherent need for more spending in Social Security, Medicare, and other areas. That spending presents a very large fiscal challenge in coming years. It's not here right now, but we'll see whether a democracy can deal with an obvious problem that's going to be present in not too many years; and the earlier we take action to deal with it, the better. But are we going to take action or not? That's the crucial issue.

Q: I know that you're a part of the Concord Coalition. Can you please comment on the work that they're doing? Also, can you comment on the work that David Walker is doing as the comptroller general?

Paul Volcker: With respect to the fiscal crisis looming out there in the future, the Paul Revere of America these days is David Walker, the comptroller general. He is absolutely dedicated to bringing the idea of the looming fiscal crisis to the attention of Congress and the American people. Maybe we have two Paul Reveres. We also have Pete Peterson pushing the Concord Coalition with a group of private individuals. This group was started by Paul Tsongas, Pete Peterson, and Warren Rudman, a Republican. Paul was a Democratic senator who once ran for president some years ago. Unfortunately, he died some years after he started the Concord Coalition. So I look at these men as the two minutemen in alerting the American public to the threat that's out there.

Q: **Why is it important for Americans or people who are not involved in the financial industry and/or economics to understand these issues?**

Paul Volcker: It is always difficult to answer that question because it seems that these issues are small and abstract in comparison to people's day-to-day problems of making a living and going to work. Well, they no longer seem abstract when it comes down to people maintaining fiscal discipline and paying for Social Security and Medicare. But the greatest challenge for democracy is to be able to effectively cope with problems that are pretty clearly out in the future but require some action, discipline, and restraint today. That's the test we're going through. And, as people get a better understanding and education about some basic economic issues, the democracy will be better able to cope with those future challenges.

Q: **What are the consequences of not being successful in this endeavor?**

Paul Volcker: In the future, there will be all kinds of consequences and uncertainty if we don't deal with these problems. But when I look back on my lifetime, it is obvious that letting inflation get a little bit out of control and not dealing with economic problems effectively in the '70s led to a very uncomfortable crisis. We don't want to have to go through big recessions again to teach people fiscal responsibility. Instead, we should anticipate what needs to be done while maintaining the growth of the economy. And the threat will always be an unstable economy and an unstable currency. And that's not just destructive to economic life, but it can be destructive to America's position in the world, which to me is the greatest concern.

Q: Although you cannot resolve it, can you comment on the government spending versus raising taxes?

Paul Volcker: Sure. The big ideological fights in this country concern the best way to deal with some of these problems. One side says, "Reduce taxes; make governments smaller; governments are inefficient and ineffective." The other side says, "Look, we have to be responsible and respond responsibly to some of these challenges by raising taxes." My view has always been we ought to make government as efficient as we can. In some cases that may mean a smaller government, but in other areas it might mean a consensus, particularly in some programs that are maintaining the national defense. Regardless, it's going to take money. And in order to satisfy people and get problems resolved relatively efficiently and effectively, then we have to pay for it with taxes. In my opinion, we do not have a very good tax system. It's confused, complicated, frustrating, et cetera. I hope that the next president reforms taxes and makes them a little more tolerable so people can support the spending we have to do.

Dr. Alan Greenspan

Dr. Alan Greenspan served as the chairman of the United States Federal Reserve Board from 1987 to 2006. During his tenure, Dr. Greenspan steered the U.S. economy through the Black Monday stock market crash of 1987, the dot-com boom of the 1990s, and the subsequent bubbles in stocks and housing. Criticized by some, revered by others, Dr. Greenspan is still seen as a leading authority on U.S. economic and monetary policy.

Q: In your opinion and from the data that you've seen over the last few years, are Americans saving less than they used to and if so, why do you think that might be?

Alan Greenspan: Well, it depends how we define savings. As far as your average American household is concerned, they would argue that they're saving more than enough—or at least until recently they would have said that. The reason [for that mind-set] is they've looked at their 401(k)s, and they've looked at the value of their homes, and they've looked at their assets generally—and while we economists may say that capital gains do not finance real capital investment and standards of living, the average household couldn't care less.

So up until very recently, you will not find any real concern on the part of American households that they're not saving enough; indeed, they have been very happy with what they have. The problem, however, is that that essentially was a mixture of capital gains on homes, stocks . . . on a whole variety of other types of assets [including] their income. The result, basically, is that as those wealth effects begin to reverse, people are going to perceive that they are indeed not saving enough, and hence a significant increase in the amount of savings out of income is going to give a much larger set of numbers that economists are going to feel far more comfortable with. It hasn't happened yet—savings excluding capital gains is actually very low, close to zero. Ordinarily, over the years that is 5, sometimes as much as 10 percent. I don't think we're getting back to 5 or 10 percent immediately, but I do think as the wealth effect as a substitute for savings begins to diminish, our savings rate will start to rise significantly.

Q: Why is a lack of savings problematic? How would you explain that to someone who thinks, "I'm living pretty well and I have my 401(k) and everything seems fine"? What does a lack of savings create in the long term?

Alan Greenspan: When you think in terms of the economy as a whole, you have to realize that if the output of an economy—or in household terms, the amount of income [available] is all consumed, [then] we're not accumulating the types of assets which we find productive over the years. Every advanced economy invests a significant amount of what it produces. It ploughs it back in the way of capital assets—meaning factories, equipment, all forms of capital—which essentially make the standard of living rise, because as technology and capital increase, an hour's worth of effort on the part of a person has (over the generations) been increasing, producing more and more in the way of goods and services. So that the issue is, for the national economy overall, unless you plough back or invest a significant part of your production, you will not have growing standards of living.

The comparable measure with respect to households is that if you don't save adequately, you are wholly dependent upon the income you are getting—which, incidentally, indirectly will rise because other people are saving and investing. But as far as you're concerned, unless you put money away for nest egg purposes, for retirement, for a variety of other purposes, you will find that you are living an extraordinarily precarious existence. Savings is the buffer which is the gap between disaster and prosperity.

Q: Let me follow up with the criticism or critique of someone like Dr. Ron Paul who says that Americans don't save for two reasons. One is because they choose not to, and another is

because there's a false sense of wealth. Many Americans feel richer than they actually are, and Dr. Paul would say that he would lay some of that blame at the foot of the Federal Reserve. You've probably heard this before from him personally. How do you respond to that? Does the Fed play any role in the last 10 or 20 years in the falling savings rate?

Alan Greenspan: By maintaining a stable financial system, a stable monetary system contributes to economic growth through enhancing stability and, most importantly, keeping inflation at a subdued level. The issue of rising wealth in the last 15 years or so is essentially a global phenomenon and one that results because of the consequences of what was seen when the Cold War came to an end. The extraordinary amount of economic devastation behind the Iron Curtain induced a very large part of the so-called Third World to move significantly toward competitive market capitalism, the effects of which are twofold: (1) a major decline in the rate of inflation, and (2) a huge increase in the propensity to save around the world, but most dramatically in those areas of the world which ordinarily save a great deal but were saving increasingly more. The effect of that was a major decline in long-term interest rates, which in turn have always had the effect of lowering capitalization rates on real estate, commercial, and on stocks and bonds, obviously. As a consequence of that, there is a sense of wealth, because the concept of wealth is not the physical things that we have per se, but what human beings perceive that those assets will eventually be able to contribute to future standards of living.

The most important issue here is wealth, in that sense, is a psychological problem or a psychological phenomenon, to the extent that you have great confidence about the capacity of physically existing assets producing far into the future, you will value those assets extremely highly, and when people talk about wealth, that's what they basically mean. Now, the Federal Reserve has had very little to do in that particular scenario and therefore Ron Paul, with whom I agree with on a number of issues, is mistaken in this area.

Q: How important is it for kids to learn at a young age the importance of saving?

Alan Greenspan: Well, remember what savings is all about: essentially putting aside part of what you produce, part of your income, to have provision for the future. In other words, people don't live only in the day that we're talking about. We're always projecting where we're going to be next week, next month, next year; we're always looking forward to what type of careers we're going to have, what we're going to learn, and how our lives are going to evolve. In other words, we don't live in the present and cannot live in the present only. Human beings cannot survive unless they create provision for the future, and a goodly part of the provision for the future is in monetary terms, and terms in which one can see what one needs as the years go on.

If you broaden this idea to the economy as a whole, without preparing for the future, and making provisions, the economy will be stagnant. It will not be rising as the United States has over our whole history, generation upon generation. It's critical—without savings, there is no future. It is critical to human beings, it's critical to a nation, and it's critical to the world at large.

Q: If there is a country that is choosing to live beyond its means, is there anything a central bank can to do to fix that, ultimately?

Alan Greenspan: If there are significant fiscal deficits or basically a lack of savings in an economy, what that will do—leaving aside for the moment what the Federal Reserve does—is to raise interest rates, because a demand for funds exceeds the supply of funds and there's nothing that one can do to prevent interest rates from rising. Now the danger is that if the Federal Reserve does not keep monetary policy tight in such an environment, and in a sense facilitate the rise in interest rates, it can do so only by expanding the money supply, ultimately creating inflation, and inflation eventually disables an economy and standards of living. So in that sense, if fiscal policy is lax or savings are exceptionally low, there is nothing monetary policy or any central bank can do about that.

All it can do is to try to protect the system from being excessively affected by what would be an irresponsible policy on the part of government.

Q: Would you add, too, that there might be some irresponsibility by individuals who choose not to save money in their own life, in their own families?

Alan Greenspan: Well, it's always a very difficult problem to make judgments about what the motives of people are. If you're in a free society, people have to choose the way they wish to live, the values they wish to implement, and it's not up to government to tell them they act should differently, with the obvious exception of being acutely aware of what the nature of rights are and what the nature of laws are. But there's very little government can do directly to affect people's attitudes. That's part of the culture. That's basically the function of society in general, of people who write books, people who think about issues, people who try to convince people about what they should and should not be doing. I've often found that one of the characteristics of a free society is that we are free to be irresponsible. I don't like that fact, but the ability to do so is an essential freedom because unless you voluntarily do the right thing it's not going to work. And if you are fundamentally an irresponsible person, no matter what government does, it'll show up in one way or another.

Q: Are you concerned about the level of foreign ownership of U.S. Treasury bonds and the fact that it's been increasing recently rather quickly?

Alan Greenspan: I'm not concerned by the fact that foreigners own a great deal of America. Indeed, one of the very important aspects of globalization is that there is a huge amount of trade amongst countries, and as a consequence of that the claims to wealth, which are a necessary concomitant of trade, grow. We in the United States own a good deal of the rest of the world, and the rest of the world owns a great deal of us, and that will continue to grow as globalization, which I think is a very powerful and positive force in a society, continues. So, provided we are dealing essentially with business, private assets, and very little government involved in this, I have no concern.

Q: Mr. Walker, he says that our country has a budget deficit problem, a savings deficit problem and a trade balance problem, balance of payments problem, all possibly made worse by leaders that are not warning us of what lies ahead financially with unfunded liabilities. Do you think that there's a tidal wave on the horizon, a tidal wave of spending that if we choose not to address and choose not to fix, it's going to make life much different for our children and grandchildren?

Alan Greenspan: There's an extraordinary event for the first time in human history about to occur, which is a tsunami of retired people as the baby boom generation over time doubles the number of retirees; and the fact that life expectancy continues to increase is going to increase that burden further. This means that the average working family, is going to have to produce, or I should say the average worker, is going to have to produce not only sufficient physical resources for himself and his family, but also for the retired people. What this essentially suggests is that unless we find a way to delimit the size of the physical resource shift that it's implicit in current law, we are going to be in very serious trouble. You cannot consume more than you produce, and what these various different deficits are suggesting is basically that we are trying to consume more than we produce. We can do that in the short run, but over the long run, it is of course impossible.

Warren Buffett

Warren Buffett is regarded as one of the world's greatest stock market investors. That said, it should come as no surprise that *Forbes* magazine named the "Oracle of Omaha," as he is called, as the richest person in the world in 2008. This savvy businessman and noted philanthropist has been the CEO of Berkshire Hathaway since 1970.

Q: How long has Berkshire Hathaway been here in Omaha?

Warren Buffett: We moved in at the start of 1962. It wasn't Berkshire Hathaway then, but this is the only office I've had since I had an office in my bedroom.

Q: Do you find things that you like and then stay there? That seems to be the case with your house and your office, and your investing philosophy is certainly that way as well.

Warren Buffett: If I'm happy with something, I don't change. I mean, if I find that I like hot dogs and hamburgers and French fries and cherry Coke, that's what I'll be eating the rest of my life.

Q: What do you say to people who say, "Oh, economic matters are too complicated, and I can't figure it out"? Why should the average American try to get a handle on these matters? Why is it important?

Warren Buffett: I think it's very tough for the average American to understand economics well, just as it's tough for them to understand physics well. It's a subject that requires some experience and thought and a fair amount of interest. And, as a practical matter, a high percentage of the population probably will not be interested in economics any more than they are in meteorology or physics or biology. Because it's important it does not mean that hundreds of millions of Americans are going to understand it well. And of course the real problem is that they all have this indirect, passing interest in it, and demagogues of various sorts can scare them with economics because it does apply to their everyday lives. But since the average American doesn't usually have the ability to, or even the interest in thinking incisively about the question, they can be subject to very superficial arguments.

Q: Why is economics fascinating to you?

Warren Buffett: I've always liked business; I've always liked investments; I've always liked economics. But I'm a disaster if you ask me what happens to a split atom or what happens to a cell within a body. Different people are wired different ways.

Q: In 2003, you wrote a story that appeared in *Fortune* magazine. Can you tell me a little about this story? Why did you write it?

Warren Buffett: I wrote an article for *Fortune* on the parable of Squanderville and Thriftville, which was designed to simplify for people the problems inherent in persistent and large trade imbalances. Economics tends to put people to sleep, and I thought that by creating a couple of islands populated by inhabitants with quite widely different activities that it might get across a point that otherwise they get lost on.

Q: What's the general thrust of the story?

Warren Buffett: Well, the thrust of it is that if you own a lot of property—in this case, an island—you can trade it for the things that you consume everyday. And you can do that for a long time, but eventually you run out of property and then you have to work a whole lot harder to provide for your own needs, but also to pay back the debts you've incurred or to get back the property you want. Short-term actions have long-term consequences that sometimes people don't think about in the short run.

Q: Is there a way to characterize our country and our philosophies nowadays?

Warren Buffett: In the last few decades, but accentuating in the last six or eight years, this country has started consuming considerably more than it produces. In other words, it's relied on the labor of others to provide things that we use day by day.

We're able to do that because we have lots of things to trade for those goods, so we can trade away little pieces of the country. And, because we're so rich, we can do it for a long time and we can do it on a large scale, but we can't do it forever.

Q: Explain that to me. Why is that?

Warren Buffett: It's like a credit card. My credit's pretty good at the moment; if I quit working and have no income coming in but keep spending, I can first sell off my assets and then, after that, I can start borrowing on my credit card. And if I've got a good reputation, I can do that for quite awhile. But at some point, I max out. At that point, I have to start producing a whole lot more than I consume in order to clean up my debts.

Q: Let's imagine for a minute that the U.S. economy is a horse and it's in a race, and the other horses are other economies around the world. How strong and how much of a favorite to win is our economy today and historically?

Warren Buffett: We have a terrific economy, and the real standard of living in the twentieth century, per capita, improved seven to one. There's never been anything like that in history. And we will have a better economy 20 years from now, and 50 years from now, than we have now. We are continuously getting more productive in the country. We have more people turning out more things. Our country has a fine future economically. You don't want to bet against the United States.

On the other hand, we are creating debts and selling off assets, which will require American citizens in the future to service those debts, and that will take some part of their output. But I want to emphasize that the output left for them will still be higher per capita than it is today. We are not spending or consuming ourselves into destitution. Americans will be living better 20 years from now and 40 years from now than they do today.

Q: Do you think that you could make an argument that Americans are living too well, or maybe beyond their means?

Warren Buffett: Well, we are using up some of our national credit card and selling off a small portion of our assets every year in order to consume more than we produce. But the value of the country goes up annually and over the decades, so we can do some of that. We can still improve the standard of living per capita, not as much as if we weren't consuming so much, but we will still be improving the standard of living. The time will come, however, if we continue this policy, when Americans will find that 2 or 3 percent of their labor every day is going to service the debts incurred by the overconsumption of the present people. They'll still live very well—I want to emphasize that.

Q: Is the fact that we're not saving as a country and the fact that there's much more foreign ownership of our bonds and our debt interconnected, and what are the ramifications?

Warren Buffett: Well, we're transferring small bits of the country—ownership of the country, or IOUs—to the rest of the world, but our national pie is still growing. In other words, we're like a very, very, very rich family that owns a farm the size of Texas, and we have all this output coming from the farm. Now, because we consume a little more than we produce, we're selling off tiny bits of that farm daily, a couple billion worth, or we're giving a small mortgage on it which we don't even notice, but it does build up over time. On the other hand, the farm is getting more productive all the time. So even though we own a little less of the farm, or we create these IOUs against it, our equity in the farm actually increases somewhat. That's why people will benefit over time. But they won't benefit as much as if they hadn't given the IOUs or sold off little pieces of the farm.

Q: At some point in the last few years, for the first time ever, you bought foreign currencies. Can you explain to me your own personal faith in the U.S. dollar? Has that faith changed or altered in the last few years? If so, why?

Warren Buffett: Both personally and at Berkshire Hathaway, we have far more assets in dollars than in all other currencies combined. So it is not like anything drastic is going to happen in the United States. On the other hand, if you give more and more of your IOUs to the rest of the world and you denominate them in your own currency, history shows that countries that do that have an interest over time in inflating and in having their currencies worth less. If I could finance all of my own consumption today by handing out something called Warren Bucks, or Warren IOUs, and I had the power to determine the value of those IOUs over time, believe me, I would make sure that when I repaid them 10 or 20 years from now that they were worth less, per unit, than they are today. So any country that piles up external debt will have a great temptation to inflate over time, and that means that our currency, relative to other major currencies, is likely to depreciate over time.

Q: What is a gold standard, and is the gold standard a viable option these days?

Warren Buffett: I do not think that the gold standard is a viable option, and I don't think that gold has magic attached to it. It is true that when you turn paper money in, what you get in exchange is more paper money. If you have a gold standard you can get some gold, but you can't do much with gold, either. Over time, people have dug up gold from the ground in far, remote areas and then they've shipped it thousands and thousands of miles and they've put it in the ground over here and hired guards to stand over it. So the real utility of gold is not high. It's been something that people turn to, but it has not been a very good investment. If you bought gold 100 years ago, it was roughly $20 an ounce. You'd have paid to store it and you'd have insured it and you'd have received no income from it at all. Your real return would be very, very poor.

Q: One of the attributes that people apply to the gold standard is that it exacts fiscal discipline on a government that uses gold as backing for its currency. Do you think that's true?

Warren Buffett: We're doing this interview in a state, Nebraska, where William Jennings Bryan said, "Do not crucify mankind upon a cross of gold." It's true that gold can act as a check on certain economic excesses, but it can act as a check, unfortunately, on economic activity, too. Its virtues become its sins, also. I do not think a gold standard would work well for the world.

Q: Can you comment on the federal debt and unfunded liabilities? Is this something that you're concerned about? Or do you think we're at a manageable level?

Warren Buffett: The net federal debt is about 40 percent of GDP. Compared to what it's been historically in this country and what it is in many other countries, it's not at an unreasonable level. And debt can only be measured in relation to income. You have 300 million Americans with great income potential. The government has a claim on that income in the future. It has whatever claim it wants, as a practical matter. Forty percent of GDP in that debt is not something that's caused us trouble in the past. I don't think it's something that will cause us trouble in the future.

Q: What do you think of the deficit reduction of the '90s and some of the financial policies of the last seven or eight years? Would you like to see deficit reduction? Do you think that piling up deficits is a bad thing?

Warren Buffett: I think keeping debt within a range of GDP makes sense. I don't think you want debt to climb to 100 percent of GDP. I don't think you want to pay off the national debt. And that means if GDP grows in nominal terms, 4 to 5 percent a year, and the national debt grows at 4 to 5 percent a year, you really haven't changed the fundamental economic dynamics of the country any more than if Berkshire is worth $10 billion and owes $1 billion and someday later it's worth $100 billion and owes $10 billion. Nothing has really changed for the worse in terms of Berkshire's credit, and the same goes for the government.

Q: Do you think that the retirement of the baby boomers will throw a curveball at this equation?

Warren Buffett: No, the demographics have worked somewhat against the standard of living for a long time. Retired people live in retirement much longer now than they did 50 years ago. But the standard of living kept improving during the twentieth century, even as demographics moved away from ideal, if you're talking about productivity. You had more and more people retired relative to the ones producing, and that's continuing. But productivity improves all the time, too, so it's a good thing when people don't have to work as hard to take care of the needs of the whole population. That's what's been happening over the years, and I think it'll continue to happen.

Q: **The speed at which globalization has happened, to the rise of China and economies, at the same time that the Western economies are getting older—is that changing the equation at all?**

Warren Buffett: What's happened, to some extent, is that China has caught on to some principles that have made this economy work so well. In 1790, there were about 4 million people in the United States and there were about 290 million people in China. They were just as smart as we were. They had a climate that was about the same as ours. They had somewhat comparable natural resources. And yet, we did enormously well over the next 217 years in improving the lives of the people here, per capita, as compared to China. Now, why did we do that? Well, we had a market system, we had a rule of law, we had equality of opportunity— not perfectly in all cases, but probably better than much of the rest of the world—and that system unleashed the potential of citizens in the United States to an extent far greater than in many countries, including, up until recently, China. And I think maybe the Chinese have caught on to some of the benefits of our system and they will unleash the potential of their people as well. And there's nothing bad about that. The fact that your neighbor lives well is not going to hurt how you live.

In this country, we have seen imports increase from 5 percent of GDP to 17 percent or so of GDP in the past 35 or so years. And yet we have 4.5 percent unemployment and we have a very, very prosperous country. So it's a good thing for us. What is not good is the imbalance between imports and exports. We've actually increased our exports from 5 percent of GDP to about 11 percent of GDP. The rest of the world is buying more and more of our goods all the time. But at an even greater rate, we're buying more and more of theirs. That's not good. More trade overall is good as long as it's true trade. If it's pseudo-trade, where we're buying but not selling, I do not think that's good over time.

Q: Is there a way to correct the trade path that we're on, and if so, what is it?

Warren Buffett: It's complicated. I reluctantly think that it probably requires some governmental policies that will lead to imports and exports actually increasing, but coming much closer to balancing imports and exports. I think that's advisable. I don't think the world comes to an end if it doesn't happen this year or next year, but piling up more and more and more external debt and having the rest of the world own more and more of the United States may create real political instability down the line, and increase the possibility that demagogues come along and do some very foolish things.

Q: You've said before that manufacturing is not the ideal business, but securities is, and sort of like losing the productive capacity of the companies. Am I getting that right?

Warren Buffett: Yes. If you go back 100 years, a very high percentage of the people worked on farms. And if you'd said to people at that time, somebody's going to invent an automotive engine, and tractors will replace horses, and you'll need fewer people and you'll have combines and planters, undoubtedly there would have been all kinds of scary headlines saying, "Eighty Percent of Farmers to be Unemployed." People would have asked what they were going to do, and would have expected the world to come to an end, and that they'd all be sitting around. That isn't what happens at all.

What happens is that you get more productive. People are freed up to go up into other things. We didn't have motion pictures back 100 years ago. That industry employs a lot of people now. It's not a blessing to the individuals, and there ought to be a big safety net for the people that get hit hard in their specific industries. But it's a blessing when fewer people can accomplish the same goals. The railroad industry, at one time, employed a million people in this country. Now there's about 200,000, and they're hauling far more freight than they did when they employed the million people. If you'd predicted 40 or 50 years ago that 800,000 people were going to lose their jobs in rails, all of the rail workers would have formed committees and looked for congressmen to protect them and that sort of thing. But in the end, that's what capitalism's all about: finding ways that fewer people can do the same job, so that the people released can turn out even more goods and services that people want.

Q: **Would you say that, just in your approach to business, a higher percentage now comes from services? Or does a higher percentage of the business opportunities come from financial services?**

Warren Buffett: Manufacturing has gotten more productive at a rate faster than most service industries have. If you look at a philharmonic orchestra from 50 years ago and now, there probably hasn't been a big change in productivity. There hasn't been much change in productivity, for example, in higher education. The output compared to the input of hours has not improved dramatically. On the other hand, if you look at a ton of steel, if you look at a freight car moving, if you look at a car produced, you'll see enormous increases in productivity. So in manufacturing, we now get more and more goods with fewer and fewer people. But that leaves those people available to do other things that we want them to do, whether it's engage in heavyweight fights or play in the philharmonic or do all kinds of things, and we still have as many cars and tons of steel and freight cars moving as we had in the past. But that's all to the good. That's what's improved the standard of living in this country.

Q: **So you're not concerned, then, by the impact of lowering wage rates from other competing economies?**

Warren Buffett: Overall, we're better off if we can get somebody else to do the things they do best, and we do the things we do best. And, like I say, in the last 35 years or so we have managed to get huge increases in the standard of living while we import about

17 percent of our GDP as opposed to 5 percent, and people are living better and we've got 4.5 percent unemployment.

But economics is not simple stuff. To help people really understand it is not simple, and there are so many people that want to make it simple for their own purposes, or who have got some particular crusade they're on. We came fairly close to the whole system imploding in the 1930s because of economic conditions. People became very responsive to communism in this country. They became responsive to Huey Long. They became responsive to the Townsend Plan in California. When people are scared about economics, they'll listen to whoever is the most persuasive.

Q: Is that the rise of demagoguery?

Warren Buffett: It really is. One thing I don't like about the consequences of sustained large trade deficits is I think it makes the potential for demagoguery and really foolish policies more likely over time. When you think about the history of this country, our economic policies have been pretty darn good. I mean, any country that delivers a seven for one increase in per capita living in a century has done an awful lot of things right. It's never happened before in mankind. If you go back three or four hundred years ago, nothing has really changed. But, of course, you and I live far better than John D. Rockefeller lived. We can attend the World Series. We can stay cool in summer and warm in winter far easier than he could. We can move around the country in a fraction of the time he could. All kinds of benefits have been showered upon us by the system, essentially. So it has worked out pretty well. There are always problems, but you want to make sure that you don't throw out the baby with the bathwater.

Q: Could you just talk about your business philosophy, and what is appealing to you when you see a business? What is it that you're looking for when you are looking to grow your business?

Warren Buffett: In businesses, we're looking for an entity that has durable competitive advantage; somebody that not only is doing well now, but will do well 10 or 20 years from now. In capitalism, when you have a wonderful business, it's like having an economic castle. And the nature of capitalism is that people want to come in and take your castle. It's perfectly understandable. If I'm selling television sets, there's going to be 10 other people who are going to try and sell a better television set. If I have a restaurant here in Omaha, people are going to try and copy my menu and give more parking and take my chef and so on. So capitalism's all about somebody coming and trying to take the castle.

Now, what you need is you need a castle that has some durable competitive advantage—a castle that has a moat around it. One of the best moats in many respects is to be a low-cost producer. But sometimes the moat is just having more talent. If you're the heavyweight champion of the world and you keep knocking out people, or if you're Steven Spielberg and can turn out great motion pictures, you've got a competitive advantage as long as you can keep doing it. It has enormous economic value.

We're looking for that institutionalized. We're not looking for the best brain surgeon in town. We're looking for the Mayo Clinic. We want an institution that, regardless of the person in charge, will maintain that competitive advantage over the decades. We hope we find that in some businesses, and then we try to get the best person that we can to run them. Usually, it's the person who's been running them.

Q: Are you always right, or do you make mistakes?

Warren Buffett: No, we make mistakes. It wouldn't be any fun if we didn't make mistakes. If I played golf and on every one of the 18 holes I hit a hole in one, I wouldn't be playing golf for very long. You have to go into the rough occasionally to make the game interesting. Not too often, though.

Q: Your father was a politician. Can you talk about the role of leadership in our country?

Warren Buffett: When you have 300 million people in a country, and you act through representative government, and that government controls 20 percent-plus of the resources of this enormously rich country, it's very important who you have in positions of leadership. It's important who you have in the legislative body and it's very important who you have as the head administrator of the country. You want someone who can see beyond the next mountain, and who can get people to follow him to the next mountain, because the populace wants to be led but they have to believe in the leader. That was dramatically illustrated when Roosevelt came in early 1933. We had a country with enormous horsepower, but the motor wasn't working. And it was turning out a very small fraction of the horsepower it was capable of. I don't know what the population was then, but it was well over 100 million people, and we had the plants and we had the soil. We had the people. And the machine wasn't working. It took leadership to get that machine to function again as it was capable of functioning, and that meant all the difference in the world.

You needed inspiring leadership then, something people believed in. The same is true in wartime and it will be in the future. The nice thing about our country is that even when we have had poor leadership, we've still done pretty well. I've always said in investments, that you really want to buy a company that's so good that an idiot can run it, because sooner or later one will. We've had 43 presidents now, and all 43 haven't been homerun hitters, but the country's done awfully well. Sometimes it's done well in spite of them and sometimes it's done well because of them, but it's really nice to know that we've got a machine that works so well, even if we don't have the best of leaders at all times. We still ought to try and have the best leader we can.

Q: Why do you always refer to U.S. bonds as risk-free investments?

Warren Buffett: They're not free of purchasing power risk, but they will always be paid in dollars.

Q: Can you just explain to me, as an investor, what you use the bond market for?

Warren Buffett: On balance, we like only businesses. Aside from your own personal talents, a good business is the best asset there is. I mean, the best investment you can make is in yourself.

If you have a 300-horsepower motor and you're only getting 100 horsepower out of it, you want to develop whatever skills are needed to make yourself the most effective human being. But beyond that, the best investment is a good business, one that has a durable competitive advantage and that will be around 10 or 20 or 50 or 100 years from now, turning out something people want at a profit. The U.S. government bond is absolutely certain to be paid. It's just total nonsense when people talk about the U. S. going bankrupt. I mean, the U.S. government will always pay its debts. The purchasing power of the dollar you receive is likely to be less than the dollar that you invested, so you have a purchasing power risk. But you don't have a payment risk with U.S. government bonds. So we would rather own a good business [with U.S. government bonds] which is likely to flourish almost under any circumstances and where, if there's a lot of inflation, we'll earn just as much in terms of real dollars as we would today. But you should not be afraid of government bonds in terms of being paid.

Q: Would you see a problem if somewhere like China, for instance, stopped putting so much money back into the bonds?

Warren Buffett: People get very confused about what will happen if, say, the Chinese or other countries dump their government bonds. If we buy $2 billion more of goods today than we sell to the rest of the world, which is more or less what happens, the rest of the world gets $2 billion worth of something, don't they? They get these little claim checks called U.S. dollars. They can exchange those U.S. dollars for U.S. government bonds, they can buy stocks here, they can buy real estate here, but they have to buy something.

So let's say the Chinese have $1 trillion worth of U.S. government bonds. Let's say they decided to sell them. If they sell them in the United States, they get dollars. What do they do with the dollars? They have to buy some other asset in the United States. They can trade those government bonds for stocks, but that just creates more demand for stocks and less for bonds. But that's happening every day for other reasons.

Now, they also could sell that trillion dollars to the French and get euros in exchange, but now the French would own them. If they dumped foreign assets on the United States, they get other United States assets. Countries can trade them around among themselves. If the British prefer to have dollars and the Chinese prefer to have pounds, you will find them making an exchange. But the Chinese—or any other country—can't dump their U.S. government bonds and have some terrible depressing effect on the United States because in exchange they'll get dollars, and what do they do with the dollars? They put them in banks or something of the sort. They buy stocks with them. They buy real estate. So it's exactly like saying, "If I've got a billion dollars worth of government bonds and I want to sell them, well, I'll get a billion dollars worth of cash and I've got to buy something else." And that something else may be my government bonds.

But the most important question in economics is, "And then what?" After all, you can't do just one thing in economics. Anything you do triggers another corresponding action. So if somebody says to you, "The Chinese are going to sell a trillion dollars worth of government bonds," then just say, "And then what? What do they get?" They get a trillion dollars worth of cash if they sell them in the United States. They put the cash in bonds here, or they put them into other bonds. They put them in stocks, real estate, or something of the sort.

What does happen, of course, is if they pile up more and more assets abroad, we have to pay them interest on that. We have a servicing cost, and that's where 2 or 3 percent of the GDP of the country could go 10 or 20 years from now, and I think that can be politically very unstable.

Q: How so?

Warren Buffett: If the American worker were told by a politician 20 years from now that, when he works 40 hours, an hour and a half of that every week is going simply to service the debts incurred by the previous generation because they overconsumed, I think that he would say, "I'm not interested in doing that anymore."

Let's take an extreme example. At the time of the Revolution, we'd send somebody over to King George, and he'd say, "Listen, this fight is hardly worth it. A lot of people will be killed. Why don't we just make a deal with you? We want our independence. We're kind of a pain in the neck anyway. So why don't we just give you 3 percent of our output forever, and you give us our freedom?" Now, King George might have liked that, and the American colonists might have liked that. We weren't producing that much anyway. It saves you going to war, maybe getting shot and killed. So the first generation would say, "It's a fair deal." Three percent royalty to the English, we get our freedom, and nobody gets killed. The next generation might even be okay with this.

It wouldn't work now. If we were giving 3 percent of the output of the United States to England for freeing us 220 or however many years ago, we'd have fought a war with them over it or we'd have repudiated it.

That's an extreme case, obviously, but if 15 or 20 years from now, 2 or 3 percent of the GDP is being paid abroad merely to service the debts or the ownership of assets that have been incurred because we're overconsuming, that will be politically unstable. Many years ago, when we lent a lot of money to various emerging countries and were having trouble getting paid back, somebody said that they found it very hard to imagine some Philippine or Thailand worker spending a couple of extra hours every week in the hot sun merely so Citicorp could increase its dividend twice a year. At a point, people just say, "To hell with it." It's much easier just to inflate your way out of it. If you're in a South American or Asian country that owes money in dollars, it gets very binding to pay back in dollars. But if you owe it in your own currency, you just print more currency. And we have the ability to print more currency. We can denominate debt in our own currency, whereas many countries can't because people don't trust them.

Q: China is the largest consumer of U.S. debt right now. If they were to slow down the purchasing, then the Treasury has to

increase the interest rate in order to raise the money that they need. Is that right?

Warren Buffett: Yes. Hypothetically, let's say that right now China may be running a trade surplus with us of $250 billion a year. Part of that surplus, they used to finance a deficit they run with the rest of the world. In other words, their total trade surplus is less than the $250 billion they're running with us. Now, they're also running a trade deficit with the rest of the world. So, some of the surplus with us goes to that. Some of the surplus is used to buy U.S. assets. In this hypothetic situation, we'll say they're putting the whole $250 billion in U.S. treasuries each year, so they are a net buyer of $250 billion in U.S. treasuries. Now, let's say they decide they'd rather buy $100 billion a year of U.S. treasuries. That simply means they put the other $150 billion in other assets that they buy here. They might buy stocks, they might buy businesses, and they might buy real estate. If they buy those stocks, bonds, and real estate, they hand that $150 billion to those people for those assets, and those people can go buy the Treasury bills. If I quit buying bonds today and start buying stocks, or if I quit buying stocks and buy bonds, it's very hard to measure exactly what effect that will have on stock or bond markets, because there's somebody on the other side of every transaction. You always have to say, "And then what?"

Q: Are we going down a road where the trade deficit is really going to become dangerous?

Warren Buffett: I think it will have political effects at some point. It will decrease the rate of gain in the standard of living for the average American over time. In my opinion, it will not turn it negative under any circumstances I can foresee, but it does reduce the rate of gain in the standard of living that American workers will experience.

Q: If you can imagine you're eight or ten years old, and you are hopping in your little boat that's your life, what are the things that set you on the kind of choice that you've sailed?

Warren Buffett: I was extraordinarily lucky. The odds were almost 50 to 1 against me being born in the United States. In 1930, of all the live births in the world, one out of 50, roughly, was in the United States. And then I was born to a couple of parents who cared a lot about me, who believed in education, who took good care of me, and I was wired to do well in a certain part of a market system that pays off enormously in a rich capitalist country. I'd been born a few hundred years ago, it wouldn't have paid off the same way. If I'd been born in Bangladesh, it wouldn't have been paid off the same way. I didn't have anything to do with that wiring. I could have been wired to play chess, and there's no money in chess. It would have required just as much brain power and hard work, but that's not where the market system paid off. I happen to be in something called capital allocation or asset allocation, and in a very rich capitalist system, asset allocation pays off in a disproportionate way to any real contribution to the society. I've been very lucky that way.

Q: Do you see money and capital assets strictly as a sort of a strategic tool that you can use to create more? How do you view money?

Warren Buffett: Well, money is a claim check on the output of others in the future. If I have a pile of dollar bills or if I have a pile of stock certificates or a pile of bonds, those represent claim checks which I or a charity or my descendants or my spouse or whoever can use to exchange for the goods and services produced by others. Somebody else will work for that. If I wanted to, I could hire thousands of people to sit everyday and paint my portrait, you know? And they would be employed, and I could use these claim checks and I could look for the perfect portrait of myself. I would never find it, because I don't look like Arnold Schwarzenegger, but I could keep looking for the guy that would try and make me look that way. And I could keep handing out these claim checks, and I would command that person's services the rest of their life. They wouldn't do anything else for society at all. Or I could build myself a wonderful pyramid. I could say, "Why should people have to go to Egypt to see one of these things? So, I'll spend all of these claim checks I've got and we'll have thousands of people in loincloths, like the original cast in the Cecil B. DeMille production, and they'll haul these blocks of granite and we'll build a pyramid and make people forget all about Egypt." And that would command the services of other people. So you can exchange these little pieces of paper for other people's goods and services in the future. And the wisdom with which you do that depends very much on the individual. And some people build pyramids, and I hope other people engage in cancer research.

Q: **Early in the Lowenstein book, which you didn't cooperate with, he makes the statement that when you were 26, you were already trying to figure out what you were going to do with the money that you hadn't made yet. I think that leads to, later in your life, an idea of progressive taxation. I believe you just donated a large sum of money to the Gates Foundation. Could you just speak a little bit about your beliefs on making money, and your obligation to your family and society?**

Warren Buffett: I didn't cooperate with Lowenstein, but I didn't block him either. There's a woman writing a book now that I'm cooperating with. As I said, I was lucky in being in the right place at the right time with the right equipment, and a market system that had enormous amounts of capital assets. Just the crumbs falling off the table would make me very rich. And the question is, what do you do with all of those claim checks? My family and I have had everything we could possibly need, you know, for the last 50 years. But, also 50 years ago, my wife and I decided that, beyond taking care of ourselves, there was no reason to set it up so that the next 25 generations of little Buffett kids could keep using these claim checks so they didn't have to do anything to contribute to society. There were better uses for those claim checks. One way or another, the money was going to go back to society. Philanthropy is the logical way to do it. The question is, who would be best at using those claim checks to benefit the six billion people around the world? I decided that the five foundations that I'm allocating the claim checks to do a first-class job of that, and so far I'm very pleased with them.

Q: What does life look like in a country where there isn't a strong economy, where they haven't figured out how to get the horsepower out of the horses?

Warren Buffett: Well, the world went no place economically for centuries and centuries and centuries. And finally along came a system that really unleashed and enhanced human potential. We started figuring out how one person could get an awful lot accomplished in terms of turning out goods and services for other people. The ratio was one to one between the individual and the output. We learned how to make people far, far more productive, whether it was Henry Ford in developing the assembly line or all kinds of things that happened in this country. When you think of what one person could deliver in the way of agricultural output 200 years ago compared to what they can do now, just think of the human capacity that's been freed up by the various developments in agriculture and manufacturing. You know, it's been a marvelous time to be alive. It really wasn't a whole lot better to live in the fourth century B.C. than the fourth century A.D., but it's been a lot better to live in the year 2007 than it was in the year 1807.

Q: What do you say to someone who says, "Well, sure, there's a lot of winners with capitalism, but boy, we've created so many losers"?

Warren Buffett: Well, there are enormous disparities in terms of how the benefits of this society have been distributed. The disparities have gotten wider and our tax system has favored enormously the rich. But even those on the low end are doing far better than people on the high end were doing 100 years ago. There're many, many things that a person earning a normal wage in this country can do and enjoy that John D. Rockefeller couldn't do and couldn't enjoy. So a rising tide has lifted all the boats, but it's lifted the yachts a lot faster.

Q: Is that a good thing or a bad thing?

Warren Buffett: I think it's a bad thing. Our tax system has gone very much awry, particularly in the last 10 years. It wasn't this way 50 years ago, but I am now treated as sort of an endangered species by the government. They want to make sure nothing bad happens to me, so I get a tax rate of 15 percent, counting payroll taxes, virtually, on a very large income. The average American is paying a higher tax rate than I and most members of the Forbes 400 are paying, if you count payroll taxes.

Q: Do you think that the pendulum might swing back the other way for the benefit of the country?

Warren Buffett: Well, we'll see. That depends on political developments. I don't think there's any urge in the present administration to have the tax system change and tilt away from fellas like myself, but the world has changed many times on taxes over the years. If you read the history of the tax code, for the last 90 years or so, there have been a lot of swings in both public opinion and activities in Congress. The one thing I can promise you is it'll be different 20 years from now.

Q: Do you think supply-side theories are 100 percent effective and efficient, or does it depend on where we are in the world?

Warren Buffett: I think that the market system generally works pretty well. And I think a rule of law helps enormously, and I think equality of opportunity is enormously important. You've got to have a way for the Jack Welches or the Bill Gateses or the Andy Groves to get into the positions that they should be in, where they're very good at using resources. And we have had a system in this country that's done a far better job in that respect than around the world. So you want a system where Mike Tyson is fighting for the heavyweight championship and Jack Welch is running General Electric, but you don't want Mike Tyson to be running General Electric and Jack Welch in the heavyweight ring. Government allocation of resources has tended, too often, to misallocate, and I think a market system does a pretty good job of allocating. But I also think you need a better distribution of the magnificent amount of goods and services that are turned out by the system.

Q: Do you think your grandchildren are going to live in a great country 50 years from now? What do you hope for your grandchildren and what do you see?

Warren Buffett: Well, 50 years later, I really hope to be around myself and be the world's oldest living man. I would love the idea of living 50 years from now if we can somehow solve the dilemma of weapons of mass destruction.

Q: And what does life look like for your grandchildren do you hope, and what do you really honestly think?

Warren Buffett: Economically, my grandchildren will live better than I lived, even if they earn a tenth of 1 percent of what I earn now. The average American is going to live better 10 years from now, 20 years from now, and 50 years from now.

James Areddy

James Areddy is a China correspondent with the *Wall Street Journal*, based in Shanghai. He covers the financial markets, the banking system, the currency in China, and various other financial issues—basically, the bread-and-butter type stories for the *Wall Street Journal*. He and several colleagues recently won the Pulitzer Prize for international reporting and international news. His particular contribution was about riding on the train to Tibet and about how China's economic juggernaut is rattling on in one of its more western provinces.

Q: Why is the Shanghai Bureau important? And where does their importance fit in the global economic story?

James Areddy: China's probably the biggest global economic story going right now. It affects everything from big business, Wall Street, and down-home America to countries all over the world. You can go anywhere and see Chinese people and Chinese exports. Whether it's bicycles or high-air refrigerators or freezers, you certainly are feeling the effects of China pretty much anywhere. Every company wants to sell and be here because it's the world's biggest consumer market, 1.2 billion people.

There's a lot of nervousness around the world about what that means for people's jobs and what it means for their incomes. Perhaps *anxiety* is a better word than *nervousness,* because there is a lot of opportunity here. There are more and more foreigners pumping into China. They all bring in money, they've all got investment ideas, and they see China as the new West, as really the untapped frontier. It really is an economic miracle, taking place right now. It is a fascinating story from every possible angle.

Q: If you were able to go back a thousand years and look at what's happened in China in the last 15 years, how would you say life is different today than it was decades ago?

James Areddy: What's happening in the world's most populist country is that it's transforming into a normal economy and country much like those everywhere around the world. This is a system that for many years was closed off to the rest of world, and didn't want to have anything to do with people outside. China called itself the middle kingdom and saw itself as the center; there was no reason to leave. Two hundred, three hundred, four hundred years ago, when Westerners started arriving on Chinese shores, they found many of the kind of opportunities that people are sensing today, but China never really opened up to those. China, since 1949, went through economic calamity, political upset, was secretive, and was closed down to the rest of the world for many years. Only in the early 1980s did China start to recognize how the world was changing, and it wanted to be part of the world. It really did open up, it really was allowing itself to interconnect with the world in every way.

Clearly the biggest impact has been economically. You can see people who years ago not only didn't have any access to material goods, whether it's a bicycle or a television, but they didn't even have money to buy those things. If those existed, they were given by the state. (People obtained coupons from their companies to have a new bicycle.) As money started to flow into the economy, as people started to have money, there was a shortage of goods. In more recent years, China has started to make lots of things, so much so that it is exporting them.

It is a highly competitive environment here because people sense a new opportunity and the government has stepped back. Now the Chinese are able to do what they want—they can start businesses, buy what they want, and increasingly, go where they want. Chinese are traveling abroad in record numbers; there's a flood into many, many countries. They are coming back with ideas, and at the same time foreigners are being allowed to come to China and set up in a way that the world really hasn't seen on such a scale for really a long time. Japan is very often used as a comparison, but Japan retained a lot of the closed-naturedness of historic China, whereas China is allowing foreign companies to come in and start factories and start selling products to its people.

Q: Although China is still a Communist state, it's not Communism like what the history books tell you. How would you describe the way this new economic model and the old political model have come together? Is this a new Communism?

James Areddy: Right. What's going on in China is very much defined by the government stepping back from society. The government's fingers are everywhere. It's in people's homes; everyone has a neighborhood committee. There's a little old lady who watches what's going on in every neighborhood, and that's certainly defined people's lives for years. It's made them a lot more reluctant to do lots of things, because there were always reports about them.

More and more, what's happening is that no one's paying attention, and that's probably the biggest change. Of course the question is, is China a Communist state or is it not? A lot of people would argue that economically it's not at all and that it's one of the most competitive economies in the world. But the truth of the matter is that the government is still party to much of what happens in the economy, and less in terms of what happens with someone's average life—who they decide to get married to, where they want to travel, what they want to buy, things like that.

Q: Can you get a handle on how big the Chinese government is and talk about it in relationship to the American government? Our government seems to be ever-growing, and the Chinese government, as you just said, seems to be becoming smaller or at least stepping back. Do you have a hunch that their government is stepping back, maybe becoming smaller? Could you compare the sizes of our government and our involvement?

James Areddy: Chinese people are worried about the same things that Americans are worried about. They're worried about their health care; they're worried about their retirement; they're worried about boosting their own incomes. They look at the government probably a little bit differently. Chinese people aren't really waiting for the government to have a lot of answers for them. It's a little unclear why that is, but they see the government stepping away from everywhere they used to be. The government used to be dictating where they worked and how they lived and things like that, and they're just not anymore. I think that Chinese people extrapolate from that that the government's not going to be involved in their retirement.

But at the same time, the government is pretty involved with lots of businesses. One of the more difficult things is trying to decide what is government and what's not government. There are a lot of companies that are quasi-government; there are a lot of people who are businesspeople but in fact are Communist party members. It's a little bit difficult sometimes to figure out where the government is in China, and that's a probably a big difference compared with the U.S.

Q: **Talk to me about Macro Economics 101. What is a trade deficit, and can you describe the trade deficit that exists today between the United States and China?**

James Areddy: China's making everything from computers to cars, and they have designs on the world's biggest economy, which is the United States. They certainly see that as a market in the same way a lot of companies see China as a market. A lot of things are made quite cheaply in China. American and Western companies are then selling those goods, whether it's computers or whether it's little plastic buckets. Anything that you find on a Wal-Mart store shelf is invariably made in China. Why is that? It's because they're cheap and they're relatively efficient; they're making good products here in China. Then, they're exporting that stuff to the U.S., and U.S. consumers are finding prices falling for lots of really basic goods. They're able to fill up their garages with lots of things that are made in China. The result: a lot of goods, a lot of stuff, a lot of ships flowing toward the U.S. In response, what China is getting out of it is a lot of money. There are a lot of dollars coming into China from the U.S., and from virtually everywhere in the world.

Q: If we were keeping score of this deficit between the two countries, where do we stand today?

James Areddy: The way people keep score on the trade relationship is often China's foreign exchange reserves. It's the amount of extra money that the government lays claim to. Sometime in late 2006 that number hit a pretty important milestone, $1 trillion, and it's continued to rise at a very, very rapid pace. That's basically $1 trillion in profit that China has earned from selling all kinds of things overseas.

Q: Some people say that if they wanted to, China could inflict a lot of pain on the U.S. Do you think that that is a legitimate concern, or do you think that China is smart enough to know that what's good for the American economy is good for the Chinese economy?

James Areddy: What scares a lot of Americans about China's growing prowess and these one trillion-plus in foreign exchange reserves is that a lot of that money is invested in U.S. Treasury bonds and in U.S. government debt. This is keeping U.S. interest rates low and house prices high and allowing the U.S. economy to continue to grow quite well. A lot of people worry that somehow China is going to suddenly ask for its money back and walk away from the U.S. economy. A similar kind of concern took place in the '80s with Japan; everyone worried that Japan would do the same thing.

At the same time, the relationship between the U.S. and Japan is a lot tighter, it seemed, than the relationship between the U.S. and China. China, for many, is a mystery at the best of times. Policy making in China is opaque. So there are a lot of concerns that China's somehow going to sell all of this debt and walk away from the American economy. But it's a little hard to see that taking place very quickly. China is a very conservative investor. They're holding U.S. Treasury bonds because they consider those to be very safe investments. They're suddenly a rich investor with lots of money and they want to be safe. They're like any rich person—they want to hold on to their money; they don't want to be poor again. It's hard to imagine some kind of wholesale pullout from the U.S. bond market, partly because China's such a big player right now. If any big player walks away from the table, that weakens the pool. China would be shooting itself in the foot by suddenly selling lots of Treasury bonds. Could they theoretically do it? Yes, but it seems quite unlikely that there would be a wholesale change very quickly.

Q: Let's just say hypothetically China divested—imagine a worst-case scenario where they said, "We're only buying euros and other currencies and we're moving away from U.S. Treasuries." Explain to me what that scenario would mean to an average American who has a mortgage and has a job. What's the domino effect of China changing its investing strategy?

James Areddy: The financial markets that we cover get very nervous about any kind of change in China's policy, and they have a very difficult time figuring out what the policy is going forward. Probably the scariest thing for them right now would be if China were to stop buying Treasury bonds. It doesn't seem very likely, it seems an almost impossible situation that they'd suddenly stop. But if they were to stop buying U.S. Treasury debt, it would likely hurt the global economy, and it would probably send U.S. interest rates higher, making it much more expensive for people in the U.S. to buy homes, to buy their cars, finance their credit card debt, all kinds of things. But it seems a very unlikely scenario that they would even stop.

Q: Is it true that what's good for the American economy is good for the Chinese economy? If so, do you see that in the stories that you cover?

James Areddy: China and the U.S. are linked economically; there's no doubt about it. They certainly share lots of the same interests, and there's bound to be a little tension between the salesman and the buyer. But at the same time, one wouldn't exist without the other one. I think, increasingly, the relationship between China and the U.S. is growing tighter, at least economically.

Q: The trade deficit: is that sustainable? Can that go on forever or at some point do you have to balance this sort of thing out?

James Areddy: One of the things that we constantly ask economists is, can the trade deficit in the U.S. be sustained? Can China continue to go on selling much more to the rest of the world than it buys? And can the U. S. continue to absorb so much more from China than it's exporting to China? There are economists lined up 10 deep on either side of that situation. There really isn't any simple answer. I don't have an answer, and we continue to ask the question because there doesn't seem to be any consensus about whether the trade deficit in the U.S. with China is a good thing or a bad thing, a sustainable thing, a dangerous thing. No one really knows.

Q: Is it true that the *Wall Street Journal* has offices all over the world, and, if so, how important would you say this story is? Do you feel like you're covering an important story for your news organization?

James Areddy: The *Wall Street Journal* has more staff outside the United States than any other major newspaper, and China is a very big story for the paper. We see it in our reader comments; we see it from every aspect.

Q: There's world news and then there's financial news. In the financial news world, there are big stories out there, but in the financial world, this has to be one of the most important stories. Can you comment on that?

James Areddy: China is a major global story. It's an economic story and it's a political story, and the *Wall Street Journal* has one of its biggest bureaus worldwide here in China. We have more people outside of the United States than any other major newspaper, and for us, China is one of the most important stories. It goes right to the heartland of America, to Wall Street, to Washington. It touches literally everything, and it is not going to go away as a big story. Whether China goes right, whether China goes wrong—it's going to be a big story for Americans, for business, and for politics worldwide, and that's what we're doing here.

Q: The Chinese empire has been around almost forever, it seems. What did it do in 1994? In 1994, the Chinese empire seemed to have turned on a switch. What did they do that has created these massive ripples, not just in their country but in the whole world?

James Areddy: I think a lot of people look at the Chinese growth miracle as someone turning on a switch, when in fact I think it's much more the government stepping away and just allowing people to do what they would naturally do. The Chinese are very enterprising, and it's the government's decision to allow people to do what they want, to go where they want, and to basically have a lot of freedom to make various economic decisions. Anything that they want to do with money, they basically can do it. That's what the big change is. It's not someone switching on a light here in China; it's really the government stepping away and allowing people to do what they want with their money.

Paul O'Neill

Paul O'Neill says he enjoyed being the 72nd secretary of the U.S. Treasury (2001–2002), even though the job lasted only 23 months. O'Neill, who has been analyzing the U.S. budget since he went to Washington, served in the Bureau of the Budget, which later became the Office of Management and Budget in the White House.

O'Neill came to American government in 1961 as a management intern, and stayed for 16 years through the Kennedy, Johnson, Nixon, and Ford administrations. The last 10 years of his tenure were spent at what was the Bureau of the Budget, which became the Office of Management and Budget. There he became deeply involved in the issues of fiscal policy, budget balance, budget making, and helping presidents choose priorities for how we spend the nation's money. Then he moved to the private sector in 1977. In 2000, he was asked by President Bush 43 to come back to the government and be the secretary of the Treasury, which he did for 23 months before he got fired for having a difference of opinion.

Q: Budgetary challenges seem like something you're extremely well suited for. As a young person who came to Washington, what was it about this that drew you in?

Paul O'Neill: I initially came to Washington because I had been in an economics degree program at Fresno State in California, and [then] went to Claremont Graduate School with the intention to get a doctorate in economics. After a year there, the financial pressure was great, and I had a wife and two children. So I kind of incidentally took an examination and was selected to be a management intern in Washington. I really liked the prospect of that a lot, because I thought if I was ever going to apply what I'd learned, especially macroeconomics, I needed to go to Washington, because that's where the action was.

I had been interested in how nations govern themselves and how they express their priorities, and I found a natural affinity when I went to the Bureau of the Budget, which turned out to be the Office of Management and Budget. It was a great place in the early days when I was there, with probably 350 of the smartest people in the country on these issues. We decided how to help a president make priorities and how to help a president evaluate programs, and I found that really stimulating and fun. I never considered what I did to be work, even though it took most of my life for that period of time; the days were long and often it was seven days a week. I think, the last two years I was there, I was off both Christmas Days, and that was about it; the rest of the time I was on the line. I was really close to President Ford, and had gotten to know him when he was in the House and then when he became vice president. He loved using the budget as a policy-making tool almost as much as I loved working with him on it. It was really a fondness for the person and a great respect for his intellect about issues of priority setting the budget that made me really close to President Ford.

Q: What presidents have you served under?

Paul O'Neill: When I first came to Washington, John Kennedy was the president, and honestly part of the reason I came here is that I really liked the idea of doing something that's bigger than an individual person. But when I came I was a management intern— I was so far out in the woods that the only time I ever got to see John Kennedy was when I was a prop and came to stand in the Rotary Drive in front of the White House when they had foreign visitors and they needed people to fill up the driveway. Then when I moved to the Office of Management and Budget (which was still the Bureau of the Budget) Lyndon Johnson was president. I got to see the president on a fairly regular basis; I was still far away from him, but a lot closer than I had been as a management intern.

When Richard Nixon became president, I was in the upper reaches of civil service. Richard Nathan, who was recruited to be a political overseer for the human resources part of the Office of Management and Budget, selected me early on in the Nixon administration to be the point person on a lot of important Nixon initiatives, including a welfare reform. So I would go to all of the cabinet-level meetings and take endless copious notes and learn what Arthur Burns and George Shultz and Pat Moynihan and people like that thought about issues and how they expressed themselves . . . which I really found enormously valuable. It was during that time I got to really know the higher levels of a White House staff, including Nixon. I was really involved in the policy analysis and recommendations of the president about virtually everything in the government.

When Nixon left and Ford became president, he viewed the budget as a principal tool for making all kinds of policy, and myself, and the other people who were in the upper reaches of the Office of Management and Budget, spent enormous amounts of time with the president in his office or in the Cabinet room, going through every option for every program in the federal government, national defense, intelligence, every aspect of human resources and community development, and every aspect of how we raised money to pay for the things that we want. It was a time of great closeness, and he loved the idea that I knew a lot about the budget; in fact, he was fond of telling people that the only person who knew more about the budget than he did was me, which was a great flattery.

Q: Would you say that President Ford was more closely involved in budgetary matters than any other president?

Paul O'Neill: The way to compare President Ford's involvement in the budget is to look back over the years. At OMB, we had people who'd been around for a long time, and we believed that the only person in modern history who knew more about the programs and policies that are incorporated in the federal budget at a level on par with President Ford was Harry Truman. They were the only two presidents who were capable of holding a press conference with hundreds of people from the media and basically answering all the questions themselves without any reference to staff, about any detail you wanted to talk about.

Q: **What about President Bush 41? How involved was he in budgetary decisions?**

Paul O'Neill: When Bush 41 became president, I wasn't in the government, although he suggested that I ought to join his administration, which I declined to do. He did, however, make me the chairman of his Education Policy Advisory Committee, so I got to see him fairly frequently during his term. I would say his involvement in the budget was not like President Ford's, but it was in some detail. One of the things I really liked about President Bush 41 is that when he saw that in his own judgment he'd made a mistake with the idea that he would never raise taxes, as in the famous "Read my lips: no new taxes," he realized that was not the right position for public policy and had the courage to raise taxes. There was a great outcry when he did it, from people like the Chamber of Commerce, and I was so infuriated by their turning on him when he'd done the right public policy thing. I was then the CEO of ALCOA and I resigned ALCOA from the Chamber of Commerce in protest against their dissing of the president when he'd done the right public policy thing, whether they liked it or not.

And then I was out of government, although I still had involvement during the Clinton administration. I got to know Clinton pretty well when he was first governor of Arkansas. I was the president of International Paper Company and we had big operations in Arkansas. He invited me in to talk with him about a lot of things, including global climate change and education policy and all the rest. And my sense is Bill Clinton was really deep into making budgetary decisions himself. I think maybe not as deeply involved as President Ford, but deeper than President Reagan for sure, and probably more detailed into things like welfare policy than most other presidents have ever been.

Bush 43 I found practically not involved in the detailed budget discussions. Early on, he asked me to serve on a committee with Dick Cheney and the then director of the Office of Management and Budget to review budgetary decisions, but in my experience he only saw the very tip of the iceberg and for sure he could never have done a detailed description of the budget. He could have done talking points, but if you asked him questions about retired officers pay, he would have drawn a blank. In his eyes, that's not what presidents are for—they shouldn't have to know that level of detail. I think it was a deliberate decision on his part not to be very involved in the detail, and to be what I would call a "talking point president" on these issues.

Q: When you took over at Treasury, how would you characterize the financial health of the United States? Are you surprised at where we are today?

Paul O'Neill: When I moved into the Treasury as the 72nd secretary, what we inherited from the Clinton administration was an economy that had been rolling itself into a modest recession for a year and a half. By that time, the dot-com bubble had burst and the economy had slowed down, and we actually had some negative quarters that we didn't really know about until Clinton was gone and Bush 43 was in charge. But on the fiscal policy front we were in a condition where we had, for the first time in a long time, a budget that was in surplus.

I have to hasten to add that while it was in surplus, it was not in surplus on a federal funds basis. It was only in surplus because the trust funds were bringing in a lot of money and together, with federal funds and the trust funds, the Clinton administration was able to claim three years of budget surpluses, which we hadn't seen since 1969. That was a year where we were in budget surplus with the use of the trust funds. The last year I think that we were actually in surplus on a federal funds basis, without using trust fund money, was in 1960, so we'd been at this now for 47 years of basically living beyond our means—especially if you think federal funds ought to be in surplus without using the trust fund money to calculate balance.

So in 2001, when Bush 43 took over and I took over at the Treasury, we were in a total surplus condition, and arguably

(I think this was a correct argument) we needed to reduce taxes because taxes had crept up to the point where something like 20 or 21 percent of the GDP was being effectively taken by federal government. Traditionally, our level has been someplace around 18 percent or maybe 18.3. So I think it was correct to say that we could afford to have a tax cut, which President Bush 43 had run on in the 2000 election, and he set out to deliver what he promised in the election and I think that was okay. The reason that I agreed to come in as Treasury secretary was because I saw lots of things in our economy and our society that needed to be done, and I was encouraged to believe that Bush 43 was up for the difficult political things that needed to happen to make course corrections. Those course corrections still include fixing the Social Security and Medicare trust funds, and fundamentally redesigning the way the federal tax system works. I thought there was some prospect that President Bush would entertain the difficult political choices that needed to be made in order to act on these things, and I spent a lot of time thinking about these things over a period, better part of 40 years, so I was anxious to have a go at it.

Q: How did it go?

Paul O'Neill: The first part was the easiest part. Cutting taxes is always a cinch—it's only a debate about who gets the credit and how big the cut is. But then we had 9/11 and it really changed where we were. The economy was still slow, although we were actually having positive growth in the fourth quarter of 2001. But there was still a lot of energy and President Bush himself was bringing this energy that we need additional tax cuts. I honestly didn't think that was the right thing to do, because I continue to believe we needed the revenue that we were then collecting to work on the Medicare/Social Security problems. To work on fundamental tax redesign after 9/11 while worrying about whether there was going to be another attack or a series of attacks would cost hundreds of billions of dollars. So I was against further tax reductions at the time, especially as we got into 2002, as I became more concerned that we were also going to need money since it looked to me like we were sliding into a war with Iraq. I argued during the second half of 2002 we should not have another tax cut because we need the money to work on important policy issues that would shape the nation going forward, and we needed to have, in effect, rainy day money for the prospect of Iraq and another set of attacks like 9/11.

That was not a popular view, and in fact, it led to a conversation with the vice president where he basically told me, "Don't worry about further tax cuts, it's okay. Ronald Reagan proved that we don't have to worry about deficits." Which is really a shock to me because whatever you may think about Ronald Reagan, I don't think he or anyone else has proved that it's possible to ignore not just deficits, but federal debt as well. I think it is true that you can be sanguine about deficits for a short period of time, but you can't be sanguine about mounting debt for the United States of America. When we, the Bush 43 administration took over, we had something over $5 trillion, maybe $5.6 trillion worth of national debt. Today I think the number's $8.8 trillion. That's not an innocent change, it is a monumental change in the debt service that we have to do in addition to and on top of all of the other things that our country needs to do.

Q: Toward the end of 2002, you wrote a report that said that the current debt wasn't the problem; it was the debt that we are stepping toward. Shortly thereafter you were asked to leave. Can you explain to me what happened the day you were fired?

Paul O'Neill: During 2002 I found myself being at odds with where policy seemed to be going, I kept arguing that we couldn't really afford another tax cut and that we didn't need one, since the economy was doing fine. But my problems were not just differences about tax policy and social policy and fixing Medicare and Social Security. I kept asking almost every week, of the people from the CIA who briefed me, you know, where's the evidence for weapons of mass destruction? I see all of these allegations and projections of trends from 1991 and what we knew in 1991, but I didn't see anything I considered to be evidence. One of the things I've been trained to do for a long period of time is to know what you know and to differentiate that from what you suspect or what someone alleges, so I kept being a pain in the neck and asking, "Where's the evidence? There's no evidence, there's nothing I believe."

Early in the administration, at a National Security Council briefing, there were a bunch of photos put on the table and it was alleged that this satellite picture of what looked like a warehouse that you could find anywhere in the world was a production center for weapons of mass destruction. I said, I've spent a lot of time going around the world, producing goods all over the world, and have seen a lot of factories and warehouses. How can you tell me this one is a center for producing weapons of mass destruction? There's nothing here that tells you that? You may assign it that, but there's nothing here that tells you that.

One of the things I found really interesting out of this experience is that even today, people that I have a lot of regard for their intellect, like Bill Clinton, still say they believed the evidence was there. I've never had this conversation with him, but it's hard for me to believe a guy who's as smart as he is doesn't know the difference between an allegation and evidence—especially someone who's trained as he is as a lawyer. I've been astounded, this is a bipartisan thing—people on both sides don't seem to get the difference between evidence and what they call intelligence, which I would call not intelligence, just a bunch of fabrications.

So I was working my way to the margins of what endurance that people had for me, both in economic policy and in everything else I encountered. I have to admit some of the things that I said during this period probably ought to have been tempered. For example, we were struggling with trying to get the International Monetary Fund and the World Bank out of the business of effectively bailing out private sector lenders who'd given money to developing countries with the expectation that the people of the United States and other tax-paying people around the world would bail out the private sector lenders. I said (probably not very advisedly), "Before we give any more money to Argentina, we ought to make sure it's not going to go to a Swiss bank account." Which was, I admit, not very diplomatic, but it was true—and interestingly enough, in a few weeks a guy who had been the president of Argentina said, without any prompting from me, "Well it was true he had money in a Swiss bank account, but it was all his own."

So in any event, as we moved past the election in 2002 and we had this continued conversation, a really heated conversation with the vice president about what I considered to be the inadvisability of a further tax cut, I got a call, early in December. I was in my office having a meeting with a group of people and my secretary came in and said, "The vice president's on the phone and would like to talk to you." And so, as it always happens when you get this kind of a call, the people get up and go in the other room so that you can have a private conversation with the vice president or the president if he calls. The vice president said, "The president's decided to make some changes, and you're one of the changes. What we'd like to do is have you come over and meet with the president and basically say that you've decided to go back to the private sector, that you're ready to quit your involvement with the Treasury." And I said to him, "You know, I'm in the middle of a meeting here, I'll call you back in a little while."

And so the people came back into my office and we finished up whatever the topic was we were talking about, and then I called the vice president back. I said I didn't think I needed another meeting with the president, thank you very much. I thought I'd had plenty of meetings, and I thought he probably didn't need a meeting and I certainly didn't need a meeting.

And I also said to him, "You know, I've been going along now for 65 years or so and, you know, for me to say that I've decided to leave the Treasury to go back to the private sector is a lie, and I'm not into doing lies. And so what I want to do is issue a press release tomorrow morning before the markets open so that they'll have time to digest this news in case it creates any stir. I'm going to meet with my staff at 8 o'clock to tell them so they won't hear it from the media but they'll hear it directly from me, because I recruited most of these people; they've done great work while I've been here, and I want to tell them personally. And as soon as I'm done telling them, because five minutes after I tell them, somebody will call the media, I want to issue a press release that basically says I've decided to resign. And I'll send the president a note telling him I'm resigning."

And I think he was surprised by that. He didn't try to argue me out of it, I think probably because he'd known me long enough to know that it wouldn't do any good, that I'd made up my mind and that was it. So I called my chief of staff, Tim Adams, back in, and my press assistant came in and I said, "I would like to issue a statement that says I hereby resign." Well, they didn't think that was a very good thing to do, and so I wrote a little more of a note then, saying that I appreciated having the opportunity to serve and I hereby resign and that was it. And so the next morning, I came in and met with the staff, and I had an opportunity to tell them in person, face to face, all of them together, "I'm leaving. You all need to stay. The president needs help and you're all talented, thoughtful people, so my actions should not lead the rest of you to do anything except to stay and serve." And that was it. I went back to my office and latched up my briefcase and went down to the parking space that's reserved for the secretary of the Treasury, got in my car, and drove back to Pittsburgh.

Q: What did it feel like to get fired?

Paul O'Neill: Well, it's a first in my life—I'd never been fired before, I'd only been promoted to ever higher levels of responsibility. But it was okay with me because I would have really been uncomfortable arguing for policies I didn't believe in. One of the things I actually said to President Bush and Vice President Cheney when they asked me to come and have lunch with them, and to ask me to serve as the secretary of the Treasury, was that I had reservations about doing this. And one of the reservations I had was that, having been the CEO of a very big corporation for 13 years and the president of a very big corporation for the period before that, I wasn't sure how easy it was going to be for me to knuckle under when I thought the policy was wrong.

The thing I didn't know is how difficult it would be to knuckle under if you thought the policy was not well vetted, that it was decided on the basis of ideology instead of what was right for the country. At that point I really thought the decisions were not being made on the basis of what was right for the country, they were being made on the basis of what was right for getting reelected. It's probably altruistic, but I thought for a long time we need presidents who are so devoted to doing the right thing with and for the American people that they're prepared to lose for their values and to hang their values out in public for everyone to see them.

Q: **Very few people know as much about budgets as you do. And as far as your work in the private sector, some said it was miraculous what happened at ALCOA. Do you think that the advice that you gave the administration, if it were a different administration, with different management styles and techniques, that there may have been a different ending to your story at Treasury?**

Paul O'Neill: There are times when I find I'd rather not be right; I wish it were true that we didn't have to fix Social Security and Medicare, and we didn't need to fix the structure of the tax system. However, the issues that I argued for and about over a long time are still there, and they're worse now. The passage of time is not going to fix these problems. The fact that our 10,000-page tax system is an abomination and actually lends credence to the idea that we're not an intelligent people hasn't improved with the passage of time. We have several thousand more pages than when I came in 2001, in the federal tax code, and by the best estimates we're undercollecting what people are supposed to pay by $300 or $400 billion a year. This is all because of complexity and the insanity of this thing that we now call our "revenue raising system" in this country.

It's going to take a president with real courage to provide the leadership to make it simple, to make it transparent so that people pay their fair share. If you think about it, right now, the undercollection that's represented by that $300 or $400 billion is like a 15 percent surcharge on the rest of us. You know, Medicare and Social Security could be fixed in a really wonderful way if we could elect a president who would tell the people some fundamental truths. One fundamental truth is this: The federal government doesn't have any money that it doesn't first take away from the people—pretty straightforward and simple.

Now the other important truth is this: I believe that in a just society, especially one that is as wealthy as we are, when people get to be 65 years old they should have financial security. That means not just the money to pay for your daily bread and your normal living expenses, but for your health and medical care needs as well. The only way to do that is to save, and right now we're living in this condition where we don't really save Social Security tax money, we don't really save Medicare tax money—we're spending it all. And in order to get on top of this notion of financial security for people when they get to be 65, we actually have to save.

I'll give you some numbers to make the point. If we were to say that we want people to have a $1 million annuity when they get to be age 65, this is what we would have to do: If we put $23,000 in an account on the day of birth for every of one of the 4 million kids born in the United States each year, and we had a 6 percent compound return rate, which is below the norm since 1929, every person would have actually over a million dollars by the time they get to be 65, which would be an annuity for $82,000 a year for 20 years, which is longer than the expected life span when you get to be 65.

Now people will say, well we have to take into account inflation and all that, and that's true. But this notion illustrates the point that if we as a society decided that we were going to save $92 billion a year, which is what it would take to put this notion into effect, we could in effect go a long way toward guaranteeing financial security and money to pay for the health and medical care needs when every American gets to be 65, without regard to whatever they did in their lifetime, so that we can make good on this idea of guaranteeing there is something to being an American, and the current generation saves the money to make it come true.

Where does the $92 billion dollars come from every year? From we the American people. To put it in context, this year our total spending is going to be something close to $3 trillion, and in fact, the money that hopefully we're going to save when we stop doing Iraq would be more than enough to fund a fully saved program to guarantee fiscal security and financial security for individual Americans, every one of them. This is not a family thing—this is if you're an American, you as an individual will have financial security when you get to 65. This is a doable proposition now, but there's a transition problem. In order to do this, we're going to have to figure out to pay for the generation now living that's got Social Security and Medicare entitlements as we work our way through this problem.

And there are ways to do that, including fundamentally fixing our health and medical care system on a bigger basis than Medicare alone. I spent lots of time working on issues of our health and medical care system, and I think the data would support me when I say that if we simply did well, extremely well, at everything we already know how to do in health and medical care, we could simultaneously improve the outcomes for our population and reduce the cost by 50 percent a year. Which is to say, instead of spending $2 trillion a year on health and medical care now (upwards of 16 percent of our GDP), we could spend $1 trillion a year and have a better outcome. That's a longer story; it's a difficult proposition to improve how we practice medical care.

Q: **Let's revisit the conversation that you had with Vice President Cheney prior to you being fired. Can you discuss the difference of opinion that you had in regard to tax cuts and deficits?**

Paul O'Neill: Sometime after the election—it must have been mid-November—there was a meeting of the Economic Policy Group, including the vice president. As we sat at the table in the Roosevelt Room, we talked about where we were and where we were going. If I remember right, Glenn Hubbard made a presentation that was displayed on the screen at the front of the Roosevelt Room and showed where we were going and what different tracks looked like and GDP growth and the rest, including the effects of the proposed third tax cut. I made the argument, which I had been making over and over again since maybe June or July, that it was not advisable to have another tax cut because of the need to fix Social Security and Medicare and to have some money to smooth the fundamental redesign of the tax system. We needed to have in effect rainy-day money in the event that we had another 9/11 event—and at that point it looked like maybe we were going to go to Iraq, and it was not going to be cheap to do that.

So I argued that we should not have another tax cut because the economy was going to be in positive territory and doing okay through the next couple of years anyway without another tax cut, and there were all of these other compelling reasons not to risk a deficit and not to risk adding more to the national debt. And the vice president basically said, "When Ronald Reagan was here, he proved that deficits don't really matter and so it's not a consideration or a good reason not to have an additional tax cut."

I was honestly stunned by the idea that anyone believed that Ronald Reagan proved in any fashion, certainly not inconclusive fashion, that deficits don't matter. I think it is true on a temporary basis that a nation can have a deficit and have a good reason for having a deficit. I think the Second World War there was no way we could avoid having a deficit, but when we came out of the Second World War we started running budget surpluses again and did that through the '50s and into 1960. It's interesting, it's really only been in the last 40 years or so that we've accepted the notion that it's a bipartisan thing that we don't have to have fiscal discipline.

A year ago there was this signing ceremony in the Rose Garden for the new Medicare prescription drug entitlement, and it's going to cost us trillions of dollars. This event was not unlike any of the others in the Rose Garden on a nice sunny day, with the president sitting at the signing table with a bunch of grinning legislators behind him taking credit for this "great gift" they're giving the American people. But none of their money was going to get given to make this happen, because the federal government doesn't have any money that it doesn't first take away from the taxpayers.

There was no mention of the fact that this in effect was a new tax on the American people, and we didn't know how we were going to pay for it. It was only grinning presidents and legislators taking the credit for a gift, which strikes me as a ridiculous continuing characteristic of how we do political business in our country.

Q: If we couldn't afford it, why did we give it to the people?

Paul O'Neill: If you can get 51 percent of the people in the Congress to agree with the President's leadership initiative to say we ought to do this, that's all it takes. And I think it's regrettably true there are a lot of people who don't understand that when they get a gift from the American people, it's from the American people and it can only be paid for with taxes over time. I think the confusion is aided and abetted by the fact that it doesn't feel like we're paying for it. It's a lot like running up credit card debt: As long as you can pay the interest charges on your credit card debt, you can live way beyond your means. In fact, we as a nation are living way beyond our means, and for a period of time, there's no doubt we've demonstrated you can get away with it. But I think we only need to look at the fate of other countries who've lived beyond their means for a long time to see you inevitably get into trouble.

If you look at Germany in 1923, they got to a point where their currency was so worthless that you needed a wheelbarrow to haul the currency that was needed to buy a loaf of bread. You get inflation where people stop investing in your national debt, when they say, "We're not going to loan you money because you're not going to be able to pay it back." It's the same thing that happens to individuals and families. When you get extended to the point that you can't service your debt, you're finished. You know, so you go through a calamity—either you go through a terrible inflation, which is a way of having a national bankruptcy, and you destroy accumulated income and wealth, and in fact you have a taking from all the people because suddenly their financial assets are worth nothing. You know, are we going to have that right away? No. But should the people who are in positions of political leadership know that and anticipate it and do something about it for the American people, you bet—and now is the time to begin doing something about it.

One of the difficult aspects of this debt problem is that it's not very transparent to people who are unschooled in fiscal and monetary policy. In a way, this problem's a little bit like the famous example of if you throwing a frog into boiling water. If you throw him into the already boiling water, he jumps out right away. But if you put the frog in the pot of cold water and turn the heat on under it, the frog will let itself be boiled because it doesn't respond to slow increase in temperature. Our debt problem is something like that. If we wait until we have a calamity and financial markets shut us off because we've exhausted their belief that we can service additional debt, it's too late. This is a problem that we need to deal with without letting the heat be turned up some more.

I would hope we can demonstrate we're intelligent people that don't wait until they create a calamity in their country before they deal with problems that are obvious to anyone who's ever studied economic policy and fiscal policy and monetary policy. You only need to look around the world to see places like Argentina, Turkey, and Germany after World War II whose governments have effectively achieved a meltdown condition. Knowing this can happen to modern nations, we should not let it happen to ours.

Q: What would you say to Americans who think economics is too complicated to get their head around? Why is it important for people to try to understand this and get a handle on it?

Paul O'Neill: I think it's really important for the American people to understand the basic principles that are involved in these issues. Otherwise it's pretty difficult to make an intelligent choice about who should lead the nation. What do you want in a president? Are you happy to just have someone that seems to be charming and charismatic, or do you want someone that will make a difficult decision, or help us to make difficult decisions that are in the long-run interest of the people? I would argue we need to elect people who have deep values and leadership characteristics that are probably expressed by a person who will tell you, "I'm going to come and I'm going to tell you the truth about some things that you may not want to hear, but that you need to hear. I'm going to do my best to make them simple enough so that you can understand why we have to make some difficult choices."

I believe this is not all a bitter medicine that we need to take. I believe there are things that we can do as a nation that are good for the long-run condition of our nation, that reinforce the value structure of our nation. For example, to assure that when people get to be 65 years old, that they have financial security. That is also consistent with becoming a truly saving nation, which is something we need to do.

Q: **Just going back to tax cuts one last time, do you have any thoughts on why people say, "Well, it goes back to the Reagan thing: Supply-side theory says that tax cuts are all good because it's all going to work its way through the system and it's all good." Does that hold water? Does supply-side theory work under certain conditions but not all conditions?**

Paul O'Neill: You know, I believe that it's possible—not easy, but it's possible—and for sure it's desirable to have a simple tax system. I hate that the titles that get put on these things, but the idea of people paying, say, 15 percent or 20 percent of their income on a no-nonsense basis with no deductions and no credits has a lot of appeal to me. I believe simplicity is our friend in having a tax system that really works, and I think it's also true the lower the tax rates, the better. But a modern nation like ours does need to collect money to pay for our needs that we share together, such as national defense or interstate highway system.

I also believe that in a just nation, all of the people who have means help to pay for the things that people who don't have the means need. So, that if you have a very low income and you can't meet your fundamental living needs, then we the people should give those people money. Now our tax code has been used and abused with tax credits and dependency allowances and the rest to deal with this problem. I would much prefer that we did all of this on top of the table, partly because when you use the tax system for our social program purposes, people with very low incomes are left out. In order partly to adjust for that, we have a refundable tax credit which was instituted several years ago during the Clinton administration; it got some momentum and it's been carried forward. I would much prefer that we be grown up enough so that we faced the fact that some people need financial help from the people of the United States and we should write them a check.

And similarly, you know, we have tax deductions for mortgage credit because we believe (and I think this is a correct belief) that it's a valuable thing for people in the United States to own their own home. But I wouldn't do it with a tax credit or with mortgage deductions. I would do it by deciding how much do we want to encourage people, and then I would write them a check. I would write them a check so that we do all of our financial business on top of the table instead of by stealth, instead of by discriminating among people based on their income level. I'd much rather help people in a straightforward fashion that has no obfuscation, no mystery, and no inequity because people with lower levels of income can't use credits and deductions.

Q: You and former Federal Reserve Chairman Alan Greenspan have been friends for quite some time. How did that come to be?

Paul O'Neill: I got to know Alan Greenspan in 1969 because he was the chairman of the Transition Group for Economic Affairs for the Nixon administration and I was in the Office of Management and Budget. I got to know him then, and over the years, even after I left the government and he came back to be head of the CEA in the Ford administration, we worked really hand-in-glove during that time. After we both left the government, before he became the Fed chairman, I saw him in other settings. He was the president of a firm called Townsend Greenspan, I was in International Paper, we were both still interested in public policy. Then he was on the board of International Paper and I became president during that time. Also, I got recruited to be on the board of ALCOA and Alan

Greenspan was on the board of ALCOA, and had been of counsel and a board member at ALCOA for a long time. So our friendship was long-standing and around lots of issues, both public and private.

Q: Correct me if I'm wrong—he's the person who might have made the deciding phone call when you were weighing whether or not you wanted to come to Treasury?

Paul O'Neill: Yeah, that's true. When I was thinking about whether I should come to the Treasury, I had met with the president and the vice president in Washington at the Madison Hotel. I told them I would call them the next day and let them know whether I was going to accept or not, but I needed to talk to my wife first. So I went to New York for a board meeting, and I was at the hotel that evening after the meeting with the president-elect and vice president-elect, and Alan Greenspan called me there. They had called him, I guess, and asked him to call me and tell me how important it was that I come to the government and how much he would enjoy working with me again in a direct way.

And I appreciated this, but I thought it wasn't going to make any difference because my wife's opinion was a lot more important. And she didn't think I should do it, but was okay with me doing it if I thought it was the right thing to do. She was pretty sure it wasn't the right choice, and as this has often turned out in life, she was right and I was wrong.

But in any event, early in the administration, we started working on a policy formulation, including the shape and dimension of a tax cut. Alan was deeply involved in those conversations and, of course, had a lot of standing with people in the Congress and in the nation, because he was looked at as an honest broker who would have a clean opinion about what ought to be done, what ought not to be done. During this conversation, I said to Alan that I thought this tax cut was okay, but that one of the difficult things to cope with was the reality that economic conditions might change, and if they change we might wish we had some of that revenue back that we were now talking about giving up on the basis of tax cuts. I told him I thought it would really be great if he would say to Congress when he appeared before the committees that it would be of great utility to have some triggers so that in the event economic conditions turned against us and revenues fell away, that we would have those revenues back. That was an abhorrent idea, especially to the supply-side ideologues who thought no tax cuts were useful unless they were permanent, and [that it was] especially important to make cuts in the marginal tax rates.

Now I honestly agree that there's a great economic utility to cutting marginal tax rates, but I don't believe you can consistently ignore the abomination that is now our tax system and get away with endless marginal tax cuts without doing something about the base monstrosity that we have. So I thought it made sense and there was some movement in the Congress to actually put some triggers into the first tax cuts so that we would have a revenue recovery in the event the economy turned against us. There was some entertainment of that idea, but it got washed away in the rush to give people tax cuts. I think it's regrettable that that happened. Things might have turned out differently if the tax cuts hadn't gone on when the economy started working away from us.

Q: Correct me if I'm wrong—he was practically still testifying when most of the journalists had left the room to say tax cuts, tax cuts, tax cuts, and they didn't want to hear the "with prudence" part of his testimony?

Paul O'Neill: I think if you go back and review the transcript of what Alan said to the members of Congress, he gave them, as he always does, a very balanced set of recommendations about "Yes, we can afford tax cuts right now, but we need to be prudent in how we do this." But President Bush 43 had built up the momentum that his first agenda item was going to be significant and major tax reductions, and he was hell-bent to do it and there was no serious legislative impediment. It was only a question of how fast.

Arthur Laffer

Arthur Laffer is a supply-side economist who gained recognition as a member of President Reagan's Economic Policy Board. He is best known for popularizing his *Laffer curve*, an economic theory that illustrates income tax elasticity.

Q: What is it about economics that interests you?

Arthur Laffer: Economics is all about human behavior. It's the allocation of resources. It's where prosperity and people's happiness really emanates. It's a wonderful, wonderful field to be involved with.

Q: Why don't we start with tax cuts? Why do you believe tax cuts are good for the economy?

Arthur Laffer: Sometimes tax cuts are good for the economy, and sometimes they're not. You obviously have to have taxes to collect the requisite ward revenues, so that government can do what it's supposed to do. But sometimes governments behave excessively and raise taxes way beyond what they should. Then tax cuts are really beneficial. The U.S. today is a lot better off than we were, let's say, when John F. Kennedy took office in 1961. At that time, we had the highest federal marginal income tax rate, 91 percent. And *that* had been lowered from almost 93 percent by Harry Truman. So, you know, it's crazy, but taxes can get way out of hand if people don't understand them.

Let me explain to you tax cuts and explain to you what you want to look at. Let me just do it simply by looking at the capital gains tax today and historically. If we were to lower the federal capital gains tax rate, the evidence suggests that revenues would rise. In fact, almost every time over the past 30 or 40 years that the federal capital gains tax rate has been lowered, revenues increase. Almost every time the federal capital gains tax rate has been raised, revenues decline. If you collect fewer revenues by raising the tax rate, what on earth is your reason for raising that tax rate? Not only are the people who invest worse off, but those people who are the beneficiaries of government spending are also worse off. It's a lose/lose situation. There is no argument I can think to ever oppose cutting the capital gains tax rate if you number one, collected more revenues and, number two, made people who invest better off. That's a win/win for everyone.

But even if the cut in the tax rate did not increase capital gains tax receipts, you still might make it a no-brainer, a win/win for everyone. For example, with lower capital gains tax rates, you're going to get more investment, more output, more employment, more production. You'll have more sales taxes, more income taxes, more payroll taxes—all sorts of other taxes will increase. Even if you don't collect more revenues from the capital gains tax itself, you may, in fact, collect more revenues for the federal government in total.

But even if you collect fewer total revenues in the federal government from a cut in the capital gains tax rate, you still might make it a no-brainer. For example, a lot of government spending is predicated on needs tests, means tests, and income tests. You have unemployment benefits, you have food stamps, and you have supplemental security income. But if you cut the capital gains tax rate and increase output employment and production, that should lead to a reduction in government spending. So even if the shortfall in revenues is there, you might have an induced reduction in spending that would more than offset the shortfall in revenues, and you would actually have a reduction in total debt. That would still be a no-brainer for cutting the capital gains tax rate.

Even if the federal government debt increases, there are state and local governments that will benefit by the federal capital gains tax rate reduction. They'll collect more taxes. They'll spend less. If the total amount of debt, federal, state, and local, is reduced, I see no argument on God's earth as to why you wouldn't want to cut the capital gains tax rate.

Even if that's not true, even if all debt goes up, you still want to look at the time pattern of this debt. Let's imagine, for a moment, that I build a factory based upon a presumed tax rate of 10 percent on corporate profits. The day I finish that factory, the tax rate goes up, from 10 percent to 90 percent. Do I tear the factory down? Of course not. I don't tear it down, but when things wear out, I don't replace them. It takes a long time to create a capital stock, and it takes a long time to destroy a capital stock. Supply and demand elasticities are very much greater after a long period of time than they are immediately. Even if the immediate impact of lowering the capital gains tax rate is to increase federal, state, and local debt over time, when those elasticities become greater and greater, that debt will fall, and, in fact, you might even get surpluses.

When you look at the overall picture, you want to consider the discounted present value of all future debt. That is the essence of the Laffer curve [the relationship between tax rates and tax revenue collected by governments]. The Laffer curve is not the end-all and be-all for cutting tax rates. You really want the government to benefit society. If you create more output, employment, and production, you may still want to even have larger deficits because it's great for society.

You should not use the Laffer curve as your tax criteria. The last thing you ever want to do is maximize tax receipts in a society. You want your tax rates way below that point. It's not simple, or not easy. You've got to think it through very, very carefully. In certain areas, where you have the capital gains tax rate and higher taxes on personal income, there are very strong feedback effects. On other taxes, you don't have those same strong feedback effects. The political issue today is what to do with the highest marginal tax rates, such as inheritance, capital gains, and dividends. I would argue that those are the exact areas in which you get the most feedback effects and in which you're most likely to be into the prohibitive range of the overall Laffer curve. If people try to raise the highest marginal tax rates on the rich and lower them on the poor, believe me when I tell you they're going to destroy the economy and they're going to create huge deficits.

Q: Can you talk about it in a personal way?

Arthur Laffer: If you're talking about the time value of debt, that's a little complex and arcane. The point I'm making is that you never can tax an economy into prosperity. If you want to create growth, people have to have incentives to grow. You can create growth to get yourself out of a deficit problem.

In the 1980s, we saw the country overrun by Fabian socialists. Tax rates were out of control, inflation was out of control. When we took office, the prime interest rate was 21.5 percent. Can you imagine that? Tax on what they called unearned income was 70 percent. In 1978, Steiger-Hansen had cut the capital gains tax rate but, before that, it was at 35 percent on nominal capital gains, not real capital gains. The effective tax rate on real capital gains prior to 1978 was probably well over 100 percent for many, many years. These were seriously bad taxes and structures.

We tried to cut tax rates and put in a sound monetary policy. That was Paul Volcker all the way, and he did a great job. Ronnie Reagan did a great job on fiscal policy, on regulatory policy, and on trade policy—we had tariff cuts. It was great. We grew the economy like mad and we grew our way out of the fiscal crisis. And that's exactly what you're supposed to do. It was Reagan and Clinton who really created the surpluses at the end of the Clinton era.

Clinton did a great job when he was president. He pushed NAFTA through Congress against his own party and against the unions. He put in welfare reform, the idea that you actually have to look for a job before you get welfare. He cut government spending as a share of GDP, by three and a half percentage points, more than any other president ever had done. He signed into law the biggest capital gains tax rate reduction in our nation's history, exempted owner-occupied homes from any capital gains taxes. That's amazing. He got rid of the retirement test on Social Security. He reappointed Reagan's Fed chairman twice. Yes. In his first two years, he made a huge mistake on the personal income tax and he pushed through a bill that cost

him the House, the Senate, the governorships, and the state
legislators. He then switched and became more Reagan than
Reagan and was a great president for the last six years of his term
in office. I'm a huge fan of Clinton.

Q: Can you tell us about the crisis you inherited when you went into office?

Arthur Laffer: I told my mom, "Mom, you can't believe it. I just
wrote a speech for Nixon and he used every single word. Well, he
did make two little changes. Everywhere I had 'is,' he put 'is not'
and everywhere I had 'is not' he put 'is,' but other than that, Mom,
it's exactly my speech." Nixon did all sorts of things wrong: the
import surcharge, the wage and price controls, the huge increase in
social spending, the doubling of the capital gains tax rate.

But, to my way of thinking, Nixon's biggest problem was going
off gold. I am a strong advocate of sound money. I believe that
it's basically the Fed's responsibility to guarantee the value of the
dollar; to make sure we don't have inflation. Nixon wanted us
to go off the gold, which led to the high interest rates and hyper
inflation of the '70s and very early '80s. In fact, it really was a
global phenomenon.

There was one person whose side I was on. Paul Volcker and
I worked on going off gold—that was our task—but both of
us shared a view that we needed to keep on the gold standard
to provide discipline to the monetary authorities. And,
unfortunately, we lost the battle. They went off gold and you can
see the consequences: the devaluation of the dollar back in the
early 1970s. But when Volcker came back in later as Fed chairman,
it was just spectacular what he did. He and Ronald Reagan were
the two instruments of the prosperity of the '80s.

Q: Could you characterize the environment that led to Nixon wanting to devalue the dollar?

Arthur Laffer: In the 1970s, we had all sorts of economic
problems. Inflation was rising. We had a weakening of the dollar
through Johnson and Nixon. Even before Johnson, we had a
weakening with Kennedy. There were all sorts of restrictions on

trade. You may remember that Kennedy had a problem with France on the dollar and then, when Johnson came in, he, too, had them. We had the Buy America program, the interest equalization tax, the voluntary foreign credit restraint program, all of these things aimed at improving the trade balance, the capital balance of the U.S. And, throughout this whole period, we had reduced our reserves of gold and we really had not used gold as the discipline that it should have been. That's with the Bretton Woods agreement.

When we came into the 1970s with Richard Nixon, I was very involved—as you may know, I was the first chief economist at the OMB when it was formed. In fact, I joined the government in October 1970. I was George Schultz's right-hand person back then, his economist. My first job was a trip to China. I was in charge of mainland China for the White House, which, for a kid my age back then, was pretty cool.

Q: How old were you?

Arthur Laffer: I was 29, maybe 30. At that time, we wanted to devalue the dollar and the French did not. John Connolly was our union representative and he was discussing this with Giscard d'Estaing, and Giscard d'Estaing was trying to explain to Connolly why they really could not allow the U.S. to devalue the dollar. This was just before the Smithsonian Accord. He said, "Mr. Connolly, I don't know if you understand the program from the standpoint of France, but you see, sir, we hold the dollars in reserves and, therefore, if we allow you to devalue the dollar against the French franc, we will suffer the capital loss on the reserves in France. That is what will happen."

And with that, Connolly takes his unlit cigar, swirls it in his mouth, puts his foot up on the table with boots on, points that cigar at Giscard, and says, "Well, hell, Giscard, we have more dollars than you do." And, of course, everyone bursts out laughing.

But going off gold and devaluing the dollar was a very big mistake. It caused a decade of hyperinflation, high interest rates, and the collapse of the world economy. We raised tax rates dramatically under Nixon and we devalued the dollar. We caused this hyperinflation. It was a double whammy, and it led to one of the worst 15- or 16-year time periods in the U.S.

After the Kennedy go-go 1960s, the Dow Jones Industrial Average peaked in February 1966 at just about 1,000. Sixteen and a half years later, in August 1982, the Dow Jones Industrial Average was about 800. Ouch. In 16½ years, the nominal value of America's stock market fell by 20 percent, and that doesn't count the trebling of the price level during that period. The average annual real rate of return from February 1966 to August '82 on the Dow Jones Industrial Average was minus 8 percent per annum compounded annually. That bear market was caused by Nixon's devaluation of the dollar and by high taxes and by restrictions on trade.

In the '80s, we reversed those policies. Paul Volcker brought us back to sound money. Ronald Reagan gave us tax rate reductions and we had a prosperity that had not been seen on planet Earth for a long, long time. We cut tax rates, we had sound money, we had free trade, and we had minimal regulations. All the four grand kingdoms of macroeconomics were put in the right place. The Dow Jones Industrial Average in August 1982 was at 800. Today it's at 13,500. That is a bull market. In the '80s, we would have given our right arms to have an unemployment rate as low as 6 percent. We've had the long bond yield fall to 4.5 percent. When the long bond is at 4.5 percent, the gods truly love you. We've had a tremendous prosperity. I'm going to say it here and I say it seriously: If they reverse those policies, if these tax increasers try to raise taxes on the rich and have unbridled monetary expansion, or if they try to restrict imports or stop illegal immigration or try to reregulate the economy, believe me that the film will play backwards. You're going to get a mini 1960s/'70s period again. It's a catastrophe that they're proposing.

Q: **What was it like be a part of the administration as you argued successfully for the tax cuts? At the same time, can you talk about how Paul Volcker restored sound money?**

Arthur Laffer: I watched the world go to hell in a handbasket under Richard Nixon. I liked the people there, but for everything

I believed in, everything I thought was sound economics, the opposite was done. Under Nixon, we had the import surcharge, we had the doubling of the capital tax gains tax, we had the unhinging of the paper currency, and we had Social Security and tobacco. We had all of this stuff happening under Nixon. That was part and parcel of one of the worst periods in U.S. history.

Before Reagan, I had done a lot of work with Bill Steiger on the capital gains tax rate reduction. I was very involved with Proposition 13 in California in 1978. Then you got Paul Volcker in 1979, and Ronald Reagan in 1980, with all of the policies of the tax cuts, sound money by Volcker, free trade, and deregulation. It was just a beautiful era. Paul Volcker clearly knew what he was doing on monetary policy and was spectacular. George Schultz, Milton Freidman, Ronald Reagan—all of our group—really knew what they were doing on economics. It was much more fun. I didn't have to bear the consequences of my own actions.

One time period that was very tough, and we deferred the tax cuts. As you know, the tax cuts were phased in. If you know they're going to cut tax rates next year, what do you do this year? You defer all the income you can. By phasing in the tax cuts, we created the recession/depression of 1981–1982. If you think this is revisionist history, go back and read my piece in *Barons* in 1981, where I talked about how we were going to have a deep recession/depression in '81 and '82 because we phased in the tax cuts. That was the only time period that was really, really tough. The president had been shot by Hinckley, and he was in a very different frame of mind than he was when he was really healthy. I was really, really concerned that Bob Dole, George Bush Sr., Dick Darman, and Dave Stockman—what I call the anti-Reagans—were going to convince the president to reverse the third year of the tax cut. As it so happened, he didn't waver. He stuck with it, and you can see how the film played. It was just a beautiful era, and I really enjoyed being there. It was loads of fun.

Q: In the early 1980s, you actually stopped the rise of the size of the federal government. The size of the federal government

grew from 3 percent GDP in 1913 and by 1980 it was at 20 percent and rising rapidly. Ever since the policies that you worked for in the 1980s were enacted, we have been at 20 percent or lower. Can you talk about that?

Arthur Laffer: The best way of reducing federal government, in my view, is to make it unneeded. When you have lots of people unemployed, when you have lots of people hungry and times are really awful, it's really very hard for the government to resist the temptation of government to come in and try to solve the problem. The government can't solve the problem by writing a check, because that check comes from workers and producers. It doesn't come from the tooth fairy. But the temptation is for the government to try to do it.

The history of the Great Depression is a classic case. Roosevelt, with the New Deal, did nothing to reduce the depression. Amity Shlaes's new book [*The Forgotten Man*, HarperCollins, 2007] clearly makes the case that they added to it. During the Great Depression, we raised the highest federal marginal income tax rate from 24 to 83 percent. We put in state and local income taxes and sales taxes. Is it any wonder it was the longest, deepest depression ever? You can't solve a depression by raising taxes.

With Reagan, it worked so nicely because by cutting the tax rates and creating the prosperity, it really reduced the need for government. The other thing that reduced the need for government, if I may be so bold, is that Ronald Reagan really understood the Soviet Union. He used an old Jack Kennedy line that the best form of defense spending is always wasted. Whenever you find yourself in a situation where you're required to use your military hardware and prowess, that is a clear sign that you didn't spend enough. Reagan used defense initiatives with regard to the Eastern Bloc and the Soviets. He and Lady Thatcher literally collapsed the Soviet Union and thereby reduced the need for us to have as big of a defense establishment as we otherwise had. It was a perfect combination of creating the prosperity and destroying the Soviet Union through a strong defense that really led to us being able to control federal government expenditures. Now we've got to figure out a way to control state and local expenditures, but that's a story for another time.

Q: Okay. Talk about deficits. Do deficits matter?

Arthur Laffer: During the Reagan era, the deficits were very, very large. That was the only way to bring back the prosperity. Are deficits bad per se? No. Are they good per se? Absolutely not. If I'm willing to lend to you at 2 percent, risk-free, and I can borrow from you at 5 percent, risk-free, how much should I borrow? I should borrow all that I can. It's a guaranteed spread. Now, reverse those numbers. I'm lending to you at 5 percent and borrowing from you at 2 percent. How much should I borrow? Zero.

Borrowing is neither good nor bad. It's a tool. You really want to look at the spread. When we came in in 1980, '81, our country was in the trash heap of history. We had a really underperforming economy. We were just like a venture capital or private equity firm. We took over this company that had been run into the ground, and of course we needed to borrow money to be able to cut the tax rates, to put the executives back, and create incentive plans to control inflation. The deficits went up but, in my view, that led to lower future deficits and a control of government debt and also control in government spending.

Q: You talked about the Clinton era. That led to the closing of the debt clock. Has that mood of fiscal discipline reversed itself in recent years?

Arthur Laffer: Clinton did exactly what you're supposed to do as president during his eight years. When you have a really prosperous economy and everything's going pretty well, do you need to spend all of that money and have huge deficits? Absolutely not. That's when you pay down your debt. Clinton even ran surpluses in the federal government. He did a great job. If you look at the national debt as a share of GDP, or steady-state interest payments as a share of total GDP, it really dropped like a stone.

Now, take George W. Bush. He comes into office on January 20, 2001. He won the election in 2000. The markets had peaked in March of 2000 and there was an incipient nascent recession coming on that was really serious. In addition to that, eight months after he's in office, you get the attack on America and this huge need to increase spending for security. Here he has a recession and the need for security. What's the guy supposed to do? Raise taxes on the last three people working? I don't think so.

Clinton provided Bush with a fixed fiscal flexibility to be able to do what was right in 2001, 2002, and 2003, given the circumstances of our country. Bush, quite appropriately, cut tax rates to stimulate the economy after the huge market crash of 2000, 2001, and 2002. He did that correctly and he increased security spending dramatically. Both of those were necessary for the health of our country. Without Clinton's control of spending and reduction of the national debt as a share of GDP, Bush never would have been able to do that. It was a perfect one-two punch. Now we've had the deficit come way back down again. It's, what, the fifth smallest budget deficit in the last 45 years? When you have prosperity and economic growth you should pay down the debt or at least let it grow much more slowly than the economy. But I thought the Clinton/Bush era was perfect from the standpoint of economics.

Q: The deficit has gotten out of control. We just crossed the $9 trillion mark. You now have a wave of populous support for tax cuts. What would happen to the deficit if you raised taxes?

Arthur Laffer: You've got a national debt of $9 trillion. Bill Safire's comment on this, he called these numbers *megonumbers.* He spelled it M-E-G-O, which he claimed stood for My Eyes Glaze Over. That's a lot of money.

Would you like to see that number start coming down again? Of course you would. There are two ways that we talk about doing that today: number one, by controlling government spending, and number two, by raising tax rates. Controlling government spending has lost favor in the Congress. You have a Democratic House. You have a Democratic Senate. You have all of these national health schemes. They aren't really willing to address the spending issue, which is what really needs to be brought down.

So they are talking about raising tax rates, especially tax rates on the rich.

I'm going to use Sir Robert Peel's phrase here: If they raise tax rates on the rich, they are going to be thwarted in their expectations of revenues. There are no tax rates that I can think of that fit more into the prohibitive range of the Laffer curve than tax rates on the rich. Capital gains, upper income brackets, dividends, inheritance taxes: If you raise those, not only will you not reduce the deficit, you're going to explode the deficit. You'll cause people to be unemployed. You're going to cause huge amounts of harm, hardship, and suffering in the U.S., and you're not going to reduce the deficit. These people are on such a bad path.

The way you bring the deficit under control is not by raising tax rates. The way you bring it under control is by controlling spending, and, unfortunately, in the last eight years, the U.S. has lost its direction in trying to be economical in government spending. These guys are going to come in and try to increase spending and raise taxes on the rich and, if they do that, mark my words, you are going to see a tragedy in the U.S. economy of biblical proportions. Balancing the budget by cutting spending is wonderful. Trying to balance it by raising tax rates on the rich is ridiculous and is pandering.

Q: Is there a time when tax cuts are bad things?

Arthur Laffer: Sure. There are lots of times when tax cuts are a bad thing. You need to have tax rates sufficient to collect the requisite revenues to provide government services. You need defense, you need welfare, and you need all of these other programs. You do need them, I think. I'm not a Libertarian. All tax, except for sin taxes, do damage. Sin taxes are good because they exist not so much to collect revenues as they do to stop you from doing things like alcohol and tobacco. Those taxes don't hurt the economy, but all other taxes hurt the economy. All taxes are bad so, in a tax system, you want to collect the requisite revenues while doing the least possible damage you can to the economy. You want to develop a tax code that's the least harmful tax code.

To my way of thinking, that's a true flat tax. That's what I'd like to see: a real flat tax, Jerry Brown's flat tax, that 13 percent flat tax. Do you remember that one in 1992? That is the perfect tax code for the U.S. economy. You get rid of all federal taxes except for the sin taxes and, in their stead, have two flat-rate taxes. No deductions, no exemptions. Implement a flat tax on personal unadjusted gross income and a flat tax on business net sales. If you did that with the static revenue situation, you would be able to collect enough revenue—no Laffer curve in this one—to match all federal revenues with a tax rate of about 11 percent on each. That's what you really need to do today to make sure you do the least damage with your taxes.

Q: Is it correct that you moved to Nashville because of the tax situation?

Arthur Laffer: That's true, I did. Taxes were a very important part of my consideration. As a Californian, my highest marginal tax rate was 10.3 percent and, with the problems with the alternative minimum tax, it probably won't be deductible for very long. Here in Tennessee, there is no state income tax at all. You don't have a preferred item that you're deducting, and therefore, you don't even come close to your AMT, either. It's a great place to live: great housing and great people. Not that California isn't terrific—it is, but it's really fun here.

Q: Can you talk about David Walker? He and Paul Volcker think that the political system is broken, because you have the people who want to cut spending on one side and the people who want to raise taxes on the other side.

Arthur Laffer: The Concord Coalition. I'm not a member of it, and I do disagree with it when they talk about raising taxes, but the Concord Coalition is completely correct on wanting to control government spending. If the Concord Coalition, with Walker and Volcker, were to be able to be successful and get rid of all of this pork, it would be spectacular.

Would you like my solution? Whether you like it or not, I'm going to tell you. If a congressman or a senator does something that causes harm to the United States, what happens to that person's salary? Nothing. If a congressman or a senator does something that promotes economic growth and prosperity and a bull market, what happens to that congressman or senator's salary? Nothing. It makes no sense whatsoever that, no matter how these people behave, their compensation is unrelated. We need to do what corporate America does. If you saw two companies, exactly identical, and Company One had a CEO who had no stock options, owned no stock, and was paid a fixed salary, and Company Two had a CEO with a very small salary and a lot of stock options, which company would you prefer to invest in? Of course you want to invest where the people who make the decisions are incentivized to make good decisions. I want to put Washington, D.C., on commission.

Let me give you a hypothetical. Let's say that you elect a new congressman, a new senator. The day he or she takes office, you give that person $5 million worth of stock. He or she is allowed to keep all the capital gains, tax-free, and is held personally liable for all the capital losses. I guarantee you these people would vote differently. The reason that you have these misdirected policies by these silly politicians is they are not incentivized to vote in the correct way. If you told them that their salary would grow dramatically if the stock market or the economy performed, they'd never go for these stupid policies they vote for. They'd never go for these pork barrels. They'd never go for this pay/go stuff. They'd do what was right for America. But the reason they don't do what's right for America is there's nothing in it for them.

Q: I haven't heard that idea. Did you make that up?

Arthur Laffer: That's what I've been doing for 30 years. That's the ultimate supply side. No other supply-side reform would be necessary if you did that one.

Q: What's the story about the Hôtel de Crillon?

Arthur Laffer: Back in the 1970s, when we devaluing the dollar and doing the Smithsonian Accord and Camp David, our delegations would go to France and meet at the Hôtel de

Crillon. I took my wife-to-be at the time to Paris and I wanted to propose to her in Paris. Now, I'm a huge Francophile and I love the country. Hôtel de Crillon Hotel is *the* hotel in Paris. I went there and tried to get the room that I'd had during the olden days and I couldn't remember what room number it was. They said, "Oh, don't worry, Dr. Laffer, it's room . . . ," whatever it was. I said, "Goodness, how do you remember that?" He said, "Because that's the only room that was bugged." I think they may have been joking, but it was a riot. I did propose to my wife there and, unfortunately, she did not accept. She said she'd think about it. It took her six weeks to make the decision.

Q: Yeah, the napkin, because I think that now has sort of stretched into a story of its own.

Arthur Laffer: My classmate at Yale, a good, good friend of mine, is Dick Cheney. He's a spectacular person. He's a fine, decent, wonderful guy and a great public servant, one of the greatest I know. I used to have dinner once a week with Don Rumsfeld when Nixon was having all of his problems. Spiro Agnew was gone, and Ford came in as vice president and I would have dinner, alone, with Don Rumsfeld. He was an ambassador to NATO and then he came over here as chief of staff for Ford and we'd have dinner. And every now and then, we'd invite someone to join us.

At the Two Continents Restaurant, right next to the Treasury, we invited a guy named Jude Wanniski who was writing for the *Wall Street Journal* at the time, and Dick Cheney, who was Don Rumsfeld's deputy chief of staff. It was during the time that Ford had that silly, silly program called Whip Inflation Now, the WIN program. It was just an acronym for a 5 percent tax surcharge, which is just goofy, silly, sparkle-headed stuff, but they did it.

What I was trying to explain to him there at the restaurant was that a 5 percent tax surcharge will not lead to 5 percent more in revenues. It may lead to 4 percent more in revenues. It may lead to 3 percent, but it may also cost you revenues because there's always the feedback effect. When you raise tax rates, you reduce the incentives for doing an activity and, therefore, you shrink the tax base. How far that base shrinks given the tax rate increase is an empirical question and depends on how long you're willing to wait.

I was explaining that, and I supposedly drew the curve on the restaurant napkin. Now, I can assure you it was not the Two Continents' Restaurant where I did that, no matter what Jude Wanniski wrote two years later, because my mom was a lovely, lovely lady and she taught me, "Arthur, never, ever, ever draw on cloth napkins," and they had cloth napkins.

But the Laffer curve was what I always used in class to show students that there are two effects of tax rates. One is the arithmetic effect, which is the higher tax rate, the more revenue collected per dollar of tax base. But the other one is the economic effect: If you raise tax rates, you reduce the incentives for doing that activity and you contract the tax base. These two effects always work in opposite directions. Sometimes the arithmetic effect wins and sometimes the economic effect wins. It depends on where you are in the curve, how long you're willing to wait, and how broad the tax is. But it was a fun story that Jude wrote about in the Two Continents Restaurant there at the Hotel Washington.

Q: You mentioned you didn't think Paul Volcker had raised interest rates?

Arthur Laffer: Paul Volcker is a hard money guy. He controlled the monetary base, and Paul Volcker understood that the Fed doesn't control interest rates. They set the discount rate back then, but the discount rate followed the market; it didn't lead the market. That was not a proactive policy in the Fed. It was a reactive policy of the markets. Volcker didn't do anything to cause the 1981–1982 recession. It wasn't tight money that caused high interest rates. It was the deferral of the tax cuts. We, unfortunately, made the huge mistake of deferring those tax cuts, which postponed income, and we caused a deep recession/depression in 1981–1982. Almost everyone blames Paul Volcker for that, but that is an incorrect accusation. What Volcker did during this period was reestablish credibility in the U.S. dollar by following a price rule. He brought inflation down and interest rates down, ultimately, in the U.S. economy. He was just spectacular in monetary policy. To blame Paul Volcker for the recession of '81–'82 is really incorrect.

Q: Even at the time, he was hung in effigy. There were people committing suicide in the heartland.

Arthur Laffer: Oh, I know. It was just terrible. It's true that, when we took office, the prime interest rate was 21.5 percent. But Volcker didn't cause the inflation. For goodness sakes, he came in in '79 and, when he came in, he didn't have total control of the Fed. He was the new guy. It took him quite a while to get control of the Fed. By '80–'81, by the time we were in, he then had control of the Fed and he did a spectacular job. You can't do more than you can do. He's just the chairman—he wasn't the boss of everyone there. But as he gained control, he was able to effectuate really great policies. He did not cause the recession of '81–'82, and anyone who tells you that he did, doesn't understand the basics of supply-side economics. Period.

Q: I think you're clear. You were friends with him at that time. What was he going through when he was being blamed for it?

Arthur Laffer: I like Paul Volcker a lot personally. I think he's a neat, neat guy. I never was a *friend* of Volcker's. I was a huge fan of Paul Volcker's, but we never went out to dinner together. He and I felt very similarly about monetary policy and making sure to establish credibility in the U.S. dollar. Guaranteeing the value of the dollar was what the gold standard did. We were unwilling to go off gold and were the last ones pushed off, because we both understood the role of guaranteeing the value of the U.S. currency.

What Volcker came in and did in '79, and really much more in '80 and onward, was establish a price rule for the U.S. dollar. He was able to really bring inflation down dramatically by making sure that that price rule operates with respect to the monetary base. Volcker did not control interest rates. The discount rate followed the 91-day table. He didn't lead it, but Volcker did control the growth rate of the monetary base. He used open market operations perfectly, and you can see exactly the consequences of his policies almost 30 years later. You can see what has happened to inflation and what's happened to interest rates. We are in great shape because of Paul Volcker's revolutionary change of monetary policy.

Q: In 1971, just after the Wood Accord fell apart, the Fed enacted its dollar index?

Arthur Laffer: Yes.

Q: That, just this fall, has fallen to historic lows. It's never been as low—is that right?

Arthur Laffer: I don't think that's true.

Q: Can you characterize the value of the dollar and the foreign exchanges?

Arthur Laffer: You can look at the worth of a dollar in terms of current goods and services and see the CPI or the producer's price. That's the correct measure. You can look at the value of the dollar in terms of future dollars. There, you're looking at interest rates. That's the way of looking at the current dollar versus future dollars. Or you can look at the value of the current dollar versus foreign currencies.

Today, the value of the U.S. dollar is extraordinarily low. It's not the lowest it's ever been, but it's in the very low range. This is not a purchasing power parity problem where we are having hyper inflation. We aren't. The U.S.'s relative attractiveness versus foreign countries since 2002 has declined dramatically, but not because the U.S. has done something wrong. It's because everyone else in the rest of the world is finally copycatting supply side economics. Seventeen or 18 countries now have low rate flat taxes? They have emulated our supply side policies, and they've become far more attractive to investments. The U.S. had been the capital magnate of the world since Reagan's tax policies and Volcker's monetary policies. We had a huge capital surplus as everyone tried to invest in the United States. Warren Buffet would call that a trade deficit, but he's wrong. It's a capital surplus. Since 2002, with the improvement abroad, people have tried to move their net investments from the U.S. and more toward foreign countries. The first impact of that is that the value of the dollar falls. It's done it many times in the past, and it's happening now. It's exactly the way markets should work, because the rest of the world is doing a lot better job of being attractive to output employment production and investments. Now, as you can see, the U.S. trade deficit is starting to fall like a stone. It's gone from 6.1 percent of GDP down to 4.8 percent, and it's going to fall a lot further. Once it's gone its route, you'll see the dollar coming back in strength. There is nothing fundamentally wrong with the dollar. It's not like it was in the '70s. Far from it. That was a purchasing power parity inflation problem. This one is a relative capital attractiveness issue and it's not a problem. Foreigners are doing a great job, and we want them to do a great job.

Let me talk about the trade deficit and the capital surplus a little bit. After we took office in 1981 and cut taxes, brought inflation under control, deregulated the economy, free trade—after we did all of that, there was a huge increase in the after-tax rate of return on U.S.-located assets. Everyone wanted to invest in the United States. How do foreigners generate the dollar cash flow to buy U.S.-located assets? There are only two ways they can do it. They have to sell more goods to us and buy fewer goods from us. The U.S. trade deficit is one and the same as the U.S. capital surplus. Ask yourself the question, which would you rather have? Capital lined up on U.S. borders trying to get into our country, or trying to get out of our country? Obviously, you'd rather have it coming in.

The trade deficit is not a problem. The trade deficit is the capital surplus. It shows the relative strength of the U.S. in attracting capital. Growth companies don't lend money, they borrow money. They attract capital. The U.S. is the capital magnet of the world and there's nothing wrong with that. We are not squandering our kids' or our grandkids' futures with credit card consumption and engorgement. That's silly. The capital surplus is a sign of strength, not of weakness.

Let me give you an example. In Japan, because of their awful policies and their huge unfunded liabilities, you have a machine that's got a negative rate of return. You take that machine by truck down to Tokyo Harbor. You load that machine onto a ship in Tokyo Harbor. You send it over to the United States. You offload that machine in the United States. You put it on a lorry and you ship it to its location. The rate of return on that machine has gone from a negative in Japan to a positive in the U.S. By putting that machine on a ship in Japan, that's a Japanese export and a Japanese trade surplus. By offloading that machine in the U.S., that's a U.S. import and a U.S. trade deficit. The capital movement is the U.S. trade deficit and the Japanese trade surplus. That's the only way you can move capital across countries, and there's nothing wrong with moving that machine from Japan to the U.S. In fact, it's good for everyone.

Q: What about moving those machines to China? Lower wage areas?

Arthur Laffer: Nothing's wrong with moving them to China. We need to have capital allocated on a worldwide basis based upon the after-tax return to the shareholders. And if countries change their policies, become more or less attractive, people are going to move capital. That's why you have to be really competitive in the U.S.

That's why I'm so terrified about these anti-rich people and these politicians who are talking about raising taxes on the rich. Do you realize how uncompetitive that would make America? In the 1980s, when we cut tax rates, it was great, because everyone else was a Fabian socialist with massively high tax rates. It was a win/win. Now that the rest of the world's got lower tax rates than we have, if these yahoos go and raise the tax rates, it's going to destroy the U.S. economy. Everyone's going to want to pull their capital out of the U.S. and put it in other places like China and that low-wage, low-tax-rate country, France. It's scary to me when I see the Obamas, I see the Hillarys, I see the John Edwards speaking nonsense. If they have their way, we're going to have one heck of a problem here in the United States.

Steve Forbes

Steve Forbes ran in the presidential primaries in 1996 and 2000 on a campaign to establish a flat income tax in America. The editor-in-chief of *Forbes* magazine and president and CEO of Forbes, Inc., found the time in his very busy schedule in 2005 to write a book on this subject: *Flat Tax Revolution* (Regnery Publishing, 2005).

Q: Mr. Forbes, in *Flat Tax Revolution*, you spoke about how taxes breed corruption. What do you mean when you say taxes breed corruption?

Steve Forbes: Well, the Federal Income Tax Code is the biggest source of corruption in Washington. Politicians know it's a source of power because of its complexity. If you sit on a tax-writing committee, you're going be guaranteed political contributions for your election cycle. As a result, half the lobbying revolves around trying to put changes and amendments into the tax code. Each bill has literally hundreds of amendments. Nobody knows what they really mean. They're for special interest, special things to change in the code which is why the code now has nine million words. Politicians love it because it's a source of power. You have to go to them to amend the code, get relief or hit your competitors. So they love it, but the American people pay a price for it.

Q: People talk about the United States as an empire. Is the U.S. an empire? Why or why not?

Steve Forbes: Well, the United States is an empire of freedom. We think of *empire* as imperialistic cultures like the Roman Empire or the Persian Empire. But the United States is different. It is an empire of the human spirit where people search for opportunities. The essence of the American Dream is allowing each of us and all of us the opportunity to discover and then develop our talents to the fullest. That is what opportunity is about. As a result, the United States is not only a large land mass and one of the most populous countries in the world; it is also a place where people from all around the world come to and then, in a generation or two, become as American as anyone else. No other entity has been able to do that. Look around the world; look at the breakup of the Soviet Union, the conflict in Lebanon, ethnic and communal fighting in other parts of the world. The United States has avoided those problems because we do have these basic principles, and when we adhere to them, we become part of the American empire.

Q: There's this great experiment in freedom, and the republic has, particularly in recent years, had an extraordinary explosion in borrowing. How much of a threat is the national debt to the sovereignty of the country?

Steve Forbes: Well, the national debt in and of itself is not the problem to the sovereignty of the country. When you add up all the assets of the nation, it's over a hundred and sixty trillion dollars. The threats are the unfunded liabilities of Social Security, Medicare, Medicaid, which account for tens of trillions of dollars, about eight to ten times the size of the national debt. That fact doesn't show up on the politicians' balance sheet. They don't want you to know what a mess they've created. If you had those kind of liabilities in the private sector, you'd be joining the ranks of Enron, marching off to whatever facility where you will be a guest of the state. That is the real problem. I believe that we can deal with Social Security and with the problems of healthcare, but that is where the real debt is and that's what the politicians don't want us to talk about.

Q: Looking back at twentieth-century America, can you point to some of pivotal moments when the United States government's monetary policy created this sort of economic mess?

Steve Forbes: I think the real turning point was probably the Great Depression. When you have warfare, the power of the government expands, government borrowings go up, and you always get hit with inflation. But up to the 1930s, the government geared back after a conflict. This happened after the Civil War.

For example, the income tax was enacted during the Civil War, but was repealed a few years later. World War I racked up a lot of debt, but in the 1920s we reduced it by a third and lowered tax rates. It's hard to believe, but in the early '20s the highest wartime tax rate was 77 percent. Then it was cut down to 25 percent. As you can see, we were still in the tradition of gearing back.

Then came the Great Depression. At the time, nobody knew why it happened. It was seen as a failure of free enterprise. The government thought the best way to recover from this disaster was the way they had historically done it after wartime. And so with Herbert Hoover's administration and later with the New Deal, the government assumed new powers to try to correct the flaws of private enterprise. This is when we had the rise of the alphabet agencies. Then, in the late 1930s, the New Deal sputtered to a halt. It clearly wasn't pulling us out of the Depression. But just as soon as it looked like this period was going to end, the Second World War broke out, accompanied by another ratcheting up of government powers. As soon as it looked like the turmoil that was caused by the Second World War was going to end, we had the Cold War. During this period, everything was done for national security. Even the interstate highway bill of the mid-1950s, which established and eventually built 40,000 miles of freeways around the country, was done in the name of national security. Education reforms were also established for national security (the government believed we needed more scientists).

So, as a result of this constant warfare we've had to fight—hot wars, Cold War, and the war against Islamic extremism— government powers have always gone up. And I think what the real challenge for the United States now is to show that we can fight these forces that threaten our basic freedoms, while simultaneously preserving our freedoms from excessive government involvement. No other states, no other nation, no other republic, no other empire's been able to do it. I think that's the challenge that we face. I think we've got to show ourselves and the world that a free people can defend their freedoms. We cannot give up more sovereignty to government bureaucracies.

Q: Given your experiences with the political system, what type of leadership would it take to put the hard choices in front of the American people? As you said, after a war we should know that we must cut spending a little bit and reduce government involvement. Yet that doesn't seem to ever happen. There always seems to be a reason why the government needs to spend more. We've heard about cutting taxes, but we've never heard about cutting spending. Why is that?

Steve Forbes: I think, to be blunt, the reason why it's been so difficult to cut back on government spending and their overinvolvement in the economy is because we've done it the wrong way. When you go after a specific government program, obviously, the beneficiaries are going to fight you tooth and nail. And beneficiaries of other programs are also going to fight you because they figure, "Boy, if they knock off that one, they're going to come after us next." We saw this happen in the mid-1990s when the Republicans took over Congress for the first time in decades. Their hard-fought efforts to ratchet back government spending lasted a little over a year. Why? I think it's because they were too limited in their ambitions and they made it sound like they were going to take something away from people or turn the tables on the big spenders.

Take, for example, one of the biggest sources of power, the tax code. If you're simplifying the tax code, people won't think you're taking something away from them. Instead, they think you're helping them. Another example is Social Security. The money is there for the current elderly, yet the real problem is for people in their twenties, thirties, and forties. So why not say, "We need to help them. We're not going to cut their benefits; instead we're going to allow them to control the money by putting it into their own personal account. There will be safeguards for it, but it belongs to them, not the politicians." People aren't going to see that as taking something away. They are going to think that the money is being taken away from the politicians, not them.

Same with health care. It's all third-party; you don't get to use it until you use it. Although health care in the workplace is counted as a fringe benefit, it's not the same thing as getting money in your pay envelope or into direct deposit. Conversely, properly structured health savings accounts would put the money directly into your account. You control it. With this system you say to a worker that he may spend $5,000, $10,000, $15,000 on his health care, but you won't see any of that money unless you go to the doctor. If you had a system where you had a high deductible policy, but you got several thousand bucks a year to go into your account and what you didn't use went into a growing tax-free account, most workers are going to think, "I'm coming out ahead."

Same with education. Why shouldn't parents be able to control where their kids go to school? Now, there's a suit just filed in my home state of New Jersey, a parent saying, "The school's failed my kid. I want to be able to take the money you spent on my kid and go to another school." Think of it this way: If an automobile company sells you a lemon car, they give you a refund and you go buy a car elsewhere. You don't give the auto company more money. The same should be done with education. The government should say, "If the school fails you, take the money and go to a school that isn't a lemon school." Again, people aren't going to think that's a cutback.

This is what leaders have to do. Use a little imagination—flanking movements instead of charting the machine gun. Bring in some artillery, bring in some air attack, and then we can beat them. I believe that leaders need to go after the big things—health care, education, Social Security, taxes. If you win there, then you have given a real blow to the leviathan. Then you can start going after other things because you've established that there's a right way to do things. People think they're coming out ahead and that they are getting something. So don't fight by the rules of the other side. You can only win if you rewrite their rules.

Q: **We grew up in a culture where we heard phrases like "A penny saved is a penny earned" or "Put it away for a rainy day." Where did this culture change in the United States? When did the shame of owing money, indebtedness, or bankruptcy evaporate and the idea of accepting massive personal or governmental**

debt become accepted? Also, do you believe this culture change is positive or negative?

Steve Forbes: Well, the key is that people must learn how to handle finances in a responsible way. Too often, the kind of consumer culture we have only focuses on the here and now, not on the future. What we should learn to build on in terms of recasting our culture is home ownership. There you're taking on debt, but you have an asset behind it, you're paying it off, it's your property.

In terms of indebtedness, people have to look at the balance sheet and make sure they have assets there. This is where having your own personal accounts for Social Security would be such a benefit because from a young age, your money's going into that account. You want to know, "How am I going to grow that account? How am I going to protect that account? How do I make sure the politicians don't wreck it for me?" Suddenly, people are going to develop a Ben Franklin–like mentality because they are talking about their own money. And don't you think that's going to start to spill over into other areas? People are going to want to talk about assets and actions that will help or jeopardize their earnings. At an early age, people will develop, build a mentality that they can accumulate and grow their assets. They will become excited to see that they worked and have something to show for it, other than just a paycheck or a trip to the movies. After a person earns their money at McDonald's, they will have something that lasts longer. Now, the words "A penny saved is a penny earned is a penny saved" will have meaning. Kids especially will be able to build this mentality at an early age.

Q: Recently, the United States has been compared to a giant ship. It has been said that sometimes it feels like the amount of debt taken on is a Titanic-like iceberg and the ship is heading toward it. Is that a reasonable analogy? Is the enormous debt that the government has created a threat to our future?

Steve Forbes: Whether it's a ship headed for an iceberg or a car headed for a cliff, when you get near the cliff, you're going to have to stop. The United States with its liabilities on Social Security and health care is unsustainable. You see huge liabilities in Europe and Japan. The question is, what do you do about it? And that is where you need a new crew or a new captain. If the people who are manning the ship can't do a good job in avoiding icebergs, you must get a new crew that doesn't keep sinking the ships. This is where we have to say, "Enough's enough. You're not doing the job. We are going to replace you and here's how we're going to change things." As free people, we have to do that. There's no point in complaining. Instead of saying, "The ship isn't doing a good job" or "The captain is about to run us into the iceberg again and sink the whole thing," we must effectively change the captain. That's what elections are about. If the captain doesn't change, it's our fault as a free people.

Q: **One of the things that we're taught is in times of war was that people have to make sacrifices. For example, during World War II kids collected newspapers and tin for the war effort, or a war tax was imposed. It doesn't seem that during this "War on Terror" that the American people have been called upon to make sacrifices. At the same time, the government doesn't seem to be making any sacrifices as the spending in nondefense areas has grown. Are we in jeopardy of essentially bankrupting America if the policies that are in place now continue?**

Steve Forbes: Well, this is where I think we need to answer the question, how do we finance this war against Islamic fanaticism, but stop crazy spending? Comparing the spending to drunken sailors is an insult to sailors. They are defending the country and they spend their own money; they're not spending other people's money. Although this is a very different type of war, one of the reasons the American people are so upset with both political parties is that they see there's no firm hand on the tiller in Washington. They read about bridges to nowhere. Here we're asking young people to go to Iraq and Afghanistan, sometimes without the equipment they need. Yet we're spending money on frivolous stuff because a politician thinks it's going to help him win reelection.

People are willing to do what is necessary to defend the country, but we as a free people now have to take the next step. It's not enough to be upset or angry at these characters. Instead, we have to say, "Who are they? Let's challenge them in a primary," just as they did with Pennsylvania state legislators who abused the public trust. Even though the challengers had very little money and weren't well known, they won. We have to take on these folks and say, "Here's what you did. You have no good explanation for it." We as a free people have to say, "It's time for you to find new opportunities."

Q: How can people better understand all the statistics that are thrown at them?

Steve Forbes: The key to understanding statistics is not to get lost in them. It's like getting lost in a jungle. To understand statistics is to cut to the chase. For instance, don't get into a debate about whether the Social Security system is going to go broke in 2050 or 2030 or 2018. Just say, "Who should own your Social Security money, you or the politicians?" Talk about it on your own terms. Don't get caught up in numbers. Discuss the basic concepts. Whose country is this? What do we have to do?

Q: Does the amount of debt service that's in the budget every year concern you?

Steve Forbes: The debt service concerns me in relation to how much of our budget goes to debt service. It's like a consumer. Let's say you earn $40,000 a year. If your debt service on your house is $10,000, historically that's okay. If you're paying $35,000 on debt service and you're only making $40,000, you've got a big problem. And so it's not the number per se. It's that you are spending all your money on credit cards and mortgage. You don't need to know what your income is to know you've got a problem. That is the way, again, you've got to fight it. Don't focus on numbers per se because you might get confused. Get to the essence the way Ronald Reagan did, the way Ben Franklin did. People remember those things.

Q: **From your point of view, what did Alan Greenspan do in the last 25 years that was great? What will people look back on and say, "What was he thinking?"**

Steve Forbes: Well, Alan Greenspan was a good crisis manager, especially when things went wrong in Asia and Russia. When we had a stock market crash in 1987, he was right in there making sure that panic didn't spread. But his greatest failure was he was like a pilot who didn't fly with instruments. He had good instincts, but if you're flying by the seat of the pants and you get some adverse weather, sometimes you're going to hit a tree. As a result, he left no legacy to a successor on how to properly conduct monetary policy. Imagine driving a car without a speedometer and without a fuel gauge. You're always going to be wondering if you are okay. Well, your instincts may be pretty good on when you're running low on gas or when you may be going too fast, but not always. So he didn't provide the speedometer, he didn't provide the fuel gauge.

What's the best speedometer, fuel gauge for monetary policy? Look at the price of gold. If it's zooming up, that means you're printing too much money. If it's crashing down in price for a period of time, it means you're printing too little money. Gold reflects the markets. Let markets tell the Federal Reserve whether it's doing its job right or wrong instead of always guessing what is the right interest rate and getting sidetracked on things that you shouldn't be concerned about. Keep the dollar value stable. Tie it to the price of gold or to a range, a little bit of flexibility. You've got to give these people something to do each day, but have that kind of gauge. Then guess what? You don't make huge mistakes like we have today with oil zooming up and other crises out there. That kind of instability hurts. We want stability, not instability. We don't want inflation or deflation.

Q: **As a holder of some dollars, is the value of the dollar starting to depreciate at a rate that is of concern to you?**

Steve Forbes: The dollar should never depreciate or appreciate. It should be stable in value. It should be fixed in value. Say a foot has twelve inches; you don't change that each day. It's a fixed measure. Same thing with an hour. There are sixty minutes in an hour, it's fixed. You don't change the number of minutes in an hour each day. The dollar should have a fixed, basic value. Gold, for all its imperfections, is like a Polaris. It's the best thing we have out there. Experience shows that. Keep the dollar stable in value and then you can focus your energies on more productive things like innovating, starting a business, building a house, being responsible, moving ahead in life.

Q: When the dollar is not pegged to any commodity, when you can just print the paper, what is the result of just expanding the dollar supply on value?

Steve Forbes: If you don't have a currency that is fixed and has a fixed measure of value, then the temptation always is to reduce the content. Politicians love to spend and they hate the idea that there's any discipline out there. So without discipline, guess what happens? You get inflation, you get chaos, you undermine it. Lenin said the best way to undermine a society is to debauch the currency because not one in a million people understand what is happening. Inflation is great for those who want terrorism, for those who want totalitarianism, for those who want chaos. That kind of chaos is the enemy of freedom. Stability is the friend of freedom; chaos is the enemy.

Q: Given that, how dangerous is our profligate spending to creating the inflation that could create chaos?

Steve Forbes: The spending is not just a monetary issue. Spending is a moral issue. You're taking money from people and wasting it. People are forced to give money to the government, presumably in return for services. As we said in our Declaration of Independence, people give money in order to secure certain rights. Period. Not to waste on all the other stuff they've gotten into. And then liberals will say, "Well, you mean you want to take away Social Security?" No, we want a system where people own the assets so they truly have something of true value there. They're not burdening other generations. They've earned it and built it so the assets are there. They can have a far better, richer retirement than they could if the politicians control their money. This is the way you avoid chaos, by emphasizing *we*. We do better when matters and money are in the hands of "we the people," and not politicians who have no sense of restraint or discipline.

Q: What do you think is the greatest threat to the stability of the United States at this point?

Steve Forbes: The greatest threat to the stability of the United States is not the kind of murderous fanaticism or terrorism that we see in the world today. Eventually, I believe that we will learn to beat it. It may take time, but we will do it as a free people. The real threat is bad ideas. A lot of bad ideas came out of the Great Depression: that government could be a stabilizer of the economy, and that government could do better than free markets. We're recovering from the devastation of the Great Depression, but bad ideas are always out there. Not fighting these bad ideas and bad conventional wisdom, are the things that can ultimately undermine a society.

Q: How big a mess are we facing with the major entitlement programs—Social Security and Medicaid?

Steve Forbes: Well, the problem with entitlements is that someday you have to pay for them. And if you haven't built the assets to pay for them, then you've got a big problem. I think that's why it is important to establish Social Security reform that doesn't appear to take something away from grandma, while actually helping younger people with their own personal retirement accounts. You change the entitlement to something where people feel they've earned it. Part of the problem with Social Security is people who are on it felt, "Well, we put money in the system, but the politicians mishandled it." These people feel cheated and deceived. Now we're finally going to tell the truth to younger people. "The money that you put in is actually yours. It's not been stolen by politicians." The truth is the only way you fight these things.

Q: In looking at history, truth is perhaps the rarest commodity on the American political scene. Does it take a crisis before American people will actually be ready for the truth and ready to act on the truth?

Steve Forbes: With human nature being the way that it is, people do not like to do unpleasant things unless they have to. Kids don't like to clean their rooms unless their parents say, "You've got to do it or you're not going to get something." That's human nature. But I think people now know that something is not right with the system. And if we get the leadership, and the people themselves say, "Here's the proper way to do it," we can deal with it. In terms of health care, people know the system seems to have higher and higher costs. Yes, we've got great new stuff coming, but it seems to get more and more expensive. Why does health care get more expensive whereas in everything else in life—the amount we spend on basic food goes down so we get more, fancier food; we have lower prices for computing power. Why can't we get some of these kind of productivity gains in health care? You ask that question and then it quickly comes back: It's because people don't control the resources. Our resources are taken from us and then we're told we're getting something back for free. It's a great gain. Take a dollar, give you back 50 cents, and you're supposed to be grateful.

Q: The idea of a flat tax that you're talking about, is that something that would help us pay off this $9 trillion that's sitting there so that we wouldn't be spending all that money on debt service and we could actually rebuild the infrastructure? Is the flat tax a good tool toward that?

Steve Forbes: The flat tax wins on all fronts. It's a great blow against political corruption and a great blow against the current system of a tax code that brings out the worst in people who are always thinking, "Do I get a deduction here, do I get a deduction there?" Instead, the flat tax enables us to do things for the right reasons instead of the wrong reasons. And finally, and very importantly, it means more economic growth. It means higher asset values. Ask yourself, why did housing prices go up starting in 1998? It's because there was a change in the tax code that, in

effect, removed the capital gains tax on your primary residence
if you sold it. Suddenly you did not have a capital gains tax. When
you remove a tax on something, the value of it goes up; very, very
basic. So by lowering tax rates, by making it simple so that people
can actually understand what's happening to them, we have a
better civil life, we have a better political life. We also have a
stronger economy, higher assets, more businesses, and better jobs
being created.

**Q: If we talk about the United States not as an ambitious empire
looking to conquer territories—in the most positive sense, we
keep the shipping lanes of the world open for trade—what is
the biggest threat to the United States? Is it this out-of-control
spending? Is it the lack of political courage? What are you most
concerned about?**

Steve Forbes: What most concerns me is not the specific problems
like out-of-control spending and the war on Islamic fanaticism.
What concerns me is that if we as a free people have the spirit, the
stamina, the orientation to do something about them. Human
nature being what it is in the world is always going to face
challenges, especially preserving freedom. Jefferson said it requires
eternal, constant vigilance. I sometimes wonder if we've lost that
vigilance. I don't think we have, so I'm an optimist. So when
specific things come along and we have an out-of-control political
culture, we as a free people have to do something about it. If we
haven't lost the spirit which founded this nation and if we can keep
that spirit going, we'll be able to deal with these problems and
pursue opportunities. So it's not specific things per se; it's whether
we as a free people can summon the will to deal with them.

**Q: Many doom-and-gloom experts say that things aren't going to
change, that people are going to continue to spend what they
don't have and make bad decisions based on the leadership
we have. Is that a fair assessment of the way the United States
seems to be going?**

Steve Forbes: Well, as a free people, we in the United States
will make mistakes. The key is do we have the flexibility, the
adaptability, and the willingness to do things to deal with things

when they go wrong? In the '60s and '70s, for example, we took a real hit from Japan. We had the flexibility to say, "What are they doing right that we're not doing?" As a result, Japan's the country that went into a 10-year recession as we moved ahead in areas of high technology and biotechnology. Japan's now just starting to come to life again.

So yes, things are going to go wrong. We will make mistakes, but the key is that we must have the flexibility, the adaptability, the can-do attitude that says, "We've got a problem here; we'd better do something about it." So rather than get doom-and-gloom message out to people, there are various other ways you can get information out there. But if you don't make the effort to get the information out and say, "Hey, [we] may have a problem here that if left untended is going to have real repercussions, unpleasant ones," guess what? The repercussion, the bad things will happen. So I'm delighted people are saying, "We have problems out there," or "Well, if this is a problem, we'll deal with it."

Q: What do you think the United States government has done best in the past 25 years?

Steve Forbes: I look to Ronald Reagan coming into office in 1981, faced with a malaise in the United States, a Cold War that was going against us, revolutions in Iran, Nicaragua, and anti-U.S. sentiments everywhere. And he said, "If we go back to our principles and have that kind of forward-looking optimism, we can do it." And in eight years, the United States economy's growth exceeded the entire German economy; just as in the last three years the expansion of the U.S. economy exceeds the entire size of the Chinese economy. Nobody knows that. We won the Cold War; people thought that was going to go forever, but we won it. Now, did we have problems in that era? Yes, but on big things, we did it right, so why can't we have that kind of Reaganist approach again? Sure, nothing's ever going to be perfect, that's not for this world, that's for another world; but by golly, we can get a lot of glorious things done with that kind of can-do American Reaganist spirit.

Q: Should we be back on the gold standard?

Steve Forbes: Should we be back on the gold standard in terms of having a pile of gold? No. All you need to do is look at the price of gold and base your monetary policy based on its price. In short, I'll pick a number, $400 an ounce. If it goes much above $400 an ounce, you're printing too much money, so soak some of that excess money you spilt and mop it up. If it goes well below $400 for a period of time, you know you're not creating enough credit for the needs of the economy, so you print a little more. You let the markets, the economy tell you what to do. You don't try to second-guess what's needed like setting interest rates and hoping you targeted it right. Markets will tell you.

Q: Is it important for the American people to recognize what this debt means to our economy in the future?

Steve Forbes: What's important for the American people to realize is that the government has, with a sleight of hand, given us a lot of obligations that we don't know we have. We know about the national debt—that's a number. We know we have obligations on Social Security and in health care that are five, seven, eight times what the national debt is, and there's no way the current system can deal with it. It's like you think you have a house, you may have bought a house, say, for $200,000. What they didn't tell you is that you've got a million-dollar mortgage on that thing. That's what the crisis is. So when people realize we've got a crisis, there are positive ways to deal with it and turn the tables on the big spenders and the politicians. That's what we've got to do.

Q: Do you sometimes feel like you're a contrarian going against the public? Do you feel that the public debate is starting to line up with you?

Steve Forbes: My role now is agitator, stirring the pot, trying to make things happen, and there are going to be times when you go against the grain. Ronald Reagan could not get elected president in 1968 when he first ran, could not get elected in 1976, but he stuck to it, and in 1980, with the same basic principles, he got in and achieved great things. So rather than see yourself as a contrarian or whatever you want to call yourself, people should see themselves as seekers of the truth or as people who are trying to do things based on basic principles. And sometimes you may find a hostile environment and sometimes you may find you've got a lot of missionary work to do, but you have to do it. That's what America's all about.

Q: As a proponent of the American people getting the truth, if you could pick one truth that they should learn about money, monetary policy, debt, gold, what would it be?

Steve Forbes: I would want people to realize that the money that the politicians spend is your money. It comes out of your pocket one way or the other. They take your money and they pay the tab and you're supposed to be grateful. Don't get caught up in the exact number; just remember it's your money. When politicians spend, they get it from you. And if they say they're going to give you a free lunch, just remember, they're using your credit card, your money. You're eventually going to be getting the bill.

Q: And once the American people have that knowledge and it has become second nature to them, if you will, what would be the right action for them to take?

Steve Forbes: The American people, as a start, should say, "Who are my representatives? Who is my state representative, state senator, congressperson, U.S. senator, governor? What are they doing and why are they doing it?" Challenge leaders in primaries, even if they're not doing the job right. Go online, write a letter to the editor, be active. It only takes a few minutes each month. By golly, that's how you get results.

Additional Resources

There are many great resources on the Web if you're interested in learning more about the nation's economy and securing your family's place within it. Here are a few suggestions for where to begin

- Peter G. Peterson Foundation: www.pgpf.org

- Agora Financial, LLC: www.agorafinancial.com

- The Concord Coalition: www.concordcoalition.org

- The CATO Institute: www.cato.org

- The Brookings Institution: www.brookings.edu

- American Enterprise Institute: www.aei.org

- Center on Budget and Policy Priorities: www.cbpp.org

- Center for Retirement Research: http://crr.bc.edu

- Choose to Save: www.choosetosave.org

- Feed the Pig: www.feedthepig.org

- Citizens Against Government Waste: www.cagw.org

- The Committee for Economic Development: www.ced.org

- US Budget Watch: www.usbudgetwatch.org

- Common Good: www.commongood.org

- The Heritage Foundation: www.heritage.org

- OMB Watch: www.ombwatch.org

- One Horizon Foundation: www.onehorizon.org

- Peterson Institute for International Economics: www.iie.com

- Progressive Policy Institute: www.ppionline.org

- Public Agenda: www.publicagenda.org

- The Tax Policy Center: www.taxpolicycenter.org

- The Urban Institute: www.urban.org

Index